DIALOG OF A VETERAN SOLDIER

Dialog of a Veteran Soldier Discussing the Frauds and Realities of Portuguese India

Diogo do Couto

TRANSLATED BY TIMOTHY J. COATES

FOREWORD BY M. N. PEARSON

Tagus Press
UMass Dartmouth
Dartmouth, Massachusetts

Front cover illustrations—Top: A Portuguese woman in India. *Bottom:* Portuguese men in India. From an original oil painting by C. Arthur Brooks and used here with his permission, based on the códice português da Biblioteca casanatense, published in *Imagens do Oriente,* Lisboa: Imprensa Nacional, 1985.

Tagus Press is the publishing arm of the Center for Portuguese Studies and Culture at the University of Massachusetts Dartmouth.
CENTER DIRECTOR | João M. Paraskeva

Classic Histories from the Portuguese-Speaking World in Translation, Volume 3
Series Editors: Timothy J. Coates and Timothy D. Walker
Tagus Press at UMass Dartmouth
www.portstudies.umassd.edu
© 2016 The University of Massachusetts Dartmouth
All rights reserved
Manufactured in the United States of America

The publisher gratefully acknowledges support from the
Fundação Calouste Gulbenkian

Managing Editor: Mario Pereira
Copyedited by Bronwyn Becker
Designed by April Leidig
Typeset in Caslon by Copperline Book Services, Inc.

For all inquiries, please contact:
Tagus Press • Center for Portuguese Studies and Culture
UMass Dartmouth • 285 Old Westport Road
North Dartmouth MA 02747-2300
Tel. 508-999-8255 • Fax 508-999-9272
www.portstudies.umassd.edu

Library of Congress Cataloging-in-Publication Data
Names: Couto, Diogo do, 1542–1616, author. | Coates, Timothy J., 1952– translator.
Title: Dialog of a veteran soldier : discussing the frauds and realities of Portuguese India / Diogo do Couto ; translated by Timothy J. Coates ; foreword by M. N. Pearson.
Other titles: O soldado prático . English
Description: Dartmouth, Massachusetts : Tagus Press at UMass Dartmouth, [2016] | Series: Classic histories from the Portuguese-speaking world in translation ; volume 3 | Includes bibliographical references and index.
Identifiers: LCCN 2016011003 | ISBN 9781933227726 (pbk. : alk. paper)
Subjects: LCSH: Portuguese—Asia—History. | Portuguese—India—History. | Portugal—Colonies—Administration—History. | Public administration—Portugal—Colonies—Corrupt practices. | Portugal—Colonies—Defenses. | Portugal—Colonies—Commerce. | Asia—History.
Classification: LCC DS33.7 .C6813 2016 | DDC 954/.78025—dc23
LC record available at http://lccn.loc.gov/2016011003

This first English translation of
Dialog of a Veteran Soldier is dedicated to two veterans
who, like Diogo do Couto's main character, are wise,
experienced hands, never afraid of speaking the truth:
Professors Francis Dutra (professor emeritus, the University
of California at Santa Barbara) and Douglas Wheeler
(Prince Henry the Navigator Professor Emeritus, History
Department of the University of New Hampshire).
Both have been instrumental in promoting the
study of Portugal and the Portuguese world
in the United States.

CONTENTS

List of Maps and Illustrations ix

Foreword by M. N. Pearson xi

Introduction: Portuguese Asia and Diogo do Couto xxi

Comments on the Translation xxv
Glossary of Foreign and Archaic English Terms xxix
Maps Showing Places Mentioned in the Text xxxii
Viceroys and Governors of Portuguese Asia, 1505–1612 xxxv

Dialog of a Veteran Soldier

Letter to the Count of Salinas and Ribadeo 3

THE FIRST PART 5

SCENE 1: The Importance of Secrecy 5

SCENE 2: How Appointments in Portuguese India Are Managed in Portugal; the Many Irregularities in the Process 17

SCENE 3: The Worst Enemies of the King's Treasury Are His Ministers; How the King's Orders and Standing Instructions Are Not Followed; and Other Subjects 21

SCENE 4: Regarding the Types of Fraud in India and the Damages They Cause 29

SCENE 5: The Second Type of Fraud, Which Is Against Men, and the Destruction It Causes 32

SCENE 6: The Third Type of Fraud, Which Is Against God, and Many Other Wicked Things the Governors Do 39

SCENE 7: The Fourth Type of Fraud, Which Is Against All, and the Nature of Old Debts 48

SCENE 8: The Treasury Inspectors; Their Unnecessary Visits to the Northern Forts; and the Irregularities They Commit with the King's Accounts 57

SCENE 9: Old Payments for Soldiers; How the King Is Robbed by Them; and How to Avoid Them 62

SCENE 10: Regarding the Accounts in Goa and Other Subjects 71

THE SECOND PART 93

SCENE 1: Irregularities in Making Appointments 93

SCENE 2: The Importance of Truth, Valor, and Gold in Retaining Portuguese Asia 98

SCENE 3: Confusion in Making Appointments 106

SCENE 4: The Red Sea Fleets; How to Select a Viceroy; the Three Traits of a Good Leader; and the Importance of Clemency 117

SCENE 5: The Importance of Generosity 128

SCENE 6: The Importance of Prudent Speech 137

THE THIRD PART 143

SCENE 1: Supplies for Portuguese Asia; Attending to Those Absent; Vice-regal Correspondence and Orders 143

SCENE 2: Fraudulent Actions of the Viceroys; the Importance of Attending to Little Things; the Cowardice of Soldiers Nowadays; and the Needs of Portuguese Asia 152

SCENE 3: To Conquer Sri Lanka or Aceh? The Importance of Conquering the Silver Mines of Mutapa 159

SCENE 4: The Wealth and Riches of Africa versus India 168

Appendix: Draft Letter from Matias de Albuquerque 181

Further Reading 189

Index 191

MAPS AND ILLUSTRATIONS

MAPS

MAP 1: The *Carreira da Índia* xx
MAP 2: The Indian subcontinent ca. 1600 xxxii
MAP 3: The Eastern Indian Ocean, Straits of Malacca and South China Sea xxxiii
MAP 4: The Western Indian Ocean and East Coast of Africa xxxiv
MAP 5: North Africa 167

ILLUSTRATIONS

The sea wall of the fort in Diu 57
Stone markers in the fort in Diu 62
Gate to the city of Diu 71
Image of St. George at entrance to the fort of Diu 98
Cannon at the fort of Diu 106
Moat of the fort in Diu 118
Tombstones in a church floor in Bassein 127
Tombstones in a church floor in Bassein 136
Façade of Church of Nossa Senhora da Saude in Sancoale, Goa 140
Front and reverse of a Portuguese *bazaruco* 152
A man wearing a doublet, jerkin, and breeches 159

FOREWORD

O SOLDADO PRÁTICO in its various versions has been known and used by Portuguese-reading scholars for many years. The most detailed exposition in English was by George Winius thirty years ago.[1] It is a pleasure to offer a short preface to this translation by Timothy Coates. As he notes, this is the first translation into any language and should make this extraordinary work more widely available. Coates's translation is bolstered by apposite elucidations, including the many (to my mind tiresome) classical allusions.

What are we to make of this text? One approach would be to sketch how it fits into colonial Portuguese literature of the time. Consider Garcia da Orta's famous *Colloquies*, a massive compilation of botanical and ethnographical material.[2] The two may well have met, for Couto lived in Goa from 1559 to 1569, while Orta had been there since 1534. His *Colloquies* was published in 1563, and he died in 1568. In 1580 he was posthumously condemned as a crypto Jew, and his bones were disinterred and ceremoniously burnt. There are both similarities and contrasts between the *Colloquies* and the *Soldado*. Both were written in the then-common dialogue form, which goes back at least to Plato. In Orta's case the interlocutor was Ruano, who may or may not have been a real person. Orta's text, though published in Goa, was best known in Europe from a translation into Latin by Clusius (1567). Couto's text, of course, remained unpublished until 1790. Orta references classical medical texts frequently, and perhaps to more purpose than Couto's demonstrations of his classical knowledge.

In this regard Couto bears comparison with Luís de Camões's famous *Os Lusíadas* published in 1572, which also is replete with grandiose antiquarian matters. These two certainly knew each other. They traveled together from Mozambique to Lisbon in 1569–70. A further similarity between Couto and Camões is that, contrary to some common misperceptions, Camões was also aware of problems in the Estado da Índia. His epic poem is frequently described as a paean of praise for Portuguese achievements, yet at the end of canto 4 the old man of venerable aspect "shook his head three times disapprovingly" and warned of the folly of the da Gama expedition. "Oh the folly of it, this craving for power, this thirsting after the vanity we call fame, this fraudulent pleasure known as honour that thrives on popular esteem." And so on and so on. Consider also a portion of a poem from Camões, translated by Atkinson, which describes Goa as "This Babylon, whence flows matter for every evil the world breeds . . . where tyranny overrides honour . . . this labyrinth where nobility, valour and learning go begging at the portals of avarice and meanness."[3] Rebelo correctly says of the *Lusiads* that "it is a poem of serious reflections on history and society that reveals a grave preoccupation with the state of the Portuguese empire and the future of the nation," and "the criticism levelled by Camões at the bad counsellors of the king, his condemnation of corruption, and other evils he detected in colonial administration are already a warning that this state of affairs could not go on for much longer without serious consequences for the empire and for the nation itself."[4]

George Winius points out many other complaints about the Portuguese administration, including a long account by Francisco Rodrigues de Silveira and several foreign visitors, notably Jan Huyghen van Linschoten and Charles Dellon.[5] It will be remembered that no less an authority than Francis Xavier was disgusted by what he found in Goa: "Everyone takes the path of 'I rob, you rob.'" Silveira's claim was an important addition to Couto's in that he pointed out that corruption was not merely a moral and financial problem, it also had ruined Portugal's military efficiency. However, his account, while possibly read in manuscript, remained unpublished until A. de S. S. Costa Lobo produced a very garbled edition in 1877.[6] As we will see, modern historians also comment on corruption in the administration.

As one reads the *Soldado*, one realizes that several themes are intertwined, though not without repetition. I need not summarize the text, which flows easily in Coates's translation. Let me just underline a few salient points. The veteran complains of a lack of administrative discipline, such as important decisions that ought to have been confidential being made available publicly or grandees boasting of their sexual exploits. A recurring theme is the difficulty of making the king aware of the problems of corruption, nepotism, peculation, and theft in the Estado. The underlying theme, a very common one in medieval European kingdoms, is that if only the king knew what his subordinates were doing he would intervene and stop the abuse. In addition, new governors bring out a host of followers with them, and they all have to be looked after for the three years that the governor holds office. Another familiar theme, then and now, is that things used to be much better. Once the Portuguese acted bravely, now they merely hang around looking for favors or sit in the entry halls of the monasteries eating the monks' leftovers. "The *Estado da Índia* was conquered with truth, loyalty, generosity, valor, and force. Now looking at its current condition, is it not the opposite of these things!" (see page 99). Indeed, the whole enterprise is in decline, and may be doomed. Judicial corruption "is the best indicator I have that Portuguese India will not endure" (see page 41). Or, "I heard a knowledgeable viceroy say that it would be a good thing if Portuguese India were lost and that it could not continue much longer" (see page 56).

Another theme is the long-standing debate over the possession of forts. Would the Portuguese have done better to be strong only at sea, rather than building numerous very expensive forts all along the Indian Ocean littoral? The first viceroy, Almeida, thought the former, telling Dom Manuel "As long as you may be powerful at sea you will hold India as yours; and if you do not possess this power, little will avail you a fortress on shores."[7] And many others agreed with this. Indeed, in the seventeenth century one of the viceroys was even looking enviously on the English position in India, for they had no forts at all.[8] However, as Couto notes, forts were built instead, many of which "have no function except to create expenses, be poorly provisioned, and stand in harm's way" (see page 160).

Two general themes in the work need to be highlighted. First, is his depiction of maladministration and corruption valid, and second, did this cause *decadência* (decay) and the decline of the Estado? As to the first, we have already quoted several contemporaries who back up Couto's claims. However, this needs to be put into context. In the later nineteenth century some historians vehemently criticized the Portuguese administration, not however that they seem to have read the *Soldado*. We can start with late nineteenth-century accounts by Protestants, mostly English but also one German, and sketch briefly what they saw as the fundamental weaknesses of the Portuguese in the Indian Ocean. The two favorite explanations were corruption and, more generally, the failure to evolve a modern official class.

F.C. Danvers wrote that "A laxity of government, and a general corruption amongst the servants of the State, in which each one, regardless of the public interests, sought but his own benefit and the accumulation of wealth, only too certainly prepared the way for the downfall of Portuguese rule in India."[9] R. S. Whiteway agreed, noting that Portugal lacked "that official class which is the backbone of efficient civil administration"[10] and pointedly praised "Albuquerque's business habits—habits that are now, as they were then, the right ones for an administrator."[11] W. W. Hunter, Richard Burton, and, a little later, Vincent A. Smith all agreed, as did a more recent author, the American F. C. Lane. The Victorians also often threw in gratuitous comments about Catholicism and *mestiços* (persons of mixed ancestry). Mixed marriages produced "a languid population of half-breeds," for example; indeed, Burton wrote, it was impossible to find in Asia "an uglier or more degraded looking race" than the Goans.[12] The German Protestant author of an 1899 account of the Portuguese in East Africa joined in the condemnation: J. S. Strandes summed up the Portuguese by saying that their "rule in East Africa was the rule of alien conquerors, based on force and destined to yield to greater strength when it appeared. It had no lasting influence whatsoever on the country, and East Africa today would appear the same even if there had been no Portuguese period in her past."[13] He echoes the British writers on the Portuguese in India when he writes that they "lost all sense of honour and propriety . . . it can scarcely be denied that rapacity, unscrupulousness and pretentiousness were the principal guides to conduct."[14]

Niels Steensgaard in his important book followed the same pattern, though not of course with racist overtones. He found the Estado to have many of the characteristics of Asian regimes of the same period, and these were strongly contrasted with the Dutch East India Company, which he found to be more "modern" and "business-like."[15]

This claim of a dichotomy between the Portuguese and the northern Europeans has been successfully attacked. One could say that at least some elements of Couto's critique also apply to the supposedly more efficient and "modern" Dutch and English trading companies. Charles Boxer, for example, years ago noted extensive "corruption" in the VOC (the Dutch East India Company), but did not attribute this as the main cause of the decline of the VOC in the eighteenth century. And he claimed that the EIC was no better.[16] Jacobs's recent excellent text rightly cautions against using judgments based on present-day standards, but does provide numerous examples of corruption in clove cultivation, cinnamon, pepper, tea, tin, and coffee. Nevertheless, corruption, she claims, was not a major reason for the decline of the company.[17] The general conclusion is that the dichotomy that Steensgaard presented is invalid. As Sanjay Subrahmanyam wrote, the Portuguese were not anachronistic medieval warriors compared with the modern Dutch.[18] So also from Glenn Ames: "Rather than avoiding the costly mistakes of the Portuguese, the Dutch had indeed come to embrace them: over-extension, huge military and administrative costs, almost constant warfare against a plethora of enemies, an obsessive desire to monopolise key commodities in the trade, and a growing primacy of imperial geo-political priorities over sound proto-capitalist practices."[19] Diogo Ramada Curto is right on the mark: Linschoten and Dellon, on whom Winius relied, "diffused the image of an intolerant Portuguese *Estado da Índia*, bloated with conspicuous consumption or sunk in corruption that was implicitly contrasted with the dynamic merchant companies and relative tolerance that was believed to mark the overseas activities of the North European nations."[20]

This is not to say that there were no problems with corruption in the *Estado*. Recent scholarship makes no attempt to gloss over the matter.[21] However, contrary to a general finding of equivalence between the Estado and the companies, George Winius claims that corruption was worse in the Estado than in any of the other colonial regimes.[22] I think the modern reader will be unconvinced, though possibly a rigorous quantitative comparative analysis would cast light one way or the other. In the meantime, I think Diogo Ramada Curto's comment that the Portuguese administration was "a system of patrimonial and personal rewards headed by the crown" can be considered to put the whole matter in an appropriate context.[23] His conclusion actually fits quite well with what I wrote some thirty-five years ago in a brief analysis.[24] It seems to me that we need to disaggregate corruption. In this article I tried to distinguish between minor peculation, this to be seen as part of any administration at this time, and wholesale theft or massive corruption, the sort of thing that Silveira complained about, where the consequences were dire, namely a loss of military efficiency. Arguably the former, relatively benign, form of corruption was more or less universal at the time, and certainly was to be found in the northern trading companies, but the more severe, and consequential, form was perhaps more endemic in the Estado than in the trading companies. The key thing is to avoid what could be called temporal ethnocentrism, that is, to judge the past through the prism of an (idealized) present. Obviously no administration in the early modern period met Weberian standards of bureaucratic norms, in short a system of legal domination in which the exercise of authority consisted in the implementation of enacted norms.

Finally, what can we conclude about the decadência that Couto depicts so vigorously? Few would argue with a proposition that by the time of the *Soldado* the Estado was indeed long past its glory days, though it may be noted that Glenn Ames wrote a book with the title *Renascent Empire? The House of Braganza and the Quest for Stability in Portuguese Monsoon Asia, ca. 1640–1663*, only the question mark casting doubt on when the decline occurred.[25] Similarly, Anthony Disney's recent text claims that the crucial spice trade to Europe was predominantly in Portuguese hands much longer than we used to think—for the whole of the sixteenth century.[26] But the consensus is that by the early seventeenth century, at least, the Estado was indeed in a state of decadência. Couto claimed that this decline was caused by the corruption and maladministration he outlined so comprehensively in the *Soldado*, and indeed George Winius follows him: "I do think that I can establish that the corruption was a real problem."[27]

To the contrary, there seems to be little doubt that corruption however defined played a minor role, if any, in the decline. No need to go into detail on this, but merely to note that Portugal, a small under-resourced country, could not compete with the larger and richer northern Europeans, most obviously the Dutch in the VOC. It was not a matter of "medieval" versus "modern" or of "corrupt" versus "honest," but rather of resources, and to an extent tactics—that is, that the VOC seems to have been more focused and discriminating in its use of force than was the Estado. Thus in a way Couto did his country a disservice, for his depiction of the Estado was arguably too gloomy, too much perhaps a product of his own tribulations and difficulties. A truer account may have located the Estado in a milieu where the administration was neither much better nor much worse than those of other entities, whether they be neighboring Asian states or incoming northern European trading companies. In any case, this debate will continue, and will now be facilitated by reference to Timothy Coates's excellent translation of a central text, *O Soldado Prático*.

M. N. Pearson

NOTES

1. George Davison Winius, *The Black Legend of Portuguese India: Diogo do Couto, His Contemporaries and the Soldado Prático: A Contribution to the Study of Political Corruption in the Empires of Early Modern Europe* (New Delhi: Concept Publishing, 1985).

2. Garcia da Orta, *Colóquios dos simples, e drogas he cousas medicinais de India*, 1563 rpt., ed. Conde de Ficalho, 2 vols. (Lisbon: Imprensa Nacional, 1891–95).

3. William C. Atkinson, *Camoens: The Lusiads*. (Baltimore, MD: Penguin, 1952), 17, 119–21.

4. Luís de Sousa Rebelo, "Language and Literature in the Portuguese Empire," in *Portuguese Oceanic Expansion, 1400–1800*, ed. Francisco Bethencourt and Diogo Ramada Curto (New York: Cambridge University Press, 2007), 375, 376.

5. Winius, *The Black Legend*, 29–57.

6. A. de S. S. Costa Lobo, ed. *Memórias de um soldado da Índia, compiladas de um Manuscripto Portugûes do Museo Británnico* (Lisboa: Imprensa Nacional, 1877).

7. Dom (or Dona for a woman) is a title of respect for nobility. Quote taken from the introduction in *The Three Voyages of Vasco da Gama*, trans. Henry E. J. Stanley (London: Hakluyt Society, 1869), xiv–xvii. Dom Francisco de Almeida made this comment in a letter to King Dom Manuel I.

8. M. N. Pearson, *Merchants and Rulers in Gujarat: the Response to the Portuguese in the Sixteenth Century* (Berkeley: University of California Press, 1976), 55.

9. Frederick Charles Danvers, *The Portuguese in India, Being a History of the Rise and Decline of Their Eastern Empire*, 1894 rpt. (New Delhi: Asian Educational Services, 1988), 1:xxxix.

10. R. S. Whiteway, *The Rise of Portuguese Power in India, 1497–1550*. 1899 rpt. (New Delhi: Asian Educational Services, 1989), 13.

11. Whiteway, *The Rise of Portuguese Power* 124n1.

12. Richard Burton, *Goa and the Blue Mountains or Six Months of Sick Leave*. 1851 rpt. (New Delhi: Asian Educational Services, 1991), 97.

13. Justis Strandes, *The Portuguese Period in East Africa*. 1899 rpt. Trans. Jean Wallwork, ed. J. S. Kirkman (Nairobi: East African Literature Bureau, 1971), 278.

14. Strandes, *The Portuguese Period in East Africa*, 269. See my *Coastal Western India* (New Delhi: Concept, 1981), 19–20; and my *Portuguese in India* (Cambridge: Cambridge University Press, 1987), 103 for discussion and sources; and Strandes, *The Portuguese Period in East Africa*, 269–72, 278.

15. Niels Steensgaard, *The Asian Trade Revolution of the Seventeenth Century: The East India Companies and the Decline of the Caravan Trade* (Chicago: University of Chicago Press, 1974), 84–94; and for a vigorous critique, see Glenn Ames, "The Asian Trade Revolution of the Seventeenth Century Reconsidered," in Charles Borges and M. N. Pearson eds., *Metahistory: History Questioning History* (Lisbon: Nova Vega, 2007), 339–52.

16. C. R. Boxer, *The Dutch Seaborne Empire* (London: Hutchinson, 1965), 225–29.

17. Els M. Jacobs, *Merchant in Asia: The Trade of the Dutch East India Company during the Eighteenth Century* (Leiden: CNWS Publications, 2006), 8, 17, 52, 80, 188, 219, 268, and 290–94.

18. Sanjay Subrahmanyam, *The Portuguese Empire in Asia 1500–1700: A Political and Economic History* (London: Longman, 1993), 270–77.

19. Ames, "Asian Trade Revolution," 348.

20. Diogo Ramada Curto, "Portuguese Imperial and Colonial Culture," in *Portuguese Oceanic Expansion*, 345.

21. See the excellent analysis in Jorge M. Pedreira, "Costs and Financial Trends in the Portuguese Empire, 1415–1822," in *Portuguese Oceanic Expansion*, especially 76–81.

22. Winius, *The Black Legend*, 68–74.

23. Curto, "Portuguese Imperial and Colonial Culture," in *Portuguese Oceanic Expansion*, passim.

24. "Corruption and Corsairs in Sixteenth-Century Western India: A Functional Analysis," in *The Age of Partnership: Europeans in Asia before Dominion* (Honolulu: University Press of Hawaii, 1979), 15–42.

25. Published by Amsterdam University Press in 2000.

26. A.R. Disney, *A History of Portugal and the Portuguese Empire: From Beginnings to 1807*, 2 vols. (Cambridge and New York: Cambridge University Press, 2009), 2:152.

27. Winius, *The Black Legend*, xi.

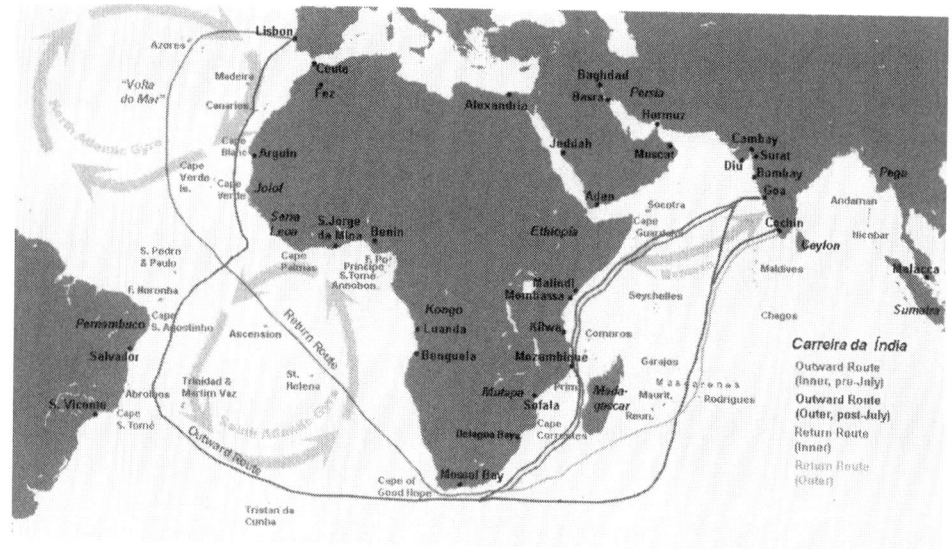

MAP 1. The *Carreira da Índia*, the maritime route connecting Portugal and India.
Source: Walrasid@Wikimedia Commons.

INTRODUCTION

Portuguese Asia and Diogo do Couto

WHEN THE PORTUGUESE arrived in the Indian Ocean in 1498, their first destination was the Malabar Coast of southwestern India. This was one of the centers of the spice trade, especially focused in Calicut. After making a number of faulty steps there and subsequent alliances with Cochin, the Portuguese realized that they would need their own base of operations. By 1510, they conquered the prosperous coastal city of Goa and the area immediately surrounding it (see maps 1 and 2). Goa was transformed into a large metropolitan hub designed along the lines of a European city. It was the capital and largest city in all of Portuguese Asia, the Estado da Índia, which stretched from Mozambique island in the southwest Indian Ocean, along the Swahili Coast to Mombasa, Muscat, and Hormuz at the entrance to the Persian Gulf. From there the Estado included Diu, Damão, the area around Bombay island, the western coast of India to Cochin and a variety of smaller towns, and Malacca, Timor, Macau and Nagasaki (see map 3). In this text, I have used the terms "Portuguese Asia," "Portuguese India," and "Estado da Índia" interchangeably to refer to this very scattered and diverse collection of outposts.

The Portuguese were able to thrive in Asian waters as middlemen, merchants, and soldiers. There was very little for them to bring from Europe to trade, other than New World gold and silver. As a result, they began a long-distance trade from one locale in Asia to another. Perhaps the most famous of these was the Chinese-Japanese trade. Leaving Macau, an annual ship would sell Chinese silk in the Japanese port of Nagasaki, in exchange for Japanese silver. The Portuguese were also horse merchants and bought horses from Persia and Arabia to sell on the Indian subcontinent. Couto references all of these lucrative businesses—the trades in silk, silver, and horses. Moreover, the Portuguese attempted to control and tax trade conducted by others in this vast Indian Ocean region, using *cartazes*, licenses or certificates that directed trade to one of their own ports, where it could be taxed. Other Portuguese left the official empire to conduct business or act as mercenaries for other powers, especially the Mughal emperors in Delhi. Still others married and became permanent members of various Asian communities. The Christian religious orders were also active, tending to spiritual needs of the Portuguese traders as well as preaching and attempting to convert local populations. It is also important to remember that even in their capital city, the Portuguese were only a small fraction of perhaps two or three percent of the total population. This was the social mix of Diogo do Couto's world in Goa, and the reader will find references to all these figures, as well as to orphans and widows.

The Estado da Índia was profitable at its peak, roughly between 1550 and 1560, well before this work was written. An economic system such as the one described above is dependent on a strong navy, well manned and well provisioned, with many ships. Without it, controlling trade was an illusion, and trade itself was greatly reduced. By the time Diogo do Couto wrote this work at the beginning of the 1600s, the economic power and influence of Portuguese Asia was in clear decline, and this is the backdrop to the urgency the reader will hear in his work.

The reader needs to be aware of the administrative structure of the Estado da Índia, since Couto makes numerous references to positions and institutions. At the top was the viceroy or governor. The reader will note that Couto always mentions both titles, giving the impression they were somehow different positions, but they were not. When occupied by a member of the nobility, the position was termed a viceroy; when occupied by a commoner, a governor. Under this official were several specialized councils that made decisions and recommendations, especially the treasury council and the council of state. The judicial system was also layered, with a judge, appellate judge, and a high court. At each fort or outpost, there was a captain, a factor (an agent in charge of trade and merchandise), and a long list of minor officials below him, such as secretary, treasurer, customs clerk, gatekeeper, and so on. At the larger and busier posts such as Diu or Chaul, these could be very lucrative positions. All positions were awarded for a period of three years, which caused two interrelated problems. As Couto points out, since each man knew he would only hold the position for three years, he had to maximize his profit as quickly and for as long as possible.

Second, once the empire started shrinking due to attacks from enemies such as the Dutch and the Omanis, the number of available administrative positions decreased. The crown, however, ignored this reality, continued to appoint more administrators than were now needed, and further compounded difficulties by appointing multiple officials to fill the same posts. Bad management thus caused a backlog and made obtaining positions more and more theoretical. The reader will find Couto addressing both of these problems in this work.

Diogo do Couto tells us a bit about his own life in this work via his main character, the veteran soldier. He was born in Lisbon in 1542. He entered royal service at the age of ten, serving Prince Luís, son of King Dom Manuel I. The next year he attended a Jesuit college, where he undoubtedly read much of the classical literature he cites in this work. In 1555, he began service in King Dom João III's household that lasted until the king died in 1557. He mentions this in the first section (see page 36), when talking about illegitimate sons of nobles whom the king does not know; he contrasts this with his own situation, writing "I spent my youth as a servant to the king, who knows my name very well." Two years later, he left Lisbon for India. In the 1560s he participated in several battles in Surat and Malabar, where he undoubtedly received some of the wounds his main character mentions. Returning to Lisbon in 1569, he visited the royal court and stayed in Portugal for two years before returning to Goa. In the 1570's he was appointed to a series of positions in the state bureaucracy, and by the early 1580s he was the captain of Tarapor, north of Bombay island. It is important to note that from 1580 until 1640, Portugal was ruled by the Spanish Habsburg kings in Madrid, and Couto makes several references to Spanish rule in this work (see 163). By 1595, he was appointed the official chronicler of Portuguese Asia and thedirector of the Goan Archives. He began writing his official history, called the *Décadas,* on the model already established by the previous historian-chronicler, João de Barros. By 1610, he learned that his first manuscript of *O Soldado Prático* was circulating in Lisbon without his name on it. He then sent two additional manuscripts of *O Soldado Prático,* the last one dated 1612. These two manuscripts, while sharing the same title as the first, are quite different. Couto altered the original from a dialog to a conversation among three people, the content is different, and the classical illusions were all added. His tone changed as well, becoming more pessimistic and biting about corruption in Portuguese Asia. Diogo do Couto died in Goa in December of 1616.

The first printed edition of the *Dialog* appeared in 1790, published by the Lisbon Academy of Sciences. It is not a coincidence that the work had to wait over 175 years before it was printed. The reader will immediately appreciate why many wealthy and powerful people in India and in Portugal did not want it to ever see the light of day. However, it was not only for this work that Diogo do Couto is known to historians; his *Décadas*, which I think it safe to say are better known, were more widely circulated. That circumstance may now change with the publication of this translation.

Nevertheless, this work caused a sensation and was responsible for the creation of a "black legend" surrounding the Portuguese empire in general and Portuguese Asia in particular. By "black legend" I mean that many a historian has pointed to this work as proof positive that the Portuguese were inept, corrupt, and inefficient in administering their empire. Such scholars argue that this explains how the Dutch, Omanis, British, and everyone else were able to wrestle pieces of it away from them. In that sense, it has a parallel with Bartolomé de las Casas's work, *Breve relación de la destucción de las Indias,* first published in 1552, which was used by Spain's enemies to "prove" Spanish cruelty and greed in their conquest of the New World, not to mention their culpability in the destruction of native peoples and civilizations. This is the famous "black legend" attributed to Spain by the Dutch and British, a legend that continues to rear its head here and there in works written about colonial Latin America, in spite of all the path-breaking research done on the spread of disease as part of the "Columbian exchange." Couto's work has been responsible for a similar amount of misinformation and a distorted understanding of the Portuguese in Asia.

O Soldado Prático was selected for translation in this series for several reasons. Most importantly, it is a classic work in the literature of the Portuguese overseas. As far as I can tell, it has never been translated, so this translation will greatly expand its readership. The work also contains an enormous amount of information about Portuguese Asia that will not be found in any other source. And the best way to kill a black legend is to confront it at its source, laying out the facts for everyone to examine and debate: this is another important reason for its selection.

This work stands in sharp contrast to another written around the same time, the epic poem *The Lusiads* by Luís de Camões. Camões and Couto were friends, and in many ways the two works are intertwined. Camões's work praises the Portuguese in their exploits and compares them to the ancient gods. Manuel Rodrigues Lapa, one of the scholars who studied and edited this work in the early twentieth century, hit the nail on the head when he said:

> *The Veteran Soldier* is one of the most honored works in Portuguese literature. It should be read after *The Lusiadas*. The two friends, Camões and Couto, created two complementary works. One sings the praise of ancient glories of the fatherland, completely oblivious to his present day. The other is an unvarnished exposé of the decadence of that time and shows us the country and empire buried in a quagmire of scandal. In this (latter) work by Couto, the love of truth is a type of vice. His hard life as a soldier taught him to face it with the same indifferent serenity that he views death. This gives the work its great value.[1]

Comments on the Translation

This work was written during the last half of the sixteenth century, and Couto tinkered with corrections and additions for another twenty years or more. The manuscript from which this translation is based is dated 1612, and parts of it were drafted by Couto himself. Because he wrote this work partially in an effort to demonstrate his education in the classics, not only is it filled with references to antiquity, but also the style of his writing is characterized by the formal, educated language of his day. As the reader will quickly note, the format is that of a conversation among three people, a common literary framework at the time. In reality, however, the work is a monologue by the veteran soldier with occasional interjections from a nobleman and crown official. My effort has been to translate this work into modern colloquial English that is readily understandable to university-level students or the general reading public, with minimal reference to footnotes (though there are a number of them) and no need for outside reading. This has been quite a task, first to translate a Portuguese work written four hundred years ago into modern English, and then to make it readable. My guiding thought at all times was to convey what Couto meant rather than produce a literal translation. Sometimes this was easy. For example, when an English expression yields more or less the same idea as a Portuguese one, such the phrase, "the apple does not fall far from the tree"—an English idiom that appears as well in the Portuguese. Sometimes my task was more challenging. One of Couto's favorite constructions was the double negative. A good example of this occurs in the first section, scene 9, paragraph 11: "This is really a curse of the Portuguese that someone who is not a member of the nobility is not listened to or appointed to do anything." That sentence now reads: "This is really a curse of the Portuguese that commoners are ignored and never appointed to do anything." Couto's incomplete phrases and unclear references also made the translation a challenge. For example, in the first part, scene 10, paragraph 70, where Couto's narrator says, "I believe that man of the Danube when he spoke before the Roman Senate," we can only guess that he was referring to Julius Caesar. In the third part, scene 1, paragraph 3, I had to assume that Couto omitted a word when he wrote, "They enter Goa's harbor with so much celebratory cannon fire that no one could hear it," and I therefore altered the text to read, "that even the deaf can hear it." My task was to unravel what Couto wanted to say and then state it clearly.

Naturally, some of Couto's vocabulary would not be used or is rare today. One of his favorite words, "vituperative," for example, occurs rarely in the twenty-first century. I use it here and there but also replaced it with "denigrate" or "harshly criticize." Couto also had nothing but disdain for the underlings who were at the beck and call of the high and mighty. I used a variety of terms for these folk: toadies, lackeys, stooges, and so on. Finally, there is the usual problem of altering Portuguese syntax to make it sound like English. The Portuguese language is fond of very long sentences, often with numerous interrelated clauses and phrases that would never be allowed in English. All these had to be trimmed and refashioned.

The work opens with a "cover letter" to the Count of Salinas and Ribadeo, a member of the Council of State. His position gave him the ear of King Dom Philip III, and he was obviously someone in whom Couto placed a great deal of trust and hope. In the letter, Couto refers to his veteran soldier (the protagonist), who is about to tell the count things he will hear from no one else, and emphasizes how important it is to listen to this unique voice. What follows is the work in three parts, divided into a total of twenty scenes. Each of these is focused on one general subject, although Couto's text wanders here and there and frequently inserts long passages that are only loosely related to his theme.

Regarding the corruption, greed, and fraud surrounding him in Portuguese Asia, Couto told the truth as he saw it. The economic power of Portuguese Asia probably peaked before 1612, and the world Couto was witnessing was one in economic, political, and especially moral decline. This is one of the many aspects that make his work so compelling. Couto was well placed to know more than the average soldier, as the crown official frequently comments, since he was the first director of the state archives in Goa. As a result, he was sitting on top of the documentation needed to prove his charges of misadministration, which he claimed were common practices throughout the Estado da Índia. Not too surprisingly, he had a number of enemies, and the manuscript was stolen several times, as were manuscripts of his *Décadas* for the same reasons. Yet Couto never tired of the effort and sent several versions of the *Dialog* for publication.

Was Couto correct? Was the Portuguese Asian Empire nothing if not corrupt, a world where fraud ruled supreme? Such was probably not the case in reality; while it is true that Portuguese India was in decline, the Portuguese were likely no more or less corrupt than others around them, as Pearson discusses in the foreword to this volume. I believe the real issue at stake here is Couto's personality and his sense of moral outrage. I think it is fair to say he was telling us what he really believed. He appears to have been one of those rare, idealistic individuals who was truly shocked and offended that people are promoted and favored because of their connections rather than their merit. He was quick to point out that pampered lackeys obtained prized positions, while hardworking, educated, and meritorious individuals (such as himself) were left behind. So it was for Couto in the sixteenth century, and so it is in our own day. One of the many ironies of this work is that if Couto had been awarded a plum position or generous favors (which he points out repeatedly were given to friends of the viceroys), we would never have been given this detailed account of graft, corruption, and decadence in Portuguese Asia. The one consolation that he might relish is that the "pampered lackeys and nobodies" of his day have long since been forgotten, while his name and publications have endured for centuries.

Relatedly, it bears remembering that Couto deliberately paraded his education in the classics in front of his intended audience. To the modern reader, his classical allusions can be tedious and might appear to be unrelated to his main points, but they are not. He both underlines his arguments by saying (in so many words), "I know what I am talking about because I have an education in the classics," and he reminds his audience that his skills have never fully been appreciated. In addition, his use of classical examples generally contrasts the noble and selfless actions of figures in antiquity with the greed and corruption of the present rulers of Portuguese Asia. I have added brief footnotes to provide the reader with a frame of reference for the lesser known person, work, or incident in question.

This work has three modern editions in Portuguese, all of which were consulted for this translation. The classic edition of *O Soldado Prático* in Portuguese is that edited by M. Rodrigues Lapa, first completed in 1937 and reprinted several times since. A second edited version was completed by Reis Brasil and published in 2008. Most recently, a new scholarly edition was completed by Ana María García Martín and published by Angelus Novus in 2009. All three versions of Couto's work were helpful in preparing this translation. Comments in the footnotes are coded RL for items noted in the Rodrigues Lapa edition, RB for the Reis Brasil edition, and GM for García Martín. The original work has very long paragraphs that are not numbered. In this edition I have borrowed the convention used by RL and RB and numbered paragraphs for easy reference. In the original, chapter headings appear before only the first nine scenes. I have added headings to all twenty not only to make it easier to find specific topics but because in earlier versions of this work Couto provided them for each scene. Perhaps he wrote this version in haste and overlooked this detail. Finally, the letter in the appendix from Matias de Albuquerque is not part of the original work but has been added to provide the reader with a contrasting voice in this tale of greed and corruption.

As the reader will appreciate, translating works written at the time of the King James Bible is challenging. Obviously, I am responsible for any errors or linguistic detours that may appear. I am very grateful to João Vicente Melo (Department d'Humanitats, Universitat Pompeu Fabra, Barcelona), who carefully read the original text and my translation and made numerous helpful comments and suggestions. My co-editor in this series, Timothy

Walker, carefully read my final draft; his editing has made my text much easier to read. I have no doubt that future translations of this work will amend and correct any mistakes I may have made. On two occasions, my students at the College of Charleston in History 350: The Portuguese Empire also assisted me by reading and commenting on drafts of this work. By incorporating their feedback, I trust the text will be clearer, and for their efforts I am most grateful. My copyeditor at the University Press of New England, Bronwyn Becker, helpfully forced me to clarify problematic passages. I also want to send a special *obrigado* to Frank Sousa, director of the Saab-Pedroso Center for Portuguese Culture and Research at the University of Massachusetts Lowell. Frank immediately appreciated the importance of this project and was instrumental in getting it started. I also deeply appreciate the support of the Calouste Gulbenkian Foundation, which made this project possible.

Glossary of Foreign and Archaic English Terms

almude	liquid measurement of about 17 liters
alqueire	measurement used for dry goods of 25 to 33 pounds
arroba	unit of weight of 32 pounds
bahar	Indian measure of weight, varied by region between 141 and 330 kilos
bazaruco	a small coin made of different metals used in Portuguese Asia
breeches	men's shorts that came to the knee
candil (plural *candis*)	unit of measure of 20 *alqueires* or approximately 500 pounds; also a gold coin worth 400 *réis*
cartaz	safe-conduct pass issued by the Portuguese directing a ship's captain to trade in a Portuguese-controlled city
Casa dos Contos	chief accounting house
chatim	Indian merchant
corja	a unit of 20

cruzado	during Couto's lifetime, a *cruzado* was a silver coin minted in Portugal worth 400 *réis*
dobra	a Portuguese gold coin
doublet	a snug men's long-sleeved jacket that buttons up the front
drachma	name of ancient as well as modern Greek currency
escudo	name of the Portuguese currency in the twentieth century before the introduction of the Euro; in this text, it might refer to the Spanish gold coin of that name introduced in 1537
factory	a place where goods are stored before shipment; merchants might also live there
factor	head of a factory
fardo	a unit of weight of 42 pounds
jerkin	a sleeveless leather, metal, or cloth vest often worn over a doublet
larim (plural *larins*)	silver coin used in Persia and the Persian Gulf worth 60 to 100 *réis*; so called because it was originally minted in the Persian city of Lara
legatus, legatus legionis	general of the Roman Empire
libra	a unit of weight of one pound and a Roman coin
mangelim (plural *mangelins*)	a unit of weight of about a karat used for precious stones, especially diamonds
marco	eight ounces of gold or silver
mina	an Attican coin
mitical	weight and money used in East Africa or approximately 75 grams
nummus (plural *nummi*)	a Roman copper coin of low value

pardau	name used for two coins in Portuguese Asia, the gold *pardau* was worth 6 *tangas* or 360 *réis*; the silver *pardau* was worth 5 *tangas* or 300 *réis*.
pataca (plural *patacões*)	coins minted in Hormuz
pate cloth	a cloth made of silk and cotton
quintal	unit of weight of about 128 pounds
real (plural *réis*)	a small copper coin of little value
robaz (plural *robazes*)	Singhalese word for a specific gemstone (type unknown)
sestertii	ancient Roman coins
talent	an ancient unit of weight and a measure of used for coins as well the coin itself
tanga	silver or copper coin used in Portuguese Asia, Persia, and central Asia valued at 60 *réis*.
tostão	a silver coin worth 100 *réis*
xerafim (plural *xerafins*)	coins minted in Goa worth approximately 300 *réis*.

Maps Showing Places Mentioned in the Text

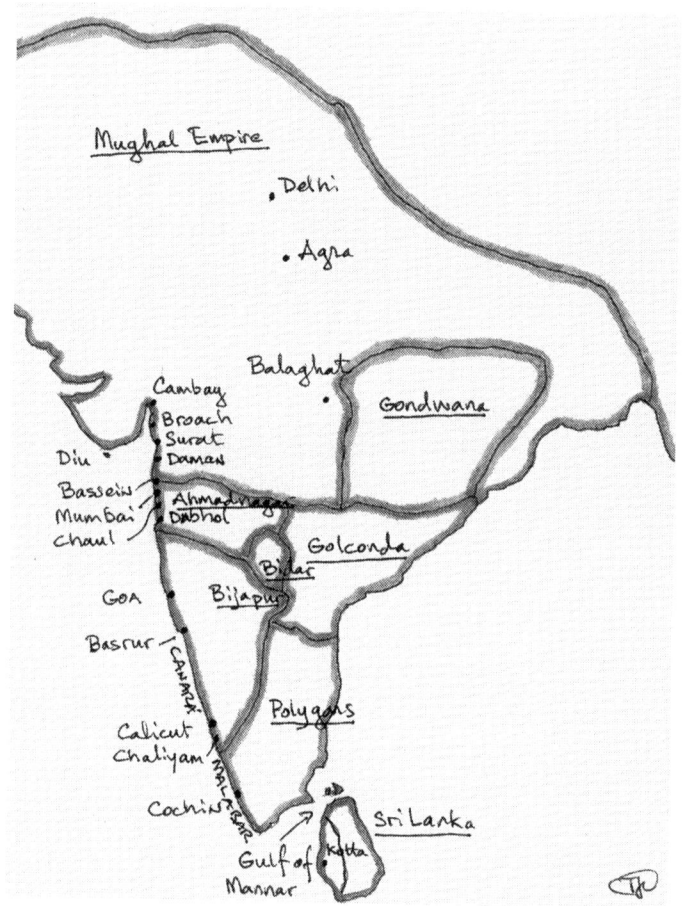

MAP 2. The Indian subcontinent ca. 1600, showing places mentioned in the text. Map drawn by Timothy Coates based on Charles Joppen's *Historical Atlas of India*, published in London in 1907.

MAP 3. The Eastern Indian Ocean, Straits of Malacca, and South China Sea, showing places mentioned in the text. Map drawn by Timothy Coates.

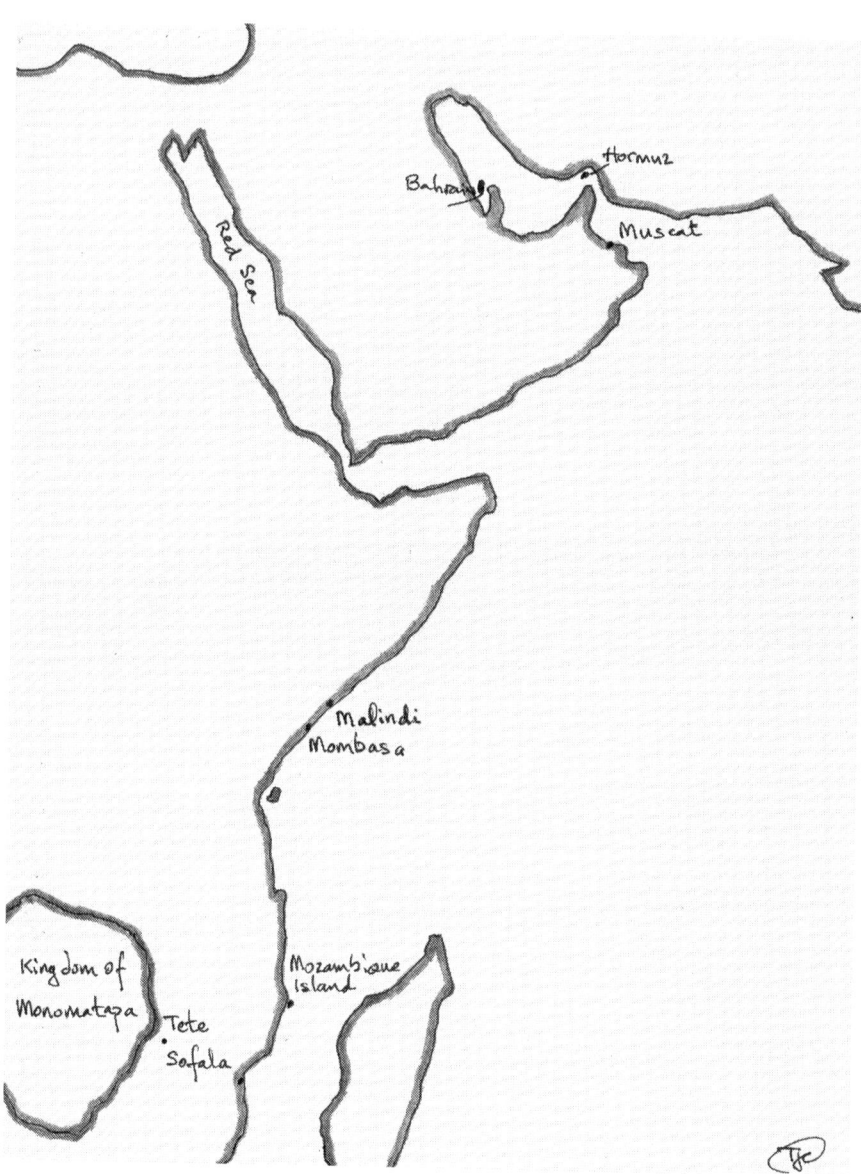

MAP 4. The Western Indian Ocean and East Coast of Africa, showing the kingdom of Mutapa and other sites mentioned in the text. Map drawn by Timothy Coates.

Viceroys and Governors of Portuguese Asia, 1505–1612

NAME	DATES SERVED
Dom Francisco de Almeida	1505–1509
Afonso de Albuquerque	1509–1515
Lopo Soares de Albergaria	1515–1518
Diogo Lopes de Sequeira	1518–1522
Dom Duarte de Menezes	1522–1524
Dom Vasco da Gama	1524
Dom Henrique de Menezes	1525–1526
Lopo Vaz de Sampaio	1526–1529
Nuno da Cunha	1529–1538
Dom Garcia de Noronha	1538–1540
Dom Estêvão da Gama	1540–1542
Martim Afonso de Sousa	1542–1545
Dom João de Castro	1545–1548
Garcia de Sá	1548–1549
Jorge Cabral	1549–1550
Dom Afonso de Noronha	1550–1554
Dom Pedro Mascarenhas	1554–1555
Francisco Barreto	1555–1558
Dom Constantino de Braganza	1558–1561
Dom Francisco Coutinho	1561–1564
João de Mendonça	1564
Dom António de Noronha	1564–1568
Luís de Ataíde	1568–1571
Dom António de Noronha	1571–1573
António Moniz Barreto	1573–1576
Dom Diogo de Menezes	1576–1578

Dom Luís de Ataíde	1578–1581
Fernão Teles de Menezes	1581
Francisco de Mascarenhas	1581–1584
Dom Duarte de Menezes	1584–1588
Dom Manuel de Sousa Coutinho	1588–1591
Matias de Albuquerque	1591–1597
Dom Francisco da Gama	1597–1600
Aires de Saldanha	1600–1605
Martim Afonso de Castro	1605–1607
Aleixo de Meneses	1607–1609
André Furtado de Mendonça	1609
Rui Lourenço da Távora	1609–1612

NOTE

1. M. Rodrigues Lapa, *O Soldado Prático* (Lisbon, 1937), 10–11.

*Dialog of a Veteran Soldier
Discussing the Frauds and Realities
of Portuguese India*

Diogo do Couto
CHRONICLER AND DIRECTOR OF THE
ARCHIVES OF PORTUGUESE INDIA

❖

Letter to the Count of Salinas and Ribadeo, the Duke of Vila Franca, and a Member of His Majesty's Supreme Council of State

T HAT WELL-KNOWN and eloquent Captain Alcibiades from Athens, in order to upstage and denigrate the Silenus games, which honored the obscene figure of Bacchus, organized an alternate set of games, which were later called the Silenus of Alcibiades.[1] These new games, in contrast to the older ones conducted under vulgar and rustic images, were performed under new statues made with great skill, discipline, and creativity; these were traits held in high esteem by the ancient Greeks.

In the same way, this poor soldier or humble servant [that is, the main figure in this work] who appears at Your Excellency's feet is such a simple and shabby figure that he might irritate those who pass him by. Examine him, Your Excellency, without judging him by his clothing, and you will find a great deal of political and moral insight, many examples, and much truth under that rustic exterior. He discusses many things that, if they were implemented would establish a society like the one just mentioned. It would be as prosperous and joyful as ancient Athens, which in the same manner, Alcibiades reformed and reorganized to reach the peak of its perfection.

For all that Your Excellency wishes to know, listen to what this veteran soldier tells you in a calm manner, without flattery or emotion. I am certain that he will answer your questions because you will hear things from him that you may not have heard from the mouths of other soldiers. He desires

---

1. Bacchus or Dionysus was a pagan god closely associated with wine. Alcibiades (ca. 450–404 BCE) was an Athenian statesman, orator and general. Silenus was a creature in Greek mythology also associated with wine. He was very smart and could reveal secrets to humans.

no more from the sufferings he had in this life than to be listened to by Your Excellency, because then you will know that the problems of which he complains can be corrected.

May the Lord protect Your Excellency and grant you a long life so that you might address the needs of this soldier and others.

Goa, January 2, 1612
Diogo do Couto

THE FIRST PART

A NOBLEMAN WHO WAS governor of India is present in the house of a crown official when a veteran soldier who served there arrives to present his petition and supporting papers [to request a pension or position in honor of his service to the crown].[1] The three have the following conversation:

SCENE 1
The Importance of Secrecy

1. Soldier: Now my request cannot fail to have a successful conclusion, as it has this great beginning of encountering Your Excellency here and now in this house. I trust that I can count on Your Excellency to support my claims of royal service to this crown official. I am really all by myself here in Portugal and have no other means except these documents to prove my many years of service and the numerous deeds that I accomplished in India. These were frequently accompanied by the spilling of my blood, shed for my faith and my king, which I do not regret. If I fail to be rewarded in this life for my deeds, up in Heaven there is one with a very generous hand who will compensate more than all the kings on earth.

2. Nobleman: How happy I am to see you here in Portugal away from that Tower of Babel [in Goa]. I know for sure that you will receive a glowing acknowledgment and generous payment for your age and services without needing to pull any strings or ask for special favors. After the king our lord appointed Your Excellency to sort through these petitions and determine their merits, it is only necessary to present your service papers and documentation. Those days are over when rewards were handed out because of favoritism or having friends in the right places. The hearts of kings are in God's hands. This is why His Majesty made the wise decision to appoint

---

[1]. The nobleman became governor of India by emergency appointment, probably at the death of the viceroy.

His Excellency [the crown official] to help those in need. My influence is not needed, and your services cannot help but be very well rewarded.

3. But now that you come here, have a seat and let us discuss what we did in India. Because of your many years' experience there and your knowledge of the people and events, I am sure you can provide a clear perspective with the independence and directness of an old hand. You are not afraid to speak your mind and are not trying flatter anyone for a reward.

4. Soldier: I kiss the hands of Your Excellency for such a great honor and the high opinion you have of me. Now all my years of travel and wanderings can be of use; I deserve to be included in this conversation.

5. Crown Official: Until now I have been quiet because I did not want to interrupt you, sir, and because I have been examining you. I have been observing your white hair, your age, facial expressions, and other characteristics. You appear different from many of the other soldiers who have come before me with their papers. You are different even from those with similar calm attitude and manner who seem to think that any assistance for their business affairs will be a long time in coming. This causes them to cast off their honor and merit and present their cases with such agitation and furor as if they were fighting their enemies. Instead of listening and responding to them, I avoid eye contact and look here and there for a place to focus my eyes to shield myself from their ranting and ravings.

6. Soldier: I can only tell you what I have seen and nothing more. When the soldiers are very deserving—I mean, because they go around until this day with such bad luck and exhausted by their many interactions with officials—they do not know what to do. Once a soldier accumulates sufficient savings, he leaves India. He brings enough to tide him over from one sailing to the next so he can return, and he finds that his petitions are answered very slowly.[2] He gets really desperate when he remembers he is in a place where he has no one to help him. Some of the money he borrowed from his

---

2. The annual sailing from Goa to Lisbon departed in December or January and arrived between June and September, depending on events along the way. The return voyage from Lisbon normally embarked the following spring, during the second half of March or early April, and arrived in Goa after six or seven months, again depending on events. Thus, at top speed and with the best of luck, a soldier could make the round-trip voyage in just under two years. From Diogo do Couto, *O Soldado Prático*, ed. Ana María García Martín (Coimbra: Angelus Novus, 2009), 62n14; hereafter GM.

friends in order to present these petitions goes to the Casa da India because of the greed of the bureaucrats, who even charge taxes on the shirt that he wears on his back.[3] In the past, these things went very well for the soldiers because the bureaucrats never messed around with the items they brought in their trunks. They brought a *quintal* of cloves, two of cinnamon, and other little things; some of it was spent in presenting their petitions.[4] Nowadays, they cannot see when they will be rewarded. They will either die of hunger here in Portugal or be forced to abandon everything and return to India without obtaining an answer. They really fear this infamous chain of events, which is pitiful when it happens. They dare not appear when called before the judge at the stated time because they think the reward will be a tiny sum or they do not think they will receive any pension at all. Everything is entrusted to the crown official, the one who slowed down the entire process. He should really be asking God's pardon as much for not readily giving a man what is rightfully his as well as for insulting his honor by making him return to India without a reward or an answer. I do not say this to make excuses for their actions but to draw attention to the misery and misfortunes that I have seen many of these fellows endure.

7. Crown Official: I am happy to hear your thoughts about this business, and you, sir, have spoken directly to the issues we were discussing. I will forgive the actions of those who have presented petitions to me until now. Since we have started discussing this business, I would like to continue our discussion for a bit, because it will help me in many things. By the way, those young lads over there should leave because much of this needs to be discussed by the Council, and its members should not hear it first from the mouths of boys.[5]

---

3. The Casa da India was the headquarters of the bureaucracy administering Portuguese Asia and its commercial hub. It was a large building located in Lisbon near the main docks.

4. Cloves (from the Molucca Islands in eastern Indonesia) and cinnamon (from Sri Lanka) were two of the most profitable spices traded by the Portuguese in Asia. Nutmeg was also valuable, while pepper was a royal monopoly. Spices were ideal for long-distance transport since they were lightweight, compact, and very valuable.

5. The kings had a number of councils to advise them on different matters such as finances, overseas colonies, etc. In 1612, the Council of State and the Council of Portugal would have advised King Dom Philip III on Portuguese matters.

8. Soldier: Nothing would please me more, since this entire evening I have been thinking about the general lack of secrecy in India. This applies to serious decisions about war as well as those regarding the administration of justice and finances. The meetings have only just concluded when their secret decisions are the stuff of gossip all over town. There is nothing more important to me right now. Even when the case is in the judge's court ready for public announcing, one knows who will be sentenced. I will add even one more thing: a High Court justice will not decide on a case until his servant receives a bribe under the table. I saw this several times, and I think this is the worst sort of injustice one could see in his lifetime.

9. Crown Official: God help me! You know that when these things happen everything falls apart—especially regarding warfare. One's enemy wants more than anything to know what his enemy is planning. This is the only path to victory. When this happens, nothing good can come of it.

10. Soldier: It is too bad but this is exactly the situation. The Samorin of Calicut, the Shah of Bijapur, all the rulers of the petty kingdoms of India, and everybody else know right away whatever decisions were made in Council.[6] They also know the details of the orders for the fleet going to Malabar and other places.[7] Numerous disasters have occurred because of this. In Dabhol and Surat, they know all about the fleet looking for ships on its way to and from Mecca and the Red Sea, as well as the timing of its arrival and departure.[8] If they can launch their ships and not get caught, they do so. If they cannot, they recall them and hide them along the shore to shelter them from attack. We make all the effort and incur expenses only to have our reputation suffer.

11. What really takes the cake is the habit of some of the nobles of the Council. They have a hobby of ridiculing each other: "So and so speaks the

---

6. Calicut was a rival coastal kingdom south of Goa; Bijapur was a Muslim kingdom not far from Goa with which the Portuguese traded (see map 2). The same councils in Portugal were duplicated in India to advise the viceroys.

7. Malabar is the name for the southwestern coastal region of India and the numerous petty kingdoms located there. Today it forms the Indian state of Kerala (see map 2).

8. Dabhol was an important trading center located between Goa and Mumbai. Surat is located north of Mumbai and was also important for trade. During the sixteenth and parts of the seventeenth centuries, the Portuguese sent fleets into the Red Sea in an effort to enforce a monopoly on trade in the greater Indian Ocean region.

truth, so and so does not," they say. They create intrigue, and they always agree with the opinion of whoever voted first. In this way, their human shortcomings are dragged into the palace. They ignore how much better it would be to uncover what is going on.

12. By reading the ancient philosophers, it is possible to see how highly they regarded maintaining secrecy. Athenians reserved the harshest penalties in their laws for those who violated secrecy. This was of such importance to them that when they were at war with Philip of Macedonia, they came upon some letters he had written to his wife Olympias.[9] They returned them unopened and did not tamper with them, despite knowing that if they opened them, they might have learned something helpful. However, they valued secrecy more than victory.

13. Diodorus Siculus writes that among the ancient Egyptians, it was a crime to uncover a secret.[10] He provides an example of a priest who saw another priest with a virgin in the Temple of Isis. This second priest trusted the first one, but all the men who had concubines were killed, as was the law. The one who discovered the secret was exiled for life. Anaxilus, the Athenian captain, when captured by the Spartans, was tortured in an effort to discover what course of action King Agesilaus had decided.[11] He responded that they could hack him to pieces, but his king's secrets they would never know.

14. The Athenians were such sticklers in guarding their secrets that Plutarch recounts in his work *De Exilio*, that an Egyptian walking down a street in Athens with something underneath his cloak was asked by an Athenian what he was carrying.[12] The Egyptian answered, "You are an Athenian, and you are asking me that? Can you not see that I am carrying something covered by my cape so that you will not know what it is?" A great believer in secrecy was Demosthenes.[13] When a friend asked him why he had bad breath, he answered, "Because many secrets are rotting in my stomach."

---

9. Philip II, king of Macedonia, lived from 382 to 336 BCE. Olympias (375–316 BCE) was one of his wives and the mother of Alexander the Great.

10. Greek historian who wrote a *Universal History* in forty volumes between the years 60 and 30 BCE.

11. Agesilaus II (401–360 BCE) was king of Sparta during the Corinthian War.

12. Plutarch (46–120 BCE) was a famous Greek historian and philosopher who lived from 46 to 120 BCE.

13. Greek statesman and orator of ancient Athens (384–322 BCE).

15. The philosopher Pythagoras instructed his students during their first two years to maintain silence in order to keep secrets.¹⁴ He believed there was nothing higher in philosophy than golden silence and guarding secrets. When the great Plato arrived at the home of Dionysius of Syracuse,¹⁵ his companion Abrias asked what he was doing. He answered that he was painting. When the king became aware of this, he had Abrias's head cut off because Abrias had discovered Dionysius's secret.

16. The philosopher Philippides decided to serve King Lysimachus on the condition that he did not want to know any of the king's secrets.¹⁶ He understood after serving in Lysimachus's guard that secrecy was a divine thing. It is of such importance that it is critical for our redemption. In the secrecy of confession, God Our Lord grants us the treasures and wealth of His glory. Only by way of this secret can we rise to see those greater things seen by the glorious Saint Paul. Eyes cannot see these, ears cannot hear them, and men's hearts cannot imagine them.¹⁷

17. Nowadays in India, as well as here in Portugal, Pythagoras has no disciples who keep silent. Everything is announced with clanging bells. Secret decisions made in Council are announced in public squares with trumpets and many similar things are done like this. The worst is the malicious gossip of wickedness, adulterous affairs, lewdness, scandal, and roguery. The very people who commit these acts are the ones who spread the gossip. When the captain, nobleman, I do not know if even the viceroy decides to dishonor a married woman, he goes around boasting about it for the entire world to know. He tells everyone about that young maiden and the affair he had with her under the pretext of marriage; then everyone in the main square knows all about it. He boasts how he fooled a rich widow with the same promise of marriage and the foolish man who was duped with a promise to marry his daughter. Immediately afterward, he walks around in the streets, showing the money he was given. He spreads the news of his

---

14. Greek philosopher and mathematician (570–495 BCE).

15. Dionysius II of Syracuse (397–343 BCE).

16. Lysimachus was a general under Alexander the Great and later king of Thrace (306–281 BCE).

17. 1 Corinthians 2:9, "But as it is written, eye hath not seen, nor ear heard, neither have entered into the heart of man, the things which God hath prepared for them that love him."

own secrets and misdeeds. These acts become his honor and nobility, while virtue and good behavior are weaknesses.

18. Now Your Graces can wonder how God can show his mercy to a land such as this. Now that I have discussed this, I would like to ask your permission to change the subject from the lack of secrecy to some other things that now come to mind. These are issues that I have noticed and are prejudicial to royal interests and to the general good of all.

19. The king orders an official inquiry and report on all his officials of justice, ministers, and captains of forts in India at the end of their terms of office. He has further ordered that these reports be sent to him sealed and held in the highest secrecy possible. As soon as these reports are started, those who fear the truth know who will be giving evidence and what they will say. They then speak ill of those who they believed testified against them, forcing the witnesses to change their testimony to favor them. Everything in India is judged by evidence. They then round up new statements from the high and mighty. These carry more weight and thus the inquiry is derailed. Or, in some cases when only suspicious testimonies are given, they then begin a second inquiry, which will void the first, and the individual is [judged] blameless and gets off the hook. Those men who gave testimony are despised, and whenever the powerful can take their revenge on those who gave statements, they do so.

20. Another example: a viceroy completes his term of office and returns to Portugal. The king orders someone with a solid reputation to conduct an inquiry on his performance while in office. If there is some secret contained within the report, something that happens infrequently, here in Portugal they are not any better. By one means or another, one of the viceroy's close friends is able to read the statements, and the cat is out of the bag. There have been viceroys who took revenge on those who testified against them. I knew several. Worse still, there were some viceroys who wrote to their friends in India saying, "So-and-so testified saying such-and-such, and so-and-so said this and that, but now I have my hands on them."

21. This is why so few men in India want to provide official testimonies; at least, I always avoided giving them. Two things I always avoided: first, publicly saying anything negative about the viceroys, and, second, providing any testimony about them. I lived by the expression about how to live in peace: "Your king—never offend nor give testimony against him."

22. Finally, I would like to conclude with one piece of advice. If I had the authority to do so, I would suggest to the king that he not order these inquiries for two reasons. It would avoid all these deceptions and intrigues; in addition, there are never any charges made against the guilty. They always go free. Only God knows how they avoid punishment.

23. Crown Official: I really enjoyed listening to all this from you. There is much substance in what you say. However, I have only this to say about the viceroys, High Court judges, captains, and other officials who are well paid will have another sort of payment in the afterlife. However, we have seen only a few embezzle the income from their positions as governors and captains. If they only had themselves to support here in Portugal, there in India they have to provide for many, who have to eat. [Yet] they do not put down roots there, and they leave no estates in India. I do not know where those many hundreds of thousands of *cruzados* disappear, the money that some bring back after holding these positions. It would appear that the Devil takes it all. Some die having taken nothing, and others live in poverty.

24. Nobleman: What you say is golden because the money from India seems to evaporate. We never see it. I want to jump in to this conversation at this point, because I have no idea where the money went that I made at my fortress and from the brief time I governed India.

25. Soldier: It is bewitched money that is transformed into lumps of charcoal. The rest of it returns from where it came. The apple does not fall far from the tree. It came by way of Hell, and by the same way it returns. The rest of it is the blood of innocents, and like the money that was paid for the son of God, it only bought a piece of worthless land used as a tomb for the dead and a nest for insects. In the same way, these others will never see inheritances come from their money. All of it will go to the graveyard, to disappear in worms and dirt. That is where most of them will end up.

26. Crown Official: We may as well drop this, as these people are adjusted to life there. There is nothing more to say, and when there is no remedy, it is then best to remain silent.

27. Soldier: Does Your Excellency really think there are no remedies? One day while I was visiting a monastery, a nobleman was also visiting. He was about to take over one of the most lucrative fortresses in all of India. He came to say goodbye. During his conversation with the brothers there, one of them said to him:

"Sir, you should remember that you are about to enter into royal service for the king, who has rewarded your deeds. In this you may gain entry into Heaven as I can by wearing this habit. With this, be content with what is yours and give to the poor and be just."

The nobleman answered, "O father, I will do what the other captains have done. If they have gone to Hell, then I will be their companion because I only go to my fortress to make my fortune." The priest refrained from repeating any more of the conversation, and he insisted that the nobleman was joking; but I swear that is what he said. The Devil took him away a couple of days later.

28. Crown Official: God save me! Such jokes are in very poor taste. With issues of the soul, we cannot take risks because the price to be paid is too high.

29. Nobleman: We will leave the soul alone. But I think he was correct in wanting to make as much money as possible because, when a gentleman returns to this country smelling of poverty, no one will look him in the face. It is better to return wealthy because then the world is your oyster, as they say. You find everything to be easy, people ask you for things, and you lack nothing. Everything that you desire comes to you. This is the nature of money, along with many other things about which I will remain silent. In brief, life is good when you are wealthy.

30. Soldier: Having a lot of money is not wealth. Wealth is found in heroic, virtuous acts and deeds; these should be the objects of desire before all others.

31. Crown Official: We have been greatly sidetracked from the original subject matter where we began, with appointments and instructions for the men. That is why, for my sake, I ask you, old hand, to return to that subject. Everything that you wish to discuss, do so with a frank and calm manner as if I were not here. Just like all people, we cannot do everything. There is no human who is so perfect that he does not make mistakes. The rulings from wise judges and the advice of experienced men allow us royal officials to have a better understanding of things of which we are sometimes unaware, because we have neither seen nor heard about them.

32. Soldier: That is the way it is, sir! From this springs the reality that kings are not aware of many important things regarding the good gover-

nance of their kingdoms. They do not see because they cannot be everywhere, and they do not discuss these matters with those who are experienced. What the kings really need are people to speak truthfully about these issues. The same thing should happen to them as happened to a king of Antioch. One night he got lost and arrived unrecognized at the home of a peasant. They began to talk about the king and all his shortcomings. The next day, his servants arrived with all the royal trappings of his office, and he would not allow them to put them on him, saying, "As long as no one recognizes me, I will be able to find someone to tell me the truth!" Just about always, royal authority either makes a person anxious about saying what he really thinks or makes him think the king will find him to be a fool. The truth can be bothersome in court, and the custom of those who do not speak it freely is to also not react to it.

33. Nobleman: That is the way it is. Do you know how this began? It started from men wanting to live for themselves and not thinking of others.

34. Soldier: I put the blame at the kings' feet because they came to prefer the company of flatterers to that of philosophers and wise men. If it were not so, we would see many examples of court favorites treated as Alexander the Great dealt with a philosopher who was frequently with him. Since the philosopher never reproached him for anything, Alexander told him:

> I am a man and because of that I will make many mistakes. You, as a philosopher, never rebuke or advise me in any way. You either do not understand my mistakes or if you do understand them, you are not my friend because you deceive me by not pointing them out. You need to leave since I do not wish to be served by you.

35. Crown Official: But if the kings did this, who would serve them?

36. Soldier: The many who would tell them the truth. When the court favorites realized that the king was irritated with flatterers, they would change their tunes and fall in line. Men usually become friends because they share the same interests. This was the case with Emperor Aurelian, who was so fond of drinking red wine.[18] Torcato also only drank red wine and planted his vineyards with grapes for red wine. This made the emperor so happy

---

18. Emperor Aurelian (214–275 CE), general and emperor of Rome the last five years of his life.

that he made Torcato the censor of Rome and guard of the Salaria Gate.[19] It is only necessary to tell the king the truth, and court favorites will realize that he wants to hear it. Then he will do for them what the emperor did for Torcato.

37. Nobleman: You are a bit mistaken in this because kings are conscious of their positions and thus are good friends of truth. They always appreciate those who speak it to them. However, if what you want to say is something else that I understand, it is not appropriate to discuss.

38. Soldier: I would say it was my error if my intention were to blame the royal personage, except for this business of tolerating flatterers and not attending to that aspect of his position. The ancient Athenians, according to Plutarch's *Life of Theseus*, called kings *anaces*, those whose prudence and vigilance guided many important matters. As a result, they were obliged to rule with such moderation and providence that they acted with nothing but goodness and virtue.

39. Others claim that this is not the derivation of the word "king"; rather it comes from a similar word that describes the sublime height of the stars ruled by the laws of nature and which attain the height of the heavens. In ancient Greek, this sublime height is called *anékas*, and *anékathen* is to act in a lofty manner. Thus the king is called "king" because divine grace has placed him at the top of humanity. Lowly and base things should not degrade his thoughts. Instead he should remember that he is in a morally upright place and be ever vigilant for virtue and honesty. He should do this to provide an example of complete honesty, faith, and other virtues for his subjects. They can gaze upon him as if looking into a very clear mirror that reflects everything perfectly with no dark spots. The king should also remember that his exalted position, above all others, demands that he should be equally vigilant to avoid saying anything unworthy of Heaven. Because of his high position, he should demonstrate that his character is closer to Heaven than to the lowliness of peasants.

40. This is not an original thought of mine. Rather, this is what many renowned philosophers say about this. When I said that the fault was with the kings, which I now say again, it is only in the sense that they fail to insist

---

19. The censor of Rome was in charge of conducting the census and supervising public morality. The Salaria Gate was one of the main entrances into Rome.

that those who speak freely to them speak honestly. This is the obligation of loyal subjects. Those who the king places in positions of authority and who have all the weight of government placed upon them are bound by the same obligations as the king has on his dignity, as I have just said. Because of this, his officials should be careful how they act. In conducting their business, they should act with the same truth and love that the king is obliged to show his subjects, who so frequently face the mouths of cannons, arrows, cannon balls, hunger, cold, and three hundred other misfortunes they daily encounter in his service.

41. This was the example provided by Jesus Christ when he ascended to his father. At that time, he entrusted his ministry to his disciples. They acted as if God were still among them, giving life to the dead, sight to the blind, speech to the mute, and providing all the other wonders of their master. In this manner, they became gods. This is what the crown official must do; he must act as if he were king, since in doing so he fulfills his obligation. He does what God would do, since the king occupies the place of God on earth and his ministers act as gods.

42. Crown Official: This description of yours is way beyond the discourse of a soldier, which you say you are. I can see that you show signs of being a philosopher, humanist, and even a theologian. These things require more contemplation than a soldier's life provides. It is not possible to carry your gun draped over one shoulder and books slung over the other. One thing will always impede the other, at least most of the time.

43. Soldier: The pen never dulled the sword. Julius Caesar was a captain and a soldier when he conquered Gaul. He fought during the day and wrote his *Commentaries* at night.[20] Alexander the Great, while he was conquering the world, always wrote to philosophers and kept a copy of Homer's *Iliad* next to his bed. The Spartan Epaminondas always brought a library with him while in the army; no one was ever able to determine which was stronger, the soldier or the scholar.[21] There were three hundred other leaders whose weapons did not hinder their brilliance. I do not say this because what Your Excellency says about me is true. It was only that I acquired a

---

20. Julius Caesar (100–44 BCE), the great Roman general and statesman, wrote *The Commentaries on the Gallic Wars* during the nine years he fought in Gaul.
21. The great general Epaminondas from Thebes lived 418 to 362 BCE.

love of knowledge when I was very young and studied the liberal arts. Books captivated me, and I read them when I was free. It is only natural for a man to want to learn, as Aristotle says at the beginning of his *Metaphysics*.[22]

SCENE 2

How Appointments in Portuguese India Are Managed in Portugal; the Many Irregularities in This Process

1. Crown Official: Let us return to our original subject matter. You blamed the men who until now have been in my position. Speaking for myself, since I am human, it is certain that I will make mistakes, and I should know what I would have to correct. You said the soldiers could be forgiven for the boastful, very forward—if not haughty—manner in which they presented their cases for awards. Their attitude was caused by their exhaustion in running from official to official. If they only realized how royal business was conducted, they would not be so upset. Even though kings have ultimate power over all men, one ultimate lordship, and one unbendable royal will, and many other unspoken traits; it is unrealistic to think they are constantly ready to conduct all manner of business demanded of them. The king's business is regulated by a schedule. That is, some months are devoted to African affairs, others for India, and still others for things as they occur. It is unreasonable to think that while they are conducting affairs related to Africa, or the treasury, or justice, that some official will appear out of the blue with the service papers of some soldier from India. What very well may happen will be that this poor timing will damage, rather than help, the soldier's claim. On the other hand, if the official does not make any decision on a soldier's petition when he meets the Council, then it seems that he is thwarting justice and delaying the appointment. It is necessary to have the patience of Job to listen and suffer.[23]

22. Aristotle (384–322 BCE) was a student of Plato and the teacher of Alexander the Great.
23. Job is one of the books of the Old Testament. A prosperous and devout man, Job was tormented by Satan with a long series of misfortunes designed to test his faith in God. In the end, Job's unwavering faith redeemed him in God's eyes. His health was restored. His lost possessions were returned to him and doubled.

2. Soldier: It is a shame that this is what happens and that the king has his schedule organized in this way. In order to give someone what is his, it is not necessary to follow a schedule. It is always the right time; at least, a good Christian king should have the time to do this.

3. I have read of pagan kings who practiced one of the requirements of Christians. Darius, the king of Persia, followed this mandate. He had a specially appointed servant who was charged with daily entering his bedroom in the early morning and saying, "Wake up, Your Majesty, and go correct the issues that God has brought you to fix."

4. From the scripture, we have the example of Christ Our Lord never delaying in making a decision. Since he came to this world for all mankind, he never delayed in delivering it to them. While walking on water, he responded to St. Peter and St. Philip.[24] While eating, he answered Mary Magdalene.[25] While walking on the road, he spoke to Zacchaeus.[26] While entering the city, he spoke to the widow's son.[27] While drinking water, he answered the Samaritan; and he even spoke to the thieves at the hour of his death.[28] At whatever time or place, he responded to petitions, made appointments, and assigned duties. This is the example he provided for kings to follow. In this position, he thought more of mankind than of himself.

5. Crown Official: Well it is true as you state, but earthly kings cannot do as much. They are made of flesh and blood and need to have time to engage in leisure. They are also subject to passions and illnesses and cannot always be engaged in the difficult business of kings. Everyone needs to relax once in a while. Everything occurs at its proper time, as the wise men say. It should be enough that the majority of their time they are working and spending less time on their diversions, which are necessary.

6. Soldier: I think the best cures for illnesses are to provide for the poor widows, the soldier with no other means, and the old gentleman. These are the people who pray to God for the king's good health. Remedies can be found in herbs and roots, but these will never bring perfection. The glorious

---

24. Matthew 14:22–23.
25. John 20:11–18; Luke 7.
26. Luke 19:1–10.
27. Luke 7:11–17; Christ raised the dead son of a widow of Nain.
28. John 4; Luke 23:32–43.

Louis, king of France, said that the poor, to whom he gave alms, were the "hounds" with whom he would hunt a place in Heaven.[29] That is what kings should be seeking.

7. Crown Official: By this way and that, kings seek Heaven. However, returning to the business of India, there are a lot of issues to decide in the three months dedicated to Indian affairs. Issues pile up. All petitioners show up, and due to the lack of time, decisions are delayed since the various plans need a lot of time for consideration. If other urgent needs come forward, such as matters relating to the galleys or other similar problems, minor issues come to a halt.[30] These things, in turn, cause the deliberations on pensions to be delayed for another year. Appointing a viceroy or some other business eats away at the king's time. The men then get no responses to their petitions. Would you blame an official for these events when they are out of his hands and there is no other time to present them?

8. Soldier: Since Your Excellency has given me permission to speak freely about all matters, you need to listen to me a moment. I say, sir, that this is all well and good if the same thing happened to the servant of the lord steward of the household, who never served the king, or if it happened to servants of the supervisor of the treasury, or of the secretary, or of the counselor, or of Your Excellency. These people sat around with their hands on their belts or sat with their legs propped up, eating the most delicious peaches and figs and taking with them the best that India has to offer. These are the people who should get delayed answers or no response to their petitions. However, what usually happens instead is that when one of these men has his papers presented at the same time as those of some old soldier such as myself, these people are awarded first. The poor soldier who was tossed about on the voyage, who faced the rain and cold in the campaigns in Cambay, the cannonballs and arrows in Malabar, Aceh, and from the Turks—he will have to bide his time.[31] He will have nothing to do but pace up and down

---

29. GM suggests Couto here is referring to Louis IX, born in 1214. He ruled France from 1226 until his death in 1270 and was canonized as a saint in 1297.

30. Providing men to row the oars on galleys was a never-ending problem for the crown. One frequent solution in Europe was to man these with convicts or sinners (sentenced by the Inquisition). Overseas, slaves were another solution.

31. The city of Cambay lies at the northern end of the Gulf of Cambay in Gujarat, India. It was a center of trade and often involved in the Portuguese-Gujarati wars

the streets of Lisbon and take care of himself by doing many things about which I will remain silent.

9. Crown Official: You are right in much of what you say here. However, these are favored appointments that cannot be avoided, since, as they say, "You scratch my back, and I'll scratch yours." My friend, now that you are speaking the truth, I will not deny it. Things happen this way because the official in this position is only human and must function in this world. He favors some because they are becoming powerful. Still others get favor because he holds them in high esteem or they have helped him. Nothing is free; to get something, you have to give something.

10. Soldier: On that account, I should blame my father. When I was a child, he took me to court to personally serve the king. I slept on top of the trunks in the king's closet. Later when I became a man, my father sent me to India as so many still do today. He thought I would be able to make my return after a number of years in royal service and be awarded with a post. It would have been better if he had sent me to serve one of the king's favorites. It is quite possible that at my age now, when I am making this request, I would have already collected the fruits of my labor and had the time to enjoy them. Now I doubt that I will, as I am old.

11. As to how to they will respond, only God knows when it will be. I could die in the hospitals in India without ever occupying the post awarded to me. I will spend my entire life never attaining that which those others whom I mentioned will enjoy, sitting on their rears resting their legs, living in estates purchased by the sweat of my labor. They have been cheating me for many years. The worst is that, when these people enter into their positions in India, the governors immediately give them favors and gifts that are

---

(1530–1535 and 1560–1561) that resulted in peace in 1615, about the time the *Dialog* was written. "Cambay" is also the term used for the region as a whole. Malabar was a particularly profitable and active region for Portuguese interaction, not all of it peaceful. The spice trade brought great profits as well as other merchants to the region, such as Arabs. The Portuguese had a contentious relationship with Calicut, the center of the spice trade until they made peace in 1588. Cochin was part of the Portuguese Empire from 1503 until the Dutch occupied it in 1663. The Sultanate of Aceh occupied the northern section of Sumatra and was an important regional maritime power, especially problematic for Portuguese Malacca.

unattainable to poor soldiers. Even though the governor saw these soldiers kill many Moors, favors go only to the governor's close friends, in spite of their great cost to the royal treasury.

12. Nobleman: To that I say: it is my fault. I am happy to hear you speak the truth in such a direct manner. These things have also happened to me, but what is a governor to do when he cannot live such a pure life, having no need for others? He has to please and reward them in order to conduct his business.

13. Soldier: I am pleased to hear this from Your Excellency because this is how I have always seen the way governors treat the royal treasury. They act not as ministers but as enemies. When they act this way, they forget that they have to repay what they have taken. This causes many shortages in Portuguese India, shortages that could be remedied with that money, such as provisioning the fleets and fortresses with their needs. Your Excellency needs to be patient, because I am going to speak about this at some length.

SCENE 3

The Worst Enemies of the King's Treasury Are His Ministers; How the King's Orders and Standing Instructions Are Not Followed; and Other Subjects

1. Soldier: One day the wife of Darius entered the tent of Alexander the Great after he had conquered all of Persia.[32] Next to Alexander was his good friend Efestion, to whom she bowed, thinking he was Alexander. After she discovered her error, she apologized. Alexander responded to her saying, "You made no error; my friend is another me."

2. From this example, it is clear that the king's friends, the viceroy, governor, or other ministers, should each act as if he were another king. He should administer, govern, and spend money just as the king himself would—that is being a true friend. But things take another turn when the governors or ministers intend to govern solely for themselves and their friends—then

---

32. Darius III (380–330 BCE) was king of Persia from 336 to 330 BCE, when his country was conquered by Alexander the Great. Darius fled from the battle, and his wife was taken prisoner by Alexander.

I think the king has no greater enemy than these people. The king could say of such people, "Is this another me or is this someone who wants everything for himself?" This turn of events is applicable everywhere.

3. We should turn from the ministers here in Portugal to those in India. Show me a viceroy who will lose one cruzado of his own in royal service in order to make another one. This is something that does not happen; rather, the money will grow in his account at the expense of the royal treasury. God knows how he does this.

4. What you will see is a governor or viceroy who initially arrives in India full of good intentions to serve the king and increase the royal treasury. It appears to all that he will redeem Portuguese India, and he will take money from some men to increase the royal funds. Somehow, four days later, everything changes because of the evil nature of the society and the diabolical nature of man. He changes his ways and secretly takes money for himself and his friends from the royal accounts as well as from individuals. I could give you many obvious and actual examples of this, but I will mention two.

5. When governors want to pay salaries, which are always done in advance, they will never leave any debts. If there are any, they will issue certificates. These are total deceptions, but I am getting off the track so I will discuss these later. These payments are not made in a currency to favor the royal treasury. Instead, they take the payments from Hormuz, where the money is more valuable.[33] In place of *xerafins*, they pay *patacas*, which run up a large royal debt. This is how they take advantage of the situation.

6. Another example: An ambassador has to be sent to Balagate or to the great Mughal, and of course he must take presents, as is the custom.[34] They make a list of what these should be, and four to ten horses will be included. The viceroy sells these from his personal stables to the royal treasury at an exorbitant price. A horse that is worth two hundred is sold for six hundred or more. Someone else's name is written on the receipt, and he receives a cut

---

33. Hormuz Island is at the entrance to the Persian Gulf. It was (and remains) a strategic point controlling maritime access to the gulf. As a result, the Portuguese established a fort and factory there to conduct and direct trade. See map 3.

34. Balagate was a kingdom to east of Goa; the Mughals inhabited the great empire in northern India centered in Delhi and Agra; see map 2.

from the profit for playing his part. This is all done beforehand, and they make a tidy sum. Here there is yet another injustice, which is when ships arrive from Hormuz with horses, the governors order that those with the best appearance be taken to their own stables and to those of their friends.[35] Setting their price has always been done by the governors and has been an enormous scandal in India.

7. Now let us continue, and we shall see how they take advantage of the royal treasury. In spending royal money, the treasury superintendent does not actually handle any money, which would be a sacrilege. The treasurer does not have the authority to handle it. The governor has this right, and sometimes he has his servants handle it. Expenses are therefore totally at his whim. The receipts for these expenses he gives to the factor or treasurer, which is their only written record.[36] Sometimes errors creep into the accounting books, which can cause a bit of work to correct, and God only knows where that money went and how it was spent. The largest part of it always goes to pay old debts, which I will discuss soon enough. These payments are distributed by the governor's toadies or agents, who are all well paid for doing this. See how his lackey gets fifty thousand cruzados, the page rings the bell, and another servant gets his share. All of this comes from the royal treasury of the king, who pays even for the governor's servants.

8. Nobleman: You have said a lot here. You know that as soon as I have taken the oath of office and received the king's instructions, I have the right to do whatever I think best, and the king then agrees to whatever a governor might do. With this authority and with all the little underhanded dealings that go on in India, I can make my friends wealthy, since they serve me and with them I represent the dignity of the office.

9. Soldier: Well, Your Excellency now shines light on a hidden issue. I wanted to discuss several things that have become huge scandals and this subject that Your Excellency mentions more so than any other. Do you know sir, what a viceroy or governor swears before the king when he takes the oath of office? It would be certain that if they remembered this, they would neither eat nor drink because I think most of them commit serious

---

35. The horse trade from Arabia and Persia was one of the many trades in which the Portuguese participated.

36. A factor was the head of the factory or trading outpost.

acts of perjury. I am saying this because Your Excellency has given me leave to speak freely.

10. Tell me sir, what viceroy or governor is so honest (and I do not say that there are not some) that in making their oaths of office they do not risk a thousand acts of perjury? First, they swear that they did not seek that office for themselves, nor did someone lobby for them to obtain it, nor did they have an agent try to obtain it for them, nor did they attempt to obtain it by any other means. In spite of this, they know full well the many ways to obtain the position.

11. Let us turn to the oaths they take to follow royal instructions, ensure that justice is carried out, and other things, which I will leave aside. Very few carry these out. The instructions are only enforced against the poor, and laws are only applied against the needy. In sum, to not wear myself out, very few governors do what the king orders. Rather, they follow the opposite course and act against the royal will and instructions. I state that nowhere is the king's will ignored as much as it is in India. Governors do things there that kings should never do.

12. What is really shocking is that there are lawyers in all the meetings who twist the meaning of the laws and regulations in such ways to enable them to do as they wish, even though they commit terrible injustice. One example of this was a case that I saw regarding a fort in India. A well-trained lawyer attempted to persuade one of the High Court judges that he could vote on a particular issue as the governor wished because the law would allow it. He added that he would give him a written statement supporting this point of view. However, because the judge was a God-fearing man, he refused to go along, and even the governor could not get what he wanted. By that one vote, the judge's side won.

13. Should I tell you what acts of perjury the governors commit, breaking their oaths once they begin to rule India? They swear with their hands on the Bible to uphold the rights and privileges of the residents of the city of Goa. The first opportunity that comes their way, they turn everything upside down and show their true intentions by failing to uphold any of their sworn duties. There are lawyers who tell them that the town's rights are interpreted in the manner that best suits the governors. I can explain better with an example.

14. An honorable older married gentleman in Goa was apprehended and

thrown in jail for some money he owed the king. The governors are always looking for such cases. If it had been a murder case, he would not have been jailed as quickly. Now that I am telling you about this case, let me state that I heard about it from someone who is familiar with such cases.

15. Right now there are a number of men in jail because of debts, while several murder cases have not been investigated as quickly as they deserved. Because of this, they say, "Do not owe the king any money and kill as many people as you like, and you will go free. I am sure no one will bother you."

16. To return to the story I was telling, the nobleman was put in jail, and he asked the city for help asserting his municipal rights. Note that citizens of Goa cannot be placed in irons except in murder cases. Even for debts to the crown, they have this right. Since they were trying to get money out of him, the withholding of such money was the nature of his crime, the High Court ordered that he could not be held in irons, as was his privilege. Instead, the court ordered that he be held in jail but not in chains. He stayed there for some time and had no rights whatsoever.

17. Now I ask you gentlemen, could the Devil himself have interpreted this provision of the law in such a manner? What does "held in irons" mean if not in jail, where everything is made of iron? I could give you so many more examples such as these that it would make me sick to my stomach, so out of disgust I will stop.

18. Now, Your Excellency says that the king grants the power to make decisions about all matters by the wording in the instructions that state at the end: "More than anything else, do what you think is in my best interest." Many fail to understand this correctly, as it actually ties the viceroy's hands and limits his power. More than anything else, the king's interest is best served by administering justice and seeing that each person gets what is his. Other important duties are to send out the fleets at opportune times, to provision them with war materials as required, to uphold the reputation of Portuguese Asia, and to defend its subjects. This provision in the instructions is needed because the king cannot second-guess what might or could happen in the future and cannot leave detailed instructions. He leaves these things for the governors and his counselors to decide.

19. However, spending from the royal treasury should only be for these things and for other usual expenses. For other things, he gives you many thousands of cruzados to distribute as favors. Even to those worthy men in

service, the majority of whom are your servants, you cannot grant money because the royal intention is to reward those who serve the king. First in line for payment are the nobility and those who live with them; he has more obligations to them than to others. However, even in this there is another great injustice when money is granted to people who never existed, then the governors or their toadies gobble up these spoils. This can only be labeled "theft."

20. In making appointments, I say you need to follow a better path. In the king's orders, he instructed the governors to appoint certain officials to post of factor or something lower. Who said that these posts could be awarded to those who serve you, when that is specifically omitted from the provision? The king's intention is to reward those who have done well and served him. Do you know how that is? If I am not mistaken, it was a declaration from the *Mesa da Consciência* here in Portugal that stated that only those who lived with the king were required to provide royal service.[37] Those who did not live with the royal court provide royal service by paying the salaries of those who live with them, a payment of so much each month. This is what is owed and what should be paid, with nothing owed in return.

21. However, the poor are robbed, as they only receive two of the four annual payments owed to them each year, one in the summer and the other in the winter. The governor or viceroy who does this has no scruples whatsoever; if I were his confessor, I would make him pay them. He who says that Portuguese India lacks funds is deceiving God, because he knows it does have them. A lot of the royal treasury is spent on unnecessary things and could be used to make these payments. As a result, I have to conclude that the governors and viceroys do not have fancy goods and never engage in underhanded business as Your Excellency says, in order to enrich their underlings. They drain the royal treasury, taking funds from the mouths of widows, orphans, poor married men, and soldiers who do not receive what is due them, distributing the money instead to their toadies.

22. All of this leads to chaos and confusion as the governors and viceroys go from one place to another seeking money for guns and expeditions and

---

37. The *Mesa da Consciência* was an advisory body to the king and his ministers. It issued opinions and today what might be called advisories or policy statements.

issuing a number of payments to family members and servants with no fear of God nor of shame of deceiving those who made the loans.

23. Crown Official: This happens like that? I am amazed that so many things go on there of which we are unaware here and the governors do not fear that one day news of these will reach the king's ears!

24. Soldier: They are not afraid of that. Do you call Your Excellency the king? These people are the kings and gods there, and the same king has made numerous provisions, one in particular that people in India will not be summoned or questioned for any reason whatsoever.

25. For certain, sir, I am sure that the king did not see that provision when he signed it, nor is he aware of it. If he did look at it, I do not think there is a king who would allow such a great injustice. If a viceroy asked for such a thing, the king would quickly remove him from office and appoint someone else. If this were to happen, I would need a safe pass to allow me to take my ship, my horse, and my estate without being summoned to court. This is something that one would expect from the tyrants in Sicily and not from the Catholic and Christian monarchs who always seek justice even when it is applied against them. In *The Chronicle of Dom João II*, we read of some sentences against this same king issued by judges.[38] This is true Christianity.

26. It is possible to see now how poorly understood this is and that the king is unaware of this provision. If he issues so many provisions for whomever, and the crown attorney can summon any of these people, which occurs daily in this kingdom and even in India, and charges are made against individuals and they manage the king's treasury; how is it possible that the governor or viceroy cannot be summoned or questioned? I do not believe that. Does Your Excellency believe that I should act as if I were a madman about this here in Portugal, talking about it until it reaches the king's ears? It would be more just, more Christ-like, if the viceroy or governor after completing his term would be judged and have to satisfy all those he owes rather than the other way around. Since in these things, the governors

---

38. Written by Garcia de Resende and first published in *Livro das Obras* in 1554. The *Crónica* cited here was not published independently until the 1750s. RL and GM note that this passage appears in chapter 94 of the work.

believe they have fooled God and the king. They conceal and omit certain things they do. I am amazed they are not tripped up by all this. They think they can cover up something so big with something so small.

27. Crown Official: What cunning cheats and tricks are these, and what frauds?

28. Soldier: I will tell Your Excellency. After a viceroy or governor completes his term, despite what is stated at the end of the announcement of his departure, the reality is that no one should seek anything from him. Four to six days before his ship is about to depart, they post large broadsides around town and in the churches stating that anyone who is owed anything should petition for it and he will be paid. Since the official already has one foot in the stirrup, no one comes forth with a claim, and the viceroys and officials produce a thousand certificates to cover their actions and mask what they are doing. All of India is scandalized, and this is how their debts and servants are paid.

29. Nobleman: Now I am sorry that I gave you such liberty to speak so freely, as I never thought that you would talk about such matters so openly. These are not matters that soldiers know about, because they are only concerned with their firearms and payments. I am resigned to this, and I feel guilty about all the other things as well. I am sure you could make a list of all the transgressions of a viceroy. You have made me recall a number of things that I had forgotten, but now that we are dealing with this material and leaving aside the other things, which I do not know how to excuse, I want to defend the honor of the governors in rewarding their servants. This does not all come from the royal treasury as you state. For the most part, what they give are opportunities, which appear daily. Rather than giving them to strangers, it seems better to give these opportunities to your friends.

30. Soldier: I do not think so. Now that Your Excellency has hit the nail on the head by mentioning the subject of deceptions and underhanded dealings, we need to expose the secrets that are unknown to the king and his ministers to demonstrate how unjust and damaging they are to the king's treasury.

31. Crown Official: I would really like to hear about that since India is another world, and the things you have mentioned have little to do with royal service, but rather with men's private interests.

32. Soldier: This takes place everywhere. Since this material is very extensive, I will summarize it as much as I can to avoid tiring Your Excellency.

SCENE 4

Regarding the Types of Fraud in India
and the Damages They Cause

1. Soldier: In India for some time now there have been four types of fraud. The first type deceives the king, the second the people, the third God, and the fourth all of these. The first, which defrauds the king, is how governors make their servants rich. This is done in many ways. For example, when someone dies without a will and no heirs, then his estate belongs to the crown. However, it is immediately divided up, and it disappears with the king receiving not one *tostão*.

2. When a Muslim or Hindu is convicted of participating in an uprising, his estate is confiscated by the town council. The edict is signed today, and by tomorrow his goods are auctioned off by the governor's servant, who had been given the goods beforehand.

3. A Jew or heretic is burned at the stake, and his estate becomes royal property.[39] It too disappears in the smoke. One person takes a thousand cruzados, another takes the houses, and a third has the garden. The fire takes the owner and his property, and you cannot even find the ashes.

4. A factor or customs official produces a bill of four thousand cruzados owed to the king. Then the account gets closed, and his secretary has all the proper documentation, which then disappears.

5. A factor passes away and his accounts are not in order. Greedy hands dip into his estate. First, they see if he owes the king anything and that disappears. Then they take his money, then his real estate, and lastly his slaves and jewels. His wife is kicked out of her house and left with nothing. In the event that her late husband does have his accounts in order, has no debts to the crown, and some later appear, the governor's servant shows up and takes everything. The widow then nearly wears out the stairs coming and going,

---

39. In Goa, the Portuguese had established a Tribunal of the Inquisition by the mid-1500s. In reality, very few people were burned at the stake, but those who were so executed also lost their entire estates.

as well as the governor's ears, but he does not return what belongs to her. He eventually returns one-fourth, and the royal treasury has to cough up the remaining three-quarters, which the governor and his servant have kept.

6. The renter of the customs house at the end of his lease owes ten thousand cruzados, and his creditors are left at their wits' end. The governor's nephew suddenly appears with a certificate awarding him three thousand, the governor's servant has another certificate for two thousand, and somebody else shows up with another certificate for so much. In two days there is not one stone on top of another for the poor creditors. If the renter puts his case before the High Court and proves that his losses were due to war and misfortune, or that others broke their contracts with him and his goods should be returned as a result, they have already been devoured in the beaks of vultures. The judges pass a provision that he pay a recalculated bill. In this way, the king gives his wealth to the servants of the governor, because when all is said and done, it is the king who has paid for everything.

7. A married man has a relative post a bond for one thousand cruzados to ensure his completion of a sentence of exile to the Molucca Islands.[40] The man flees while on the way there, and the next day the bondholder's houses are sold at auction and someone consumes the money and everything else. There are a hundred thousand such schemes as these. I am convinced that if the king wished to investigate and forced the governors to put this money into the royal treasury, he would add annually more than thirty thousand cruzados. It would be better to use this sum to pay four months' salary to soldiers in winter so they would later be available to serve on the fleets, rather than spending it on undeserving servants of the viceroys.[41]

8. Nobleman: How am I supposed to pay those who have served me since they were children if not by making them rich when I am in power?

9. Soldier: What you are talking about is governing your estate and that

---

40. Being forced to move to a distant part of the empire was a common punishment. The exile could last two, three, five, or ten years, depending on the crime.

41. "Winter" here refers to the monsoon season in Goa in June, July, and August, during which months navigation was impossible and the soldiers usually lived in groups under the protection of a captain who fed and sheltered them for the season. The Portuguese called this period winter, even though Goa is north of the equator, because the heavy rains and high humidity caused chilly weather.

of your servants. It is derailing royal government, which you promised to administer honestly, which you should do as a loyal subject, and which you took an oath to do. As the great legal scholar Masurius Sabinus stated, we are obligated to attend to the needs of three types of people above all others: first are orphans whom we should shelter, patients who will be cured in our homes, and those whose goods are entrusted to us.[42] A governor has the obligation for these reasons to be vigilant for the king's best interests, as well as for all the other reasons, and to not undermine them. You should pay your servants from your own funds. It is because of this that the king gave you rewards and funds to meet your obligations to your servants. Leave the royal treasury to meet the king's needs, which are numerous.

10. Nobleman: This would be for me to go to India to serve my friends but not myself, if I had to give them what the king gives me. Leaving that aside, there are many other underhanded ways to make my friends wealthy, ways that you have not mentioned.

11. Soldier: I did not want to mention those as they would dishonor the office of governor, but if you poke me, I will react. I am ready to tell more, if the secretary will allow me to continue, and he is not bored listening to me. I hope I am not taking up too much of his time because I am sure that he has other more important matters to attend to, matters which require his attention.

12. Crown Official: For some time now, I have not seen any other business more important than this. What I am hearing from you are issues that have been hidden from us here. Since they are unknown, the king is not able to benefit as he should. I am taking some mental notes from what you have been saying because I know they will benefit the king. So please continue your discussion as it is very helpful and hardly a waste of time. In fact, it is instructive.

13. Soldier: These things, all of them that Your Excellency has heard, are the rough, unpolished truth. They come from a simple soldier, who now that he has put his musket away can only speak the plain truth. If what I say here is restated by another and expressed differently, then Your Excellency would more clearly see the ways in which the king is defrauded. Where and

---

42. Masurius Sabinus, famed Roman jurist who wrote *The Book of Civil Law*.

why does Portuguese Asia suffer from shortfalls when it produces sufficient income to pay for all its expenses? I think it is easier to understand these things than to change them.

14. Crown Official: Now we are getting to the bottom of the truth. When it is expressed in other fancier ways and embellished, it is easy for someone to get lost in the words. For that reason, soldier, you should continue with what you have started. It is quite possible that your discourse will be more noble than the certificates of service that you brought.

15. Soldier: Truth when spoken with an agenda is not truth. For my part, when I speak it, I am not looking to be honored, because speaking the truth is the best thing in world. Now that Your Excellency has given me permission, I will continue with what I started.

SCENE 5

The Second Type of Fraud, Which Is Against Men, and the Destruction It Causes

1. Soldier: The famous tyrants Phalaris of Agrigento, Dionysius of Syracuse, Jugurtha of Numidia and others like them did not maintain their kingdoms because of their virtues, as they were cruel and inhuman.[43] Yet it was through their generosity that they ruled their subjects, never taking what belonged to them. They understood that if they were tyrants to their own subjects, or if they refused them as king, they would be rulers of empty cities and towns because their subjects would flee from them. It is the obligation of a good king to enrich his subjects because there is no king of poor subjects who can be called "rich."

2. This was why Alexander the Great ordered that a gardener be punished. He had pulled plants out by their roots, and by that we understand that kings should not destroy their subjects because by doing so they will lose their kingdoms. In the same way, a wise gardener will not pull a plant out by its roots, as it cannot bloom again later. The careful pastor will not

---

43. Phalaris, ruler of Agrigento in Sicily from 571 to 556 BCE; Dionysius I (the Elder) ruled the city of Syracuse on Sicily from 405 to 367 BCE; Jugurtha ruled Numidia from 118 to 105 BCE.

nick the skin of the sheep while sheering them. The wise and prudent king will not tyrannize his subjects to the point they have nothing.

3. The first kings of Portugal were aware of this—we think until the time of King Dom Dinis, who was most famous for this practice.[44] These kings loaned their subjects money as a matter of course, and this made them wealthier and their customs revenues grow. Despite the fact that today kings do not do this, they still want their subjects treated kindly and do not want them to be oppressed with new duties or taxes, as some governors do. (The true Portuguese spirit will always come through.) Great obstacles only make their loyalties shine. These other deceptions, which are directed toward men, which Your Excellency says do not affect the royal treasury, I feel these are even more prejudicial to it than the first type of fraud. Your Excellency will excuse me, but even though you governed Portuguese Asia, I have to say what I believe.

4. The first Christian governors of India made their rulings for the benefit of the king's subjects, listening to the petitions from the poor widow, the needy married man, the afflicted prisoner, and the injured soldier. These they quickly answer with little thought, because these are acts of true justice.[45] However, a few years ago the Devil made the governors withdraw and cease interacting with the people. By virtue of their positions, these men should be like Marcus Livius Drusus, the Roman tribune.[46] According to stories, he lived on a public square in a house that was open on all sides. A famous architect offered to remodel his house to make it more private. He responded by saying, "You would be a better friend to make the house more open. The life of an official should be visible to the public so they can see how he lives, being available by keeping his doors open at all times."

5. This is how the viceroys, treasury officials, and magistrates in India as well as here in Portugal should act. They should have their doors and their

---

44. King Dom Dinis ruled Portugal from 1279 to 1325 and was one of its most famous and able medieval monarchs. He reorganized land practices, improved agriculture, centralized the power of the monarchy, improved trade, and promoted the arts.

45. The author is making an important distinction here between those who are commonly labeled "the deserving poor" and the vagrant, lazy, and idle people who refused to work, the "undeserving poor."

46. A tribune of the Plebeians during the first century BCE.

windows not closed but rather open so everyone can see them, and they can be available at all hours to administer justice. But now because of their "serious business," which I could label by another term, the governors lock up their houses and hide themselves, conducting the business of others and with only their own people. If they reserved two days for public audiences in a month, it would be to the detriment of those who attended. I do not know what fiendish soul it was who first denied a petition presented to the magistrates of the High Court. These figures, wishing to impress others as great jurists, created something out of nothing and then noted they had great misgivings and doubts about it. When the poor petitioner awaited his response, he found his case was problematic and filled with obstacles. He then tried a more effective method, which was to see one of the underlings of the governor or viceroy and satisfy him with the customary bribe. The next day the petition was resolved in the manner he originally desired, with none of the legalistic hurdles worthy of Bartolus.[47] In this manner, the obstacles were removed because his gift erased any legal doubts and cleared the way. The law was now crystal clear and legal opinions were in his favor.

6. In another example, when a factor, customs judge, or another official wants to occupy his post and start his duties, he awaits the promised provisions from the governor. This official waits for many days and months going to the governor's house and seeing his secretary, never getting what he seeks because he does not know how to play the game. He presents his papers, which are then forwarded to the secretary who is the responsible party. These papers get stuck there like lost souls because the governors and viceroys have allowed this trickery so they can enrich their friends. Even the secretaries can be deceived. When the secretaries then speak with the governor, they deliberately omit discussing anything relating to such petitions.

7. When the official begins to realize this is a delay, he gets advice from others. He makes new appointments and brings fine carpets, finely embroidered cloth, gold chains, and other similar things to a trusted servant of the governor, who welcomes him. The official tells him he only desires justice. Then in a day or two, the official gets his position confirmed just as he wanted. This is all done to the detriment of the royal treasury because

---

47. Bartolus of Saxoferrato (1313–1357) was a famous Italian professor of law and legal scholar.

these goods only cover up what is going on. Even though the new factor or official may dip his hands into the royal treasury whenever he wishes, he has learned that arriving with his hands full will open doors.

8. This knavery also affects the royal treasury when a new captain appears, ready to occupy his fortress, and it costs him more dearly and he collects more. He issues two receipts on paper for supplies, one to come from royal funds and the other to come from the people. The chaos, tyranny, and oppression they practice should only be found among barbarians. We will discuss these at length later.

9. The list of provisions and payments that the captain takes with him includes his right to three or four thousand cruzados in income from his fortress. Instead of this, he takes ten or twelve thousand. The new captains make contracts for the goods from where they are headed, and for these they spend another several thousand pardaus from the royal treasury, which they take in hand right away. When they purchase these items, they are always of the worst quality. The captains ask that they alone be allowed to send a ship to that port, as if the ocean and its navigation were not open to all. In this they hinder the commerce of the local people who supply the forts.

10. In short, I could go on and on. These governors and viceroys issue edicts that run roughshod over the king and his subjects. I never saw any so cruelly applied as those directed at the inhabitants living in fortresses. These edicts went so far that men could not enjoy the company of their own wives without permission from the captain because some only want to enjoy the company of a select few women. I found myself in a fort where they told me that one resident complained that the captain took his wife against her will. The captain called him to his house and beat him with a stick because his complaint had made the captain's act public. Your Excellency can only imagine what other things would follow.

11. Nobleman: I cannot deny any of the things you have stated, but tell me: How could I deny a nobleman with whom I grew up and who has served the king for many years spending money? It is logical when the governor, while collecting the fruits of his labor, favors these people, even if slightly at royal expense. The king is not so naïve that he does not know all about this, nor would he want to be such a poor friend to his subjects that he would not want them to take delight in enriching themselves in these forts. Many times they turn around and spend much of this in royal

service, so he takes no notice. Ultimately, it is to the nobility to whom the king has obligations.

12. Soldier: I will respond to all that Your Excellency says. You say that you cannot deny these things to a nobleman who has served the crown for many years, spending freely from his own pocket. This is all well and good when they have sold houses in Portugal and lands that produce income so that they can arrive in India and spend these funds in royal service. However, most of them arrive from Portugal without a penny to their names or the clothes they will need. Right away, they start trying to get financial rewards from the governor or loans from established married men who helped their fathers or from someone else whose daughter they say they will marry. They spend all this borrowed money, not feeding and sheltering soldiers, but instead parading around Goa on fat horses most of the year.[48] Four months of the year when they visit Malabar, they are given a small ship and are very well provided and are awarded more money than they need.

13. How can Your Excellency say whether it was the king who spent money or the slow-witted married man who paid someone to marry his daughter, only to have her name ruined and the father impoverished? What is worse is that, from the moment they arrive in India, these men act as if the world were made for them, that everything belongs to them, and that loans made to them are owed to them because they are noblemen.

14. As it so happens, there is some sweet irony here as well, because some of these people are bastards, sons of noblemen, and most of them were raised in the backwoods. They have never set eyes on the king, nor does he know their names. These people are nobles because of some relative. When they leave the rustic farmhouses where they were raised, they come here to India, and in four days transform themselves into something grand and royal. In my own case, I had a better upbringing than these people. I spent my youth as a servant to the king in his chambers. He knows my name very well. If I were sent to a factory or fortress where one of these people serves as captain, he would treat me as if I were the rustic peasant

---

48. Horses were imported from the Middle East and were status symbols, as living in the tropics was demanding for horses and maintaining them was expensive. In fact, horses could not be raised in India at all. The Portuguese made a great deal of money in this trade, selling horses to Indian rulers in the interior.

who raised him. He plays "rob the king" at every turn; he is nothing more than an abusive thief. In a place with justice, he would be punished with a thousand deaths for the smallest of his insults. He never pays taxes on his own goods and sells the king rice, gunpowder, wood, and everything else at exorbitant rates, never purchasing them with his own money. Most of these he takes by force from merchants who come to his fort, buying them at prices he sets. He is the only one who can buy anything that arrives in his port, and he has the king and the people where he wants them. He has no fear of God or of the king, and he commits infinite other acts of tyranny, which I will tell you if you ask.

15. The pitiful factor, if he spits in church, will be excommunicated. These captains do not want the sun to shine on him, even though it is meant for all, or allow him to have water from the public fountain. The factor might have been the first to take the fortress, sustaining many injuries in the process, or the first who attacked a ship from Malabar. Meanwhile, the troublesome nobleman is untouched, as if God did not want to spill the blood of such men.

16. This problem has grown to the extent that some will not accept such positions in factories because doing so brings only infamy, dishonor, and insults from the captain. The captain is someone I cannot murder, not because I lack the will for it but because, when I finish my term, I have to render an account. Some of these men go to France, another goes to Germany; the years pass by, and I get older and clear my mind of these things to move on. This is probably enough about this subject, and if one day they ask me, I will say what I refrain from saying now.

17. Now, Your Excellency says that the king is not fooled by the tangled manner in which the viceroys make grants to nobles and captains. These officials then take their positions in fortresses. Your Excellency agrees with it, and that it is good. To all this, I respond by saying that the king is deceived more here than by anything else. If you told me that the riches of India were sufficient for all the needs of Portuguese Asia, then such a statement might be true. However, its finances are so tight that these disgraceful acts cause many hardships. Many times I saw fleets of ships that were urgently required, yet they could not be sent because of the lack of funds. The viceroys then turned for help to the poor, impoverished married men for loans and took public goods without paying for them. You could label

this "tyranny" better than "necessity." Under these circumstances, it would have been much better if the treasury had those ten thousand cruzados that were fraudulently given to the captain of Hormuz, and the other thousands that were given in to the captain of Malacca, and the other sums that were awarded for still other fortresses. These people do not make the nobles rich, but rather impoverish the state.

18. It is from this series of events that the resulting shortcomings force the governors to impose new taxes and fees. War is left to chance when individuals finance great fleets, some of whom sail on these ships. They go forth not to build forts in Chaliyam or Calicut nor to capture Surat, but to pillage the forts of the north and put the king's subjects in great danger.[49] They impose new restrictions that increase their wealth by new taxes on rice from the villages that provide it in rent.[50] By doing this, they sap the lifeblood from the people to the tune of twenty thousand cruzados, and each year the royal tribute increases. At the same time, they waste a hundred thousand cruzados inflicting injuries on Christians.[51] The worst thing is that these actions discredit the state of Portuguese India because our enemies know more about this than we do, and they dismiss the viceroys as irrelevant.

19. It would all be different if the money spent on these fleets remained in the royal treasury. God does not desire these expeditions to take place and the king does not want them either; rather, he would object to them. The king is aware of the needs of his subjects. Honor obligates the king to relieve his subjects of such tributes and taxes.

20. Darius, a pagan king of Persia, was drawing up a list of taxes and tributes for the people, and he called in some of their leaders. He asked them if the list demanded too much, and they said it was just. Nevertheless, he reduced the taxes by half. He was so generous that what his subjects considered just he found excessive. In that kingdom there were many wealthy people from whom he could have demanded large sums, but he understood that kings have the weighty obligation to support their subjects. In the scriptures, we have the speech of Ahab, the king of Samaria, and what he

---

49. Chaliyam was a small Portuguese outpost and fort built in 1531–1532 in an effort to control trade around Calicut. It was lost in 1571. See map 2.
50. One of the ways the Portuguese controlled the limited land areas they held in South Asia was to impose a rent or annual tribute from each village.
51. Some, but not all, of these tribute-paying villages were Christian.

said to the Israelites: the best and wisest course of action for a king is to sustain and protect his subjects, even at the cost of spilling his own blood.[52]

21. It was because of this love and trust that when this king was surrounded by the numerous troops of King Ben-Hadad of Syria and the king of Damascus and began to despair, his subjects came to his aid, risking their own lives. A force of thirty valiant young men went forth to spy on the enemy's campground. Once they knew the enemy was asleep, they fell on them with great force and killed many. This threw the enemy into such chaos that when King Ahab appeared with his troops his enemies were completely overrun.[53] This is how grateful subjects act! I could give many more examples, but I will not because I do not want to tire you.

22. Now coming to a conclusion about frauds committed against men, I say that he who wants to obtain a position has to speak with an open wallet and be willing to pay. This has come to the point that a relative of mine, in order to obtain a signed order awarding him his position, said that it was not possible to obtain it without first giving a trusted servant of the governor a fancy embroidered silk bedspread. This was in spite of the servant's obligation to approve such royal orders whenever they are presented to him.

23. Crown Official: I am astonished to hear such things. Around here, we know nothing of such matters. I ask you to please continue and not to interrupt what you have been telling us.

SCENE 6

The Third Type of Fraud, Which Is Against God, and Many Other Wicked Things the Governors Do

1. Soldier: Now I can get to the third type of fraud, which is against God. Many things run counter to his grace and justice. I will discuss this subject as quickly as possible because in other places, if there is sufficient time, I will fill in anything I may leave out.

2. No sooner does a viceroy arrive in India than his underlings begin to pull their dishonest tricks. The first appointments are the crown judges of the forts. There are many more people requesting these positions than posts available to sell. They then begin the negotiations, agree on a price, and are

---

52. See 1 Kings and 2 Kings.
53. See 1 Kings 20.

appointed. The sale of these judicial offices brings income to the personal servant or underling of some three, four, or five thousand cruzados. I can tell you that in one case, someone got more than two thousand for one judicial appointment, not counting little jewels and earrings.

3. These judges will rule on decisions easily, without the High Court judge examining them, as if they had many years of legal training under their belts. For some their decisions are no better than a gamble, since they cannot read or write well. Justice is poorly served by such people! Those who purchased these positions have to recoup their loss, as well as support themselves for three years.[54] They also have to save up to pay the next viceroy, who will take part in this folly. Some of these appointees are so skilled at negotiations that they obtain judicial positions at a series of fortresses, just like someone harvesting grapes from the king's vines. Whoever appears with the staff of office is a merchant. He can demand loans for business in China, as well as so many gifts that his house cannot hold all of them.[55] For he who has nothing to give, something bad will happen; he will have to pay the piper!

4. Let us leave behind the disorder and injustice that take place there and that continue with no end. In those places, it is the strong who have justice on their side, and the little guys are the only ones caught in this spider's web. It is the Jain merchant who urinates while squatting who is immediately condemned.[56] The two heathens who fought with each other, but only the one who wickedly insults the other is then thrown in jail. The rich man and his friend outdo themselves taking advantage of that heathen and take his goods by force and keep him a prisoner in his house. This is a minor thing; they can do whatever they wish. The Muslim who swore falsely on the Koran is arrested and has to pay court costs, while his friend, to whom

---

54. An important point to keep in mind is that all positions in the state bureaucracy were appointed for three years only and terms were normally not renewed because so many others were in line.

55. Business in China, especially buying Chinese silk with Japanese silver, was a highly profitable venture at the time.

56. The ancient Indian religion of Jainism teaches nonviolence toward all forms of life. Some Jains cover their mouths with cloth to avoid inhaling insects by accident, and they refrain from eating root vegetables to avoid harming insects in the ground. The reference, I assume, is to a practice that avoids harming living things.

he loaned money and who lied with his hand on the Bible, pays not a *tanga*, nor does he pay what he owes.

5. A Muslim ship captain about to leave for Hormuz does not have justice on his side in regard to a merchant with his freight charges or some other contract between them. The merchant gives him two tapestries, the captain carries some goods at no charge, and the merchant thinks this is more than just. This is also done sometimes concerning important matters, and the injured party cannot talk about it. By taking his case to the local justice, he is sure to spend all his money. If by chance he has no funds, he will not find any justice, or it will be slow in arriving. If he is owed two thousand cruzados, when the sentence is completed and his accounts are drawn up, he will have less than five hundred, and the rest will have vanished in expenses and gifts.

6. In official statements and inquiries given by a friend, who killed someone or who committed adultery, a crown judge or lawyer may change the testimony where it reads "saw" to "heard," and where it should read "yes," it reads "no." The friend receives every benefit of the defense, which will prove whatever he wishes. Whoever died, died, and his killer goes free. Even worse, if you ask one of those officials to examine what he has done and question how he could hand down such an unjust sentence, he responds in a very offended manner, "This is what the High Court justices have ordered, and I do not understand anything more." This fiend does not recall making false statements or paying to fix testimonies. Nor does he remember giving testimonies under oath, swearing he would go to Hell if they were false.

7. This is the best indicator I have that Portuguese India will not endure. In such an obvious manner the governors sell the judicial offices to those who want to buy them. The Roman Empire only started to decline under Emperor Commodus, who succeeded Marcus Aurelius, 180 years after Christ's coming.[57] He began to sell judicial and public offices for money and was the first to demonstrate this was the path to a kingdom's ruination.

8. Nobleman: It has to be this way because in India there are not enough justices and trained lawyers to fill these positions. If Peter is awarded such a position, and he is not trained in the law, what difference does it make to also give a position to John? In regard to these injustices that you mention,

---

57. Commodus ruled Rome from 177 to 192 CE.

the governor does not order these done, nor does he want to send anyone to Hell. Besides, those things that are given to my chamberlain and servant, such as embroidered bedspreads, tapestries, fine cloths, and little things made of gold or silver, these are trifles, and you can take them. There are theologians who advise me, and they say that this is selling influence or a favor and not a position. These things are necessary when there is a lack of qualified men to serve you, and even when there are enough, the theologians are right.

9. Soldier: Hell is filled with theologians who advise you that such acts are favors (if it is like this and I do not doubt that it is). What does it mean, "to sell favors"? In what earthly or divine law will you find this? The king's treasury pays me five thousand pardaus for my ship, yet I have to give three thousand in a secret bribe as a favor? This is to defame the theologians and make them into authors of thefts. The governors commit their various injustices and should not try to cite theologians as excuses because this is another sin on their heads. By doing this, they commit two grave sins, one financial and a second to their reputations.

10. When you say that these judicial positions are awarded in this manner because of a lack of qualified men, I counter by saying that, for many years now, it has been the custom that men were not sought for positions but the other way around: positions were sought for men. He who seeks such people will find them, but he does not look. The close friends of the governors would lose much if such people were found. These men would not be bribed, but petitioned and honored, because necessity should not force them to abuse the law. The Carthaginians understood this very well and ordered that everyone who wanted to become a magistrate had to be wealthy. If they were poor, they could not administer true justice, since it was possible that necessity might force them to commit some folly.

11. If the governor sought out wealthy men, because there are many of them who are fair, and gave them honors and titles, he would have people to administer justice to the poor. These are the people the king should be seeking. The king should provide, administer, and defend the rich and powerful because the poor and little people are the falcons and hawks with which the king finds Heaven.

12. Raphael of Volterra tells us that Amadeu, the Duke of Savoy, who was married to a daughter of Charles VII, king of France, said that of all the princes of his day, Amadeu was the one who most carefully tended and

provided for the poor.⁵⁸ He spent the greatest share of his wealth on them. One day an ambassador asked him about the birds and dogs he used for hunting, because in Savoy they held great hunts on horseback using birds. The duke took the ambassador to the window and showed him many poor people receiving alms from the duke's men. The duke then said that these were the birds and dogs with which he hoped to find Heaven—the words of Christ and of a very just prince! The governor and the king need to be ever vigilant and ready to ensure justice for the little people. For the powerful and the arrogant, the world is theirs. No one has to see to their needs, no one watches over them, and no one has to ensure that they obtain justice. These people normally get so much that it is an injustice for the poor.

13. Now let's look at an example of a king who favored the poor. Flavio Suintila, the son of Reccared, king of the Goths, so favored and loved the poor, was so charitable and humane to them, that he had no other name except "Father of the Poor."⁵⁹ This is a higher and more grandiose name than "king" and carries more majesty than the term "emperor." These are titles that people here on earth have invented. "Father of the Poor" is a title from Heaven, the name of God, whom we call "Father." This name inspires more charity than any other!

14. To this king-father whom we have been discussing, the Lord our God showed many blessings. He gave him a victory against the Ruccones.⁶⁰ He allowed him to defeat and crush the Romans and throw them out of all of Iberia, which he deserved to rule, including Portugal itself. Suintila ruled his empire for many years in peace and harmony because this is how God favors those who shelter and favor their poor. He was succeeded by his son Raccimer, a wicked and perverse man, uncharitable to the poor, who quickly lost his kingdoms when Sisenand took them with the help of the French.⁶¹

15. Now the poor are despised and ignored! It could very well be that this

---

58. Amadeu IX (1435–1472) was married to Yolande of Valois. Because of his many charitable deeds, the Catholic Church made him a saint in 1677. Raffaello Maffei or Raphael of Volterra (1451–1522) was a noted Italian humanist.

59. Flavio Suintila Balto (584–633) was the son of the Visigothic king Reccared I. The Visigoths ruled Iberia after the Romans and before the Arabs.

60. A northern Iberian peoples, possibly the Basques.

61. Raccimer ruled from ca. 626 to 631 CE; Sisenand ruled from 631 to 636 CE. King Dagobert of the Franks helped put Sisenand in power after he was given an enormous plate of solid gold.

is why Portuguese India is punished by the Lord our God. The governors have little to do with them. Because of the immorality and injustice of which I have spoken, the licentiousness that I see everywhere, it seems that the Lord our God has washed his hands of Portuguese Asia. Everyone lives as they wish, the Moor, the heathen, the Jew. They know that whatever offenses they commit can be paid off.

16. It was because of other injustices and licentious acts such as these that the kingdom of Castile was nearly lost under the reign of King Henry.[62] It was the time when the wonderful philosopher and important poet Hernando del Pulgar wrote those serious and weighty rhymes called the *Mingo Revulgo*.[63] He did this because he saw that all was lost; people were not living according to the rules and were acting as they pleased, not fearing God or obeying the law. It was all the king's doing, and he rebuked him by saying:

> Sleepy and still dreaming
> It will not help him to mark the sheep
> Because he does not know he has to give
> Accounts of them to each owner
> Because I will not mark them
> The Christians followers of the Messiah
> The Jews followers of the laws of Moses
> The Muslims followers of the word of Mohammed
> All get mixed together.[64]

17. By calling the king "sleepy" or "lethargic," he is suggesting that a king who does not take care of his subjects and who does not administer justice is sleeping in a foolish and careless dream. It is only natural for such foolishness to break and destroy itself. In this manner, the king or governor who destroys or squanders the wellbeing of his people is a delirious fool. If kings had to account for their negligent acts, there would not be so much disorder. If a governor were punished for what he did in India, people would hope the situation could be corrected.

---

62. Henry IV of Castile, who lived from 1424 to 1474.

63. A noted Spanish historian and author who lived c. 1430 to c. 1493 and wrote the satirical *Coplas de Mingo Revulgo* around 1485.

64. This is a very rough and literal translation of the passage, copla 10, of this work. See the commentary in J. Domínguez Bordona, ed. *Fernando del Pulgar II Letras-Glosa a las Coplas de Mingo Revulgo* (Madrid: Espasa-Calpe, 1958), 172–73.

18. The Spartans wanted to check the unjust acts of their kings so they would govern with fear of retribution from their subjects if they had no fear of God. They created *ephors*, which were new magistrates similar to the dictators of Rome. These officials had complete authority and power over princes and governors, and were created to right any wrongs done to the little people and prevent any injustices that the kings might inflict upon the people. The first to occupy this position was Elatos, 130 years after Lycurgus.[65] The king of the Spartans at the time was Theopompus.[66] He was such a good and moderate king that he agreed to this new position, being more concerned with the wellbeing and harmony of his subjects than with his own desires and preferences. When his wife rebuked him for allowing someone else in his kingdom to have more power than the king, and she argued this would undercut his son, he responded by saying his son would be stronger and rule longer when his reign was established on just laws and his subjects were not troubled.

19. These are kings who could be called "fathers of the people." Not any less praiseworthy are our most Christian kings of Portugal, who with the same zeal as fathers appoint judges to protect their people in the same manner as the ephors of Sparta. As long as this good and holy custom continued, subjects had this final recourse. But this is not the case in India, where there is a greater need for it than here in Portugal. There the viceroys and governors are supreme rulers. If there were a *Mesa da Consciência* there, they would be restrained and not able to operate so freely.

20. Returning to the passage by Hernando del Pulgar, he is telling us that everything during this time was chaotic and that it was impossible to distinguish Christians, who adore the true Messiah who has already come, from the Jews who follow the laws of Moses, or the Muslims, who follow the words of Mohammed and who is venerated in Mecca. This led to a confused blending of the three peoples, and it was impossible to distinguish one from the other because they all lived as they desired.[67]

21. Let us return to the lack of justice practiced by the governors; I will

---

65. The position was created ca. 754 BCE. Lycurgus was the famed lawgiver of Sparta, who lived from 820–730 BCE.

66. One of two kings of Sparta, 725–675 BCE.

67. Jews and Muslims living under Christian rule were required to wear some sort of identification indicating their religion. The essence of this passage is that social conditions were so chaotic that it was impossible to sort out who followed which religion.

cite another sin, which is greater than all the others practiced against God. A rich and honorable citizen dies, leaving his daughter with twelve, fifteen, or twenty thousand cruzados. One of the governor's servants hears about this and deceptively asks her to marry him, making his case very forcefully and also making many promises to the judge of the orphans and her tutor.[68] He even promises the judge that he can keep his position for an additional three years. He has ways to get his man's name into the selection process and then have him appointed to the position, even though doing so is contrary to the municipal statutes. In this manner, the young lady, the daughter of a very honorable gentleman, someone who could have married a wealthy man of some means, was married instead to a servant from the sticks, with no means or family background. Many times this has been the cause of a thousand lewd acts.

22. In another case, there was a rich orphan girl under the care of her tutor. Another of the governor's servants came to ask her to marry. The governor got involved in this business and split the money with the tutor. Of the fifteen thousand pardaus she had, she got two thousand, and they took the rest. Until now, I have never seen a viceroy take a very poor daughter of an honorable gentleman (of which there are many in India, and they have no means to get by) and help her by marrying her to one of his wealthy servants. He is only concerned with helping his servants get wealthy. The same things that I have said about orphans I can say about the rich widow who is left with villages that provide payments of two thousand pardaus. The governor marries her to one of his servants, altering the rent agreement by removing the obligation to serve the king on horseback in war. In addition to the offense committed against God by using force, he steals from the king by what he removed in the agreement. Because of this, these marriages are not made of free will but rather are creations of the governor, who controls everything.

23. Crown Official: You have told me a lot. I have heard you raise very serious issues. I do not know how the Lord our God overlooks so much that is vile. These things are happening? I tell you that I am so shocked and

---

68. The judge of the orphans was responsible for guarding the inheritance of orphans and generally supervising orphans until adulthood. The appointment was for three years, and it came with a stipend.

scandalized from hearing these things that the first opportunity I have of bringing this to the king's attention I will, and I will not rest until I convince him to strongly punish these many depraved acts, especially this business of the marriages. It is not right for the wealthy daughter of an honorable nobleman to marry this type of poor servant who is so beneath her. Really, I do not know how this does not gnaw at their consciences.

24. Soldier: Excuse me, Your Honor, but as the poets say, those who cross the River Lethe lose their memories of everything.[69] When they pass the Cape of Good Hope, most viceroys forget everything as well, and I am not sure if that does not include their fear of God and king.

25. Nobleman: I am happy to say that I never had time to become involved with any of the things you mentioned. In the few months that I governed India, I never saw any of this and never got involved in it. Had I known this about these marriages, I also would have arranged them because I have an obligation to honor those who serve me and to make them wealthy.

26. Soldier: That is true. However, Your Excellency cannot honor them by dishonoring others. You insult the man, even though he is dead, by taking his daughter and marrying her to someone you should not. If he were still alive, with the wealth he acquired by so much combat and work, with so many misfortunes, he would give his daughter in marriage to someone he selected. He would honor her and be honored by the family. The law that Solon passed, which Plutarch recounts in his *Parallel Lives*, states that no living person should be so bold as to speak ill of the dead.[70] He will face a greater penalty, in this case not by speaking ill of him but by dishonoring him and harming his estate!

27. We will leave the offences committed mainly against God, since they are against Catholic doctrine, principally the canons and decrees from the Council of Trent.[71] These state that coercion or force of any kind cannot be used for a marriage since it must be entered into by the free will of both parties. Many times the orphan girl is not old enough to consent, nor is this

---

69. The River Lethe according to Greek mythology was one of the five rivers of Hell. Those who drank its waters would forget all they knew.

70. Solon (638–558 BCE) was an Athenian statesman, lawmaker, and poet. The Greek historian and biographer Plutarch (46–120 CE) was most famous for *Parallel Lives*.

71. One of the most important councils of the Catholic Church, held from 1545 to 1563 to respond to many of the issues raised by Luther and the Protestant Reformation.

consent obtained. Because I am afraid that I have tired you, I will leave the subject matter of the fourth type of fraud for another day, since it will also give me time to refresh my memory on some things.

28. Crown Official: These things of which you speak are not tiring but rather make one cry. For your love of me, continue with this subject. I enjoy listening to you so much that the time seems to fly by.

29. Soldier: From the mouths of little people, many times God reveals huge secrets that are hidden from the great and wise. There is no higher philosophy than truth. This, spoken from the mouth of someone as insignificant as myself, has the same effect as if it had come from the wise men of the earth. I have not based this business on anything except the truth, and it is the truth that gives speech to those who cannot talk and instructs the ignorant. Because of this, I will continue with this subject.

SCENE 7

The Fourth Type of Fraud, Which Is Against All, and the Nature of Old Debts

1. Soldier: When I spoke of the deceptions against men, I mentioned the unnecessary trips the governors make to outposts in the north and the great oppression these cause the people, and the great injustices that are practiced there. Some of these I left for this section, which will deal with those deceptions that are against all; that is, they are against God, the king, and men. What does Your Grace think of the lewd and wicked acts they commit in these miserable cities they visit?

2. When a governor has settled in one of these cities, if he is not feeling completely happy, there is no lack of toadies who will tell him that so-and-so has a beautiful daughter or that so-and-so, a woman who presents some petition, is a courtesan and is available, and that another woman, whose husband is in jail, is very good-looking. These expedient contrivances are not brought to the governor's attention by just anybody, but frequently by upstanding, serious people, whose high positions make me remain silent for fear of God.

3. I have been told that there was a governor or viceroy who asked a man face to face for his daughter. This was a poor man requesting an office, and his daughter was very beautiful. This poor man told the governor, "Is this what I have to do, sir? God would never desire such a thing! My daughter

has nothing except her honor." What a slap in the face that was for the governor! That would really shake him up and make him serious and pensive. At the very least, he would have arranged a good marriage for the father's sake for his daughter. I do not recall what happened in that case. I happened to be in that city, and I heard this from trustworthy people. I do not want to say more than what I know.

4. If the governor or viceroy of Portuguese India does not have sufficient self-restraint, as did Alexander the Great, who did not want to see the daughters of Darius, because he knew that when evil thoughts prevail, reason is lost. His thoughts will be slaves to his desires, which is the most demeaning state possible. Greater glory goes to a man who has conquered himself than to one who captures large and powerful cities. If soldiers saw their leader conquered by a daughter of Cápua, as was Hannibal, they too would forget their duties.[72]

5. The ancient leaders had so much self-restraint, and they worked so hard to guide their soldiers away from lewd acts, that the goods they collected from a just war were called *castrenses*, from the Latin *castrum*. As Vegetius writes, the soldiers had to be as chaste as if they were castrated.[73] In truth, this is good advice from ancient soldiers, because an act of lust diminishes strength more than losing an arm or leg. In the same way, we see how the natural force of a tree can be damaged more by a small injury to a root than by cutting off an entire limb.

6. Because of the obligation to follow these rules and because of other great virtues, the ancients gave their soldiers blank shields. When they completed heroic, notable exploits worthy of remaining in the minds of men, they could paint them on their shields. They did not imagine that the glory of their forefathers would suffice. According to Ovid, neither their ancestries nor the great deeds of their ancestors were sufficient to make them feel noble if they were not virtuous and courageous themselves.[74]

7. This custom of blank shields on which to paint heroic escapades was

---

72. Cápua is a city south of Rome, famed for its beautiful women. One woman from Cápua was credited with seducing General Hannibal from Carthage during the Second Punic War, keeping him from attacking Rome. Hannibal lived from 247 to 183 BCE.

73. Note the word play here with *castrum* (fortified settlement) and *castratum* (castrated). Vegetius or Publius Flavius Vegetius Renatus was a writer during the late Roman Empire.

74. Ovid, or Publius Ovidius Naso (43 BCE–17 or 18 CE).

mentioned by Virgil in his book 9, speaking about Helenor.[75] He says Helenor died with a blank shield because he was killed at such a young age, too young to have taken part in a heroic act to depict on his shield. This blank shield is also mentioned by Persius in the fifth satire *candidus umbo*, where he says that a soldier who has a blank shield has completed his training.[76]

8. Captains at that time worked so hard to ensure their soldiers traveled a virtuous path that they labored to become models of virtue themselves. According to many philosophers, the surest way for those in charge to ensure their underlings seek a virtuous life is to provide an example. During the siege of Carthage, that sober and brave General Scipio Africanus was presented with a young, captured Numidian lady who was very beautiful.[77] He did not want to see her; he set her free and married her to her fiancée.[78] This self-control impressed Roman writers more than the conquest of Numidia, the liberation of his homeland, the destruction of Carthage, and all the other illustrious deeds he accomplished.

9. Along these lines, the poets liked to emphasize the importance of this: they imagined that Minos, who in Hell is the judge of the dead warriors and inquisitor of crimes, had to decide who would be honored by being in the first triumphal chariot—Scipio, Alexander the Great, or Hannibal.[79] He decided it would be Scipio, because his clemency was of greater importance than the strength of Alexander or the might of Hannibal. Scipio conquered Africa with both his words and his sword, and he never committed any act of war that was not justified. He never showed his enemies the might of Rome without first offering clemency; he never shed blood on the battlefield without also shedding tears of compassion. He conquered not only his enemies but also his own emotions, as shown with the young woman in Carthage.

---

75. Virgil, or Publius Vergilius Maro (70–19 BCE). Helenor was the son of Licymnia, a slave women, and the king of Lydia. He fought in the siege of Troy and his death is recounted in *The Aeneid*, book 9.

76. Aulus Persius Flaccus (34–62 CE) was a Roman poet and satirist.

77. Publius Cornelius Scipio Africanus (236–183 BCE), a great general and military leader of Rome during the Second Punic War. Numidia was a kingdom in modern day northern Algeria and Tunisia.

78. The original says only "married," but we know from the historical record she was married to her fiancée.

79. In Greek mythology, Minos was the king of Crete and judge of the dead in Hell.

10. As Alexander was human and prone to violence, he did not want to see the daughters of Darius, to avoid lust. Nevertheless, he was conquered by rage and by wine, so much so that he killed his best friends.[80] In Hannibal you can see these as well. Even though his exploits were great, there was an air of cruelty and tyranny about them, and they defeated him as a result. In Cápua, it was Marfisa his captive who defeated him, and his cruelty and tyranny killed him in the end because he never saw the faces of the Romans.

11. Antioch III, when he was in Ephesus, saw a priestess of the Temple of Diana who was very beautiful.[81] Realizing that he desired her, he immediately left that city. It was more important for him to restrain his desires and leave some important matters unfinished than to do something unjust and dishonest. One of the close servants of King Agesilau found it odd that the king did not want to see Megabata, the daughter of Antipater, who was a captive. He told the servant that he:

> wanted more to dominate his own emotions and become better in similar things than to take a powerful city by force. It is more admirable in a captain to see him control his own will than to take liberty from others.

12. These people were heathens who all struggled hard to conserve purity, with no concept of obligation except that to reason. These feelings cause a great discomfort for a Christian governor depraved by his cravings. These not only offend his honor and duty, but they also gravely offend God and the husband of the dishonored wife, and insult her father, her brothers, and all who know about it. In these cases, it is not only the governor who commits many sins, but also his servants who commit many others when they present the petition from the poor widow or the helpless orphan girls to pay them what is due their husbands or fathers, or when the married women who has her husband in jail for a crime or for some money owed to the crown. The governor's servants settled such cases in such diabolical and infamous manners that I am stunned. What is worse, I think they may be pleased with what they have done.

13. Crown Official: You have been quite the sermonizer here, but I have

---

80. Alexander killed one of his close friends, General Cletius, in 328 BCE. Both had been drinking and Cletius argued with Alexander.

81. Important Greek city on the Aegean coast of modern Turkey.

not forgotten that you promised to talk about old debts. I would really like for you to explain what they are.

14. Soldier: I will tell Your Grace: it is money that the king owes to Peter, to John, and to others for goods that they take in rice, wheat, fish, cord for rope, wood, nails for shipbuilding—in short, the supplies they will need for ships and royal stores. The king does not pay for the lion's share of these goods. No, I do not mean the king, I misspoke, he does not take what belongs to others. It is the governor or the viceroy who takes these things because he needs them, and he uses that reason as an excuse. Yet he is always the cause of the shortage. The poor merchants wait many years for their repayments, suffering in silence. Their last chance is to sell the paper certificate of debt to one of the governor's servants or favorites, or to a nobleman's relative, at one-quarter of its face value.

15. But there is more. When a nobleman is about to take charge of his fort, then the viceroy's favors begin. He is given a provision in old debts for ten, twelve, fifteen thousand pardaus, yet he paid only one-quarter of their value. Once he arrives at his fort, he is paid the full face value. For an old debt of four thousand pardaus, someone received one thousand, and the poor man loses three thousand pardaus, which rightfully belonged to him. The captain or the governor's agent then swallows these without any scruples.

16. Crown Official: God save me! What a great theft, what great harm this causes the royal treasury and what an injustice to these people! This is something that should be investigated and punished rigorously.

17. Soldier: Does Your Grace see how many forts there are in India? Every three years these people leisurely gorge themselves at the trough to the tune of fifty thousand pardaus, stolen from individuals, the king, and the state of Portuguese India. These will later lack basic necessities. The just and necessary thing to do is to repay these people.

18. Nobleman: What kind of friendship do you want me to offer if I do not right away offer this and other favors to a nobleman who is a friend of mine? To not give this to him is also a cruel punishment. I was not the first to do this. The nobleman would complain that the governor had withheld from him what he gave to others.

19. Soldier: Like father, like son. In the same way, the first governor did this with one of his relatives, and then it became the custom for all to do it!

Do these noblemen not have salaries? Do they not carefully cultivate loans from the living, the deceased, and from orphans?[82] Do they not buy and sell as they wish? Are they not like gods in their respective forts? Do they not take some two hundred, hundred, or eighty thousand cruzados from some? Are they not greedy sons of . . . and the ten thousand for the king in old debts, can they be overlooked? Because he who now has a hundred thousand had ninety, or who has fifty thousand had forty. They too can live like that. With the king's papers on one side and the others' on the other side, they conceal many of the state's failures. So, why not save money to avoid this?

20. When you tell me that you cannot deny gifts to your friend, a nobleman, who is about to take command of a fort, this reminds me of Antipater, who was a good friend of the great Phocion.[83] Antipater asked Phocion for something like this, and he responded, "Antipater, you cannot have me as a friend and be a flatterer, because a friend will only ask for something that is right and a flatterer will ask for everything he wants." The nobleman who sees Portuguese Asia indebted and who asks the governor for money from the king's treasury for his fort should be called a cruel enemy rather than a loyal subject. A good subject cares more for increasing the king's honor and treasury than his own. By what law or reason is a poor man not paid his due when he sold his goods to the king? He is not paid in six or seven years because you tell him there is no money. Yet, the viceroys then pay their servants and toadies hand over fist, and for that there is plenty of money? It would please God that you not take from one to pay the other because it then results in old debts!

21. These men should be like Phocion, of whom I just spoke, when he was governing Athens and had run up some necessary debts for the state. Lamaco asked him for funds for festivals and sacrifices that were normally held every now and then, and Phocion answered, "By the Gods, I swear that I would be ashamed if I gave you money, even for the sacrifices, if I did not give it to Calides" (indicating a man to whom he owed a sum of money).

---

82. The deceased and orphans had judges or guardians who protected their estates and who had the authority to use them to make loans.

83. Antipater (397–319 BCE) was a great general who served under King Philip II of Macedonia and Alexander the Great. Phocion (402–318 BCE) was an Athenian statesman.

This good governor stopped offering sacrifices to the gods in order to first repay his debts. Is it not more just for a governor to refrain from paying his relatives or servants, or even withhold his own salary, in order to first repay the poor widow or orphan for the goods he took from their fathers or husbands for the king's service?

22. I will refrain from listing the many other injustices and destructive acts suffered by the people and by the king's treasury by the visits of the viceroys to the northern forts. I am tired and even grieved by all this. I have yet to mention the visits of the treasury superintendents to the forts of the north, and how this is a great disservice to the king. I am only surprised by one thing. The viceroys do not have any interest in visiting the forts in Kanara, Malabar, and south to Sri Lanka. These also belong to the king, not just those forts in the north. Greed keeps them from seeing that others have noted the reason for their failure to travel south. More than anything it is because these places yield very little. The viceroys could easily return from these places with bolts of fine cloth, pretty jewels, and finery, but I also know they have more than their share of misfortunes. By turning their backs on the prayers of the little people, they never pass the Cape of Good Hope without regretting what they have taken. Their sons die in the hospitals. I am not sure if some have understood the reason for these misfortunes, because God never sleeps and always hears the voice of the just. Abel's blood continually demands justice from Cain.[84]

23. Nobleman: I give up. Everything you say is golden. I did not play that game because I did not have time to make such trips.

24. Soldier: But had you more time, Your Grace would have done this because your servants and cronies would have liked to get their hands on some fine cotton cloth from Bharuch and some embroidered pieces from Diu.[85] They would have convinced you to go.

25. Nobleman: I would have done it for sport. What a pity it is that we are more attracted to evil than to good!

26. Soldier: I was just going to say that, because the first viceroy to visit the north did not go looking for trinkets but for musket balls, which he found in Dabhol, when he destroyed it and the overconfident fleet of Mir-

---

84. Genesis 4:8.
85. Bharuch is an important trading city on the Gulf of Cambay.

Hocém, whom he defeated in Diu, avenging the death of his son.[86] These actions elevated and honored the name of the Portuguese and they began to expand Portuguese Asia. Lopo Vaz de Sampaio went to the north, but he went to seek out and fight the fleet of Haga Mamude, which he did and which he destroyed.[87] They went around heavily armed, and their swords were covered in blood up to the hilts. They increased the king's treasury by conquering many enemies, not by imposing new taxes on his subjects.

27. Nuno da Cunha went to the north three times. He went first to capture Bassein, second to construct a fort in Diu, and lastly to destroy the kingdom of Cambay.[88] Dom Garcia de Noronha also made this journey to prepare the fort in Diu and seek out the Turkish fleet, which was hiding from him without daring to attack. Viceroy Dom João de Castro went to the north twice, once to aid in the siege of Diu and another time to attack the kingdom of Cambay.[89] That very powerful king met him on the fields near Bharuch and offered him battle, which Dom João de Castro dared not accept. On his return to Goa, he attacked the coastline, destroying Adil Khan's outposts, destroying his well-known town of Dabhol.

28. There are many other examples such as these that show the adventurous spirit of these men. The soldiers, who were part of the initial explosion of fury and brilliance of the Portuguese, performed acts that should be remembered for all time. They were also honored and favored by the viceroys, and they too shed blood for them. At that time, you did not see the soldiers hanging around entry halls or the porches of the monasteries, eating the monks' leftovers, which I saw later. Now such valiant men are not around because times have changed for the worse, and the avarice of the governors makes them seek out a new life. Some go to China and Japan; others go to Bengal and Malindi.[90]

29. Four soldiers in royal service have acquired the local custom of not

---

86. Mir-Hocém was Amir Husain Al-Kurdi, the governor of Jeddah and admiral of the Mamluk Egyptian fleet fighting the Portuguese in Chaul in 1508 and Diu in 1509. The viceroy was Dom Francisco de Almeida and the son he lost in battle in Chaul was Dom Lourenço de Almeida.

87. Lopo Vaz de Sampaio captured the fort at Mahim, north of Bombay.

88. Nuno da Cunha captured Damão in 1529, Bassein in 1533, and Diu the next year.

89. Dom João de Castro captured Broach and took part in the Battle of Diu in 1546.

90. Malindi was a Portuguese ally and is a city on the coast of east Africa, north of Mombasa. See map 1.

wanting to leave without their captains first filling their pockets with money, and I think they did well. The rewards that they shared were given to the servants of the viceroys. The soldiers' pay, which is not given until they are about to leave, they obtained in another way. The soldiers have to eat, and the nobles who would have paid them were dead. Everything comes to an end and a bad one; however, every day this goes from bad to worse. Nowadays they only want to take, and they harvest the grapes every three years from this vine. Then another [viceroy] comes and, instead of remedying the situation, he only causes more destruction. What is worse is they care so little. I heard a knowledgeable viceroy say that it would be a good thing if Portuguese India were lost and that it could not continue much longer. No matter where he went, he heard news that all was lost. That is how he felt.

30. Crown Official: According to this, only God can fix these things the way they are going. The king can only seek out illustrious and experienced nobles that he thinks will serve him well and send them as viceroys. If they have such terrible characters that they do these things, instead of enriching the king and comforting the people, they impoverish them and burden them with additional taxes. Instead of making Portuguese Asia grow, they make it shrink. Under these circumstances, whom can you trust to lead? Here on earth there are no angels, and those in Heaven do not favor us with their help.

31. Soldier: There are many solutions but I do not want to speak of those right now. Only to the king would I speak of them, and it will cost him something. I will speak for free about everything else. Only the solutions I will sell at a good price.

32. Crown Official: Well, I am of the opinion that you will be rewarded as you wish because this is very important. I heard you claim that the treasury superintendents, who also go to the cities in the north, commit a number of injustices and disservices against the king. I would like to know what they are because the viceroys say the opposite in their letters to the king.

33. Soldier: I never saw acts that were more contrary to the king's interests, and I will explain these shortly if Your Graces are not tired of listening to me.

34. Crown Official: Nonsense, soldier! I am not tired, and in fact this conversation gives me energy and the clarity to see and understand things well enough to be able to explain them to the Council. So therefore, continue and do not stray from your original intentions.

The seawall of the fort in Diu.
Photo by Timothy Coates

SCENE 8

On the Treasury Supervisors; Their Unnecessary Visits
to the Northern Forts; and the Irregularities They
Commit with the King's Accounts

1. Soldier: Now Your Graces should pay attention, because I am about to explain several reasons why the visits of the treasury supervisors to the forts in the north are disservices to the king. The first of these is that no supervisor, or at least very few, go there on official business. They are not asked to come, and they do not ask to go. In fact, I think they may bribe someone generously to allow them to go. It is then obvious that they do not go to serve the king but to serve themselves.

2. Another reason why these men go to the forts is that the governors do not trust the factors posted there. This seems to be a case of treason insofar as it suggests they do not trust the person the king has appointed to do his duty. The reason these men make these trips is to order money, lumber, fish oil, olive oil, cotton piece goods, rice, wheat, ships, and everything else for the fleets and warehouses. Just for doing this, they receive a salary of one thousand cruzados, twenty men to accompany them, payments for their food and lodging, and a ship to take them there, five pardaus daily for food, and provisions and expenses for everything else they might need. They also get five hundred pardaus in old debts and another five hundred in debt owed by the factors in case they end up owing in the accounts they give him and other similar things.

3. The benefit these trips derive for the royal treasury is to purchase wood from the captain in Bassein at the price he wants, as well as wheat and rice; and he sends more pure-bred roosters and jeweled beds. If they buy any of these items for five pardaus, it pleases God that the ship will transport them for six, with one pardau for them. In this way, they send all the goods their owners wish, since they work for them. They run up ordinary and extraordinary expenses, every hour sending ships to take these goods to Goa at the pleasure of their owners; these profits are his gifts. In this way, the king spends ten or fifteen thousand cruzados on these things, and the supervisor who does this has expenses of three or four thousand pardaus. For these reasons, it would be better to directly purchase these goods in Goa at higher prices.

4. What really is over the top is that if you visit the home of one of these treasury officials, you will see his living room and porch filled with tailors, some making silk covers and sheets, others making richly embroidered bedspreads. Further inside the home there are silversmiths making silver goblets, tankards finished in the Chinese style, chains and bracelets for daughters and wives, and decorated boxes made from tortoise shells, silver, and coconut shells from the islands.[91] Downstairs in the shops there are highly skilled craftsmen and carpenters making all manner of couches

---

91. Coconut shells were a source of coir fiber, used for making rope, shipbuilding, and rough textiles.

and sofas, inlaid desks and free-standing inlaid closets. There is such plenty that you feel you have entered the workshop of some business rather than the home of a treasury official. Some of these officials are so wrapped up in this business that they carry depositions with them for future inquiries to be undertaken on customs officials and ship's captains. These depositions keep the more minor officials under the treasury secretaries' thumbs. In this manner no treasury official, no matter how serious his crimes, will be punished. Rather, he will go free.

5. Does Your Grace know to what extent this has spread? I heard from a nobleman, a friend of mine who was the captain of one of these forts, that in his last year in office he wanted to have the customs officials investigated in his fortress, and he wrote the governor. He had to come up with more than three thousand *dobras*, which he knew were given to a treasury official who visited there to give a deposition about them. All these officials were in his pocket. One unloaded the ships from Mecca. Its boxes of gold and silver were unloaded at night, and they bartered the payment for their duties in his house. In the end, the Devil took everything.

6. Sometimes I heard this nobleman complaining about the treasury officials. I think he may have written the king about this because, during his first year in office, the governor's term ended and a new one began. That year, three treasury officials visited his fort, which cost the royal treasury more than twelve thousand pardaus. The service they provided to the customs house was to undervalue the unique and costly pieces held there by valuing them less than their real worth. They then purchased them for the lower price, getting them cheap and costing the king a great deal.

7. In one of these customs houses, the following incident occurred. A Muslim merchant was taking a small roll of beautiful pieces of cloth, the finest available, to Mecca. These were specially ordered in Bharuch for the Turkish governors. These cloth pieces were appraised at eight pardaus each, but they were worth between twelve and fifteen. The treasury officials did this so they could obtain some at that price. The Muslim understood what they were doing and began to shout that his fine pieces of cloth were worth more than fifteen pardaus each and that the king of Portugal was being deceived in this appraisal and that he wanted to pay the customs duties for their true value. The customs officials changed their tune after they un-

derstood the merchant's reasoning. They placed a new value of ten pardaus on each piece and did not purchase any because they were ashamed. The Muslim man was willing to pay more than twice as much in taxes rather than sell some of them to the officials at much less than they were worth. I could list some hundred thousand additional cases, but I will skip them because such theft repulses me. Everything that the treasury supervisors do, the factors will also do. These are the people the king has appointed in honor of their services, and this is the honor they show, sometimes even spending more. It would be better to save treasury funds for necessities, not spend it on these charges and expenses.

8. Nobleman: Oh! This cannot be this way! That factor wanted to use the king's money to pay salaries for the captain and other debts. If he daily paid imaginary debts, nothing would get done, and the shipyards and warehouses would lack supplies.

9. Soldier: This is the greatest deception of life. I know very well that they do this because the captains are never better paid than when there are visits from the treasury officials. I know why, and so do they, but I cannot tell everything. I can only say that the treasury inspectors usually bring lists of what must be paid and purchased, and of all the other things that could be ordered from the factors, who will always want to buy things at a lower cost. However, viceroys want to provide benefits to their toadies, and by virtue of this system they give them these five or six thousand pardaus.

10. Crown Official: I think you may be correct, because the factors the king had in Flanders and in Mina are never visited by treasury officials to purchase goods required in Portugal.[92] Likewise, the factors of the forts can send a list of what they require so that it can be purchased beforehand, when it is cheaper. But I heard you talk about old payments for soldiers, and that a lot of the income of Portuguese India is tied up with them. I would like to know how that is. This is probably something like the old debts that you already discussed.

11. Soldier: Even worse! Your Grace should know that these are gaping

---

92. One of the first factories founded by the Portuguese was in Bruges, Flanders. São Jorge da Mina was another early factory, established in 1482 along the coast of West Africa in what is now Ghana.

wounds, channels that carry away the greater part of the king's money, and the sweat of the little people is like what is given to the Devil, even though they can give no more. If they do not give it, they take it by force. I do not wish to discover any more rotted fruit than what I have already described.

12. Crown Official: These things are very important because this business of who is listed in the payment books has been manipulated many times, and we need a solution to keep these old salaries from draining the royal treasury. Now I would really like to hear what you think, so I may understand it and see how this works. Until now you have been praiseworthy in the services you have offered the king, and this one is of no less importance, so do not withhold anything. I promise you that if you explain all, the king will know of the great service you perform for him.

13. Soldier: I do not want any greater honor than to see some of my suggestions implemented. Anyone who sees Portuguese India turned upside down, as I see happening, would want to do his Christian duty to help if he could—even if he could do no more than act like Solon. When he saw his native island of Salamis captured and occupied by the Megarans, he made many satirical comments about how the Athenians allowed their enemies to take his island.[93] This scandalized the leaders of Athens to the point that they passed a law that anyone who spoke about capturing the island of Salamis would die. Because Solon was so grieved at the thought of the disintegration of the Athenian state and dared not to speak for fear of this law, he pretended to be crazy. He went around the city eating charcoal and singing some verses, which for the sake of brevity I will not recite. These verses described what an insult to Athens it was that the Megarans held his island. The verses had such an impact, that the Athenian leaders rescinded the law and made him the captain to lead in the island's recapture. Thus he who suffers because the honor of his country is damaged will seek every possible solution to remedy it. So Your Grace orders me to explain to you what old salaries are; I will explain how the registration books are manipulated, everyone uses them to drain the treasury, and how the governors, captains, and official in the forts deploy them, unraveling the finances of the treasury.

---

93. Salamis lies between Athens and the nearby city of Megara, which held the island before it was captured by Athens.

Stone markers in the fort in Diu. The tablets at the left and right are tombstones, while the center stone reads, "During the reign of the most serene King Dom João IV, who ordered Fernão de Miranda Henriques, governor of the fort..."
Photo by Timothy Coates.

SCENE 9

Old Payments for Soldiers, How the King Is Robbed by Them, and How to Avoid Them

1. Soldier: First, since Your Grace has asked me, I will explain old payments for soldiers. These old payments are those due me, to Peter, to John, and to all those listed in the military registration books, totaling more than a million in gold. They are the reason all those leave Portugal to go to India, be they single soldiers, married men, or tradesmen. All of them are listed and receive their salaries wherever they serve, with the exceptions of Bengal and Malindi. Yet many of these men are deceased, and they are still listed as active in these books. Some who have been dead for twenty years are receiving salaries, which the king pays, not to them but to others, who receive it in the following manner.

2. A captain goes to take charge of his fort, and the governor gives him a provision stating that the quarterly salaries shall be paid for fifty servants and twelve relatives. The relatives receive large amounts and some of them

get paid, while the payments for the others the captain keeps for himself. In reality, he only has ten or twelve servants with him, and he keeps the additional payments. Any men who died, and the men in Bengal or Malindi, all remain listed in the book. Other imaginary people are paid by order of the governor even if they are not listed. Either due to fear or a lack of conscience, the secretary of the factory will then certify, "All the men listed were paid."

3. In the same way, the factor has certain men to whom he pays quarterly salaries. He has two such men with him and all the others get their money by other people's names. Forts on the frontiers, according to the regulations, should have three hundred to four hundred soldiers, but six hundred to seven hundred get paid. It would be a miracle if two hundred were actually present (the others all being deceased). Every day new imaginary men are created. Later, when the books are examined by the factor to calculate whom the captain has already paid, a fourth will not have signed for payment. The captains then produce signed statements from these men saying that he [the captain] should be paid their salaries. These statements then reach the viceroy or governor, who passes a provision that the captain be paid for those who have not signed the book. I know two or three captains who took in payments in cash for more than forty thousand pardaus for each of these imaginary soldiers. If this happens every three years in just one fort, how much would it be for all of them? It is certain that this is the greatest state expenditure in the budget.

4. Another example can be found in a fortress where every summer six or seven ships await to guard a convoy. They are paid for escorting twenty-five ships, but they do not accompany more than twelve or thirteen. The difference is split three ways among the captain of the fort, the factor, and the captain of the ships, and it pays for their food. These fleets then go about virtually empty-handed and are captured by pirates, which has happened several times.

5. Your Grace can now see how poorly the king is served and how his fleets are in danger. I will skip over many other similar cases that wallow in that honey pot called the royal treasury. Such cases are without end and involve those officials responsible for the registration books and those who audit the accounts. The factors are also involved in this fraud; because they pay some salaries with gusto, these payments to soldiers will then fall into

the factors' hands, some to buy expensive goods cheaply and others to pay their bills. However, these I forgive because, if they did not do these things, the poor things, how would they purge themselves of guilt?[94] The Casa dos Contos is a purgatory for the factors and treasury officials in India, and there is much to be said about that.[95] In Portuguese India, there is nothing holy, everything is rotten and filled with holes, with running sores. If you do not cut off one limb, the illness will spread throughout the entire body and corrupt it.

6. Returning now to the subject of old payments, a factor or treasurer presents his account to the Casa dos Contos, which states that he owes two thousand cruzados. Right away a provision is passed that he should pay one thousand, and the remaining thousand will be redeemed in old payments due to those who present themselves. The bill is then paid, and the old payments get collected by friends or other people—even by people who do not exist—and others who are familiar with the names in the books. The money for those who are absent or dead is subtracted. When a servant of the governor visits the fortresses of the north on an errand for his master, or when his master arrives from Portugal and visits these cities to inform them of his arrival and of the king's health, he collects at least two thousand dobras. He also collects certificates for three or four hundred pardaus in old payments for Diu or Hormuz, and these are paid as described above in good coin.

7. In another example, the doctor for the viceroy or governor submits a petition that he should be paid the back wages for the soldiers he has treated. Without having visited one of them, since all of them were in the hospital, he is paid five or six thousand pardaus in back pay. One of the secretaries of the General Registry told me, when speaking about this material, that a doctor working for a viceroy was compensated twenty or twenty-two thousand pardaus in this manner during his three years there.

8. I do not want to overlook one thing that I find unjust. In the fortresses, when the salaries are given to the soldiers, they are paid ten at a time. At the bottom of the registration book is stated the direction that one soldier

---

94. Couto is being ironic here; in other words, if they stopped acting dishonestly, they would have to reform themselves.

95. The *Casa dos Contos* was the head accounting house.

may substitute for another if his name is not listed in the book. This soldier may be paid at a reduced rate. So the poor suffering man is paid two quarterly payments, one of which he takes because no one knows that he never served in Hormuz or Diu, and the other one is a reduced payment. He is the guarantor for the one standing closest to him whose name was not on the list. This has happened to me, and that is why I speak about it with grief.

9. By these examples, everyone will see how and where the king is robbed. When the state of Portuguese India is in need, there is nowhere to turn for help because the greatest part of its income from its customs houses disappears in this smoke and mirrors.

10. Crown Official: I am pleased to hear about these things, stated so clearly. I only heard about them very briefly from higher officials. Reading the written opinions, I could never determine much, but I can now. With the zeal of a good Portuguese subject, you have explained more for your king than anyone has previously. Now that we have discussed this subject, I would like to hear your opinion as to how to correct it. In addition to your extensive experience and good judgment, I am sure some experienced and knowledgeable people there have presented their suggestions about how to remedy this.

11. Soldier: There are some on the Council who can give good advice in all matters, because they are experienced and have been there much longer than the nobles who are called to give their opinions at the council. Some of these are totally inexperienced. This is really a curse of the Portuguese that commoners are ignored and never appointed to do anything. All the other nations have more respect for age and experience in warfare than for someone's bloodline and nobility.

12. Leaving behind this material, which was good to speak about, you wanted to ask my opinion about the business at hand. In order to do that, it is necessary to ask someone else with knowledge about it, someone who is not a soldier like me. These matters are for those more familiar with the business of finances and related matters. Who can give a better overview of these than Your Excellency, who lived for so long in India as a captain, a captain in charge, and later as governor of India, dealing with all these issues? You are personally familiar with these matters and have a better understanding given your illustrious lineage and distinguished upbringing.

13. Nobleman: I do not go along with that. The upbringing and lineage

that you talk about do not provide any better reasoning than that, that you have shown. Because of the many years of experience that you have had with these matters, you clearly show the good and the bad. For that reason, continue and tell us your opinions. I will give mine when His Majesty asks me for them. It is possible that many of the things you say will remind me of things I have forgotten.

14. Soldier: Better to obey than to give up. I am still your subject, as I was when you were governor, and I will do as you order. I will tell you about the military side of things since I do not understand the details of the treasury.

15. First, I think that if His Highness intends at some point to pay what is owed he must clear up the debts in the registration books and list the living in one book and the dead in another. Once this is done, the books can be closed and placed in a chest or archives, which there should be in India for all such old materials. These would include all letters from the king, from the captains in charge of the fleets, and the forts, correspondence to and from the nearby kingdoms, missions of ambassadors, written opinions regarding conditions in Portuguese Asia, notebooks regarding the fleets with the captains' names, and everything else that would be useful for future historians. This would keep alive the name of Portugal and the Portuguese in Asia and maintain its fame in the world. The neglect of Portuguese Asia could be a long story of embarrassment for so many governors. There have been so many who lacked interest in the results of their actions. The memory of their deeds would be forever preserved in such an archives.[96]

16. However, returning to our suggestion, once this arrangement of the registration books has been completed, and all the soldiers living in Goa and the nobles who receive monthly payments to feed and house them have been registered, all the other old books should be burned. These new books should only be used in the following manner: to organize six regiments and register all the Portuguese soldiers in India. The soldiers who live in Goa

---

96. This paragraph gives us another indication of when the *Dialog* was written, because the archives mentioned here were founded by royal decree in 1595. Diogo do Couto was its first director, and many of the collections are organized exactly as he describes. Presumably, he wrote this passage before 1595 and did not change it in his final version in 1612. These collections are known today as the Historical Archives of Goa, the oldest archives in India.

should register for whatever company they wish. The oldest and most experienced nobles will be the captains, who will also have sergeants, corporals, and other officials. Each company will have a secretary who will maintain a register of those serving in the company, with their names, birthplaces, and the year they arrived. The governor in power at the time should then issue decrees to all the cities and forts in Portuguese India that the captains there should, under strict penalties, list all the soldiers present. This list would be registered by the most trustworthy local alderman.

17. When these soldiers are ready to register, the secretary will tell them the names of the captains of each militia so they can select which one they wish to join. As soon as they make their selection, their names will be registered in a book designed for this purpose as follows: so-and-so, son of so-and-so, who came to India in such-and-such a year, registered in the company of so-and-so. All of them will be registered in this manner. Once they are listed, each soldier will be notified that as soon as he arrives in Goa, he must join his company. The registration will end in all the forts, and copies of the books will be sent to Goa. Then each captain can see the list of soldiers and will immediately know who is in each company. He will know who is present and who is absent. Once these registration books arrive from the fortresses, on the appointed day the captain will come for the general roll call where there will be a master register containing the names of each soldier and his company. From this he will compose a list of each company.

18. In this way, the viceroy will know in an instant which soldiers are serving the crown and where they are living. When the soldiers living in Goa wish to leave, they will be required to inform their captains or the company secretaries, who will note in the margin that "so-and-so left Goa to join the expedition," or something else. When they return, they will immediately go to their company and have their return noted. Those who join the armada will go with their captains to be paid, and this will be noted in the book. That way, the salary for a soldier paid in Diu or Damão will be subtracted, since it will be registered in these books. Thus, those who serve will be paid, and the captain will not be able to pay fifty men unless they are with him, nor will the factor or any other official be able to pay his absent servants. This will eliminate old salaries and the ability to give salaries to others, since they will not get anything until they are present to receive it.

19. In order for this to work, it is very important that His Majesty pay monthly salaries to those who live in Goa to allow them to eat.[97] In the end, His Majesty will pay less by doing this than he did previously with the old payments given out each year in the manner I have stated. Married men in Goa and other cities should be registered in other books, which the captains should keep, sending a copy to the viceroy so that he can draw up a master register of married men, with their names and the places where they reside.[98] These men will not be paid a salary unless they serve on the armada. The current books are filled with the amounts owed to married men, men who have not served for thirty or forty years, but are still registered and continue to receive salaries. Many of these men have been dead for a long time, but they earn salaries just like the living. Others have left for China or returned to Portugal with their names still listed, and they are still due salaries. Payments for people such as these make up the greater part of this royal debt.

20. As soon as a soldier gets married in Goa, or any other outpost, he should be obliged to present himself before the secretary of the soldiers and declare that he is married, and this should be noted in the book. If he was married in Chaul and registered in Diu, he would be obliged to go to the secretary in Chaul and state that "so-and-so, son of so-and-so, of such-and-such company, was married in this fort," and this marriage would be noted in the captain's book. The secretary would be required to send a certificate to the captain or secretary of the company in Goa stating that so-and-so from that company was married so he can update his records. His name would then be added to the book of married men residing at the fort where the marriage took place.

21. In this way, it will always be clear who is a soldier and who is a married man, who is living and who is dead. Regarding deaths, the secretaries of the

---

97. Throughout the empire, the crown was notorious for late payments and for not paying salaries.

98. Couto is making a sharp distinction here between single and married men because married men did not have to serve in the military and they enjoyed certain rights not available to single men, such as holding office or wearing a cape. In theory, soldiers were all single, and therefore no married man should have been receiving a soldier's pay.

misericórdias and hospitals in all the forts will be responsible.[99] As soon as a sick soldier enters a hospital and dies, the secretary should send his name to his company secretary so that his death can be noted next to his name in the registration book. At the beginning of each month, the company secretary will list those who have left Goa, those who have married, or those who have passed away. By doing this, the dead will not be listed as living, the married as single, or the absent as present. It will straighten out the current situation and forbid one person from receiving the salary of another. People off in China will not be listed as present; Peter will not able to receive John's salary. Captains will not be able to pay more men than they command, and the viceroys will not give grants of old salaries. This would save the crown more than twenty thousand pardaus each year if payments were handled in the manner I have explained.

22. What I have said here is my opinion on this matter. It is possible that there are better ideas than what I have proposed. I will not find fault with those because I am not so attached to my own ideas that someone else's might not be better. He who believes this should follow this concept in all things. Plato in *Timaeus* says that no one was ever brought down in error by following someone else's ideas, but rather that many were derailed by following their own. St. Paul did not want to follow his own plan to go to Rome but instead followed the plan put forth by Philemon.[100] In the Bible, we see that David was a greater prophet than Nathaniel, but in the business of building the Temple, he was not so wedded to his own ideas that he could not accept those of Nathaniel.[101] Our Lord God complained repeatedly to Moses about the children of Israel being stubborn and rejecting the advice of others. For that reason, they spent their entire lives wandering, with their enemy's swords hanging over them.[102]

23. So I say that I submit these suggestions, but I am open to ideas from

---

99. The Santa Casa da Misericórida was the principal charity throughout the Portuguese world. It had chapters wherever there was a Portuguese settlement, and one of its many duties was to bury the dead. Its secretary would have been well placed to provide such information.

100. Philemon, chapter 1; Acts 10:21; Acts 23:11; Acts 27:14–16.

101. 2 Samuel 7, and 1 Chronicles 17.

102. Numbers 14.

others. If my ideas are good, do what the ephors of Sparta did when, in council, they gave a simple man, such as myself, great praise for completing a very difficult task. All of them feeling pleased, they then let the man leave the Senate and selected another very serious man who they asked to deliver the exact same praise using the same words. In the same way, drinking out of a simple clay mug improves the taste of the drink.

24. However, in all of what I have said there remains one sticking point, and that is that Portuguese India will not survive these companies of soldiers because, if the soldiers are united, they will sack and plunder the cities, rob the people, and commit all sorts of extortion. I do not know which is worse, that the king should lose what is his or the disorders caused by soldiers.

25. Crown Official: For certain, I do not think that any of those Athenians would have been able to offer a better suggestion in these matters than you have, as you also have done in all the other issues. I feel that you have a passion and spirit that is greater than others, and it encompasses more.

26. Nobleman: What you suggest cannot be such a bad thing since it was tried during the time of King Dom Sebastian, when he first sent Dom Luís de Ataíde to India.[103] He carried with him instructions to form companies of soldiers, which he did for a few days. But good things are never brought to completion. Regarding what you fear about the disorderly conduct of the soldiers, if they have honorable captains, there will be none of this. The day one soldier caused a disturbance, he would be shot. If a captain shot four soldiers, the others would fall in line. If a captain tolerated such behavior, the viceroy would throw him in irons and send him home to the king.

27. Crown Official: Even though I have been very closely following this matter about the registration of soldiers, I have not forgotten that you mentioned the account books, with which there are irregularities and corruption. I would really appreciate it if you would discuss this issue now while the sun is setting. This material is important, and I have just taken on this responsibility about India. I want to know everything and familiarize myself with what is going on there to be able to explain it.

---

103. King Dom Sebastian ruled Portugal from 1557 to 1578. He was the next-to-last king of the House of Aviz and died on the battlefield in Morocco.

Gate to the city of Diu.
Photo by Timothy Coates

28. Soldier: In order to do that, it will require more time. When I mentioned it in passing, I did not think that Your Excellency would find it of interest. But now that I have started it, I will finish discussing it as Your Excellency orders.

SCENE 10

Regarding the Accounts in Goa and Other Subjects

1. Soldier: The main accounting house in Goa is the most important one of all those in India for the king's treasury. It coordinates all the factors from all the fortresses, from the fleets, the small and the big ships, public treasury officials, and all the income from rents, which is a great sum. For this reason, it is important that honorable and truthful men, good upright officials,

administer it. All such effective administration is currently lacking. This institution is run by ten accountants with their secretaries, two supervisors, one guard, and one additional clerk with his secretary, and one chief inspector. Of these officials, the chief inspector has a salary of 330,000 *réis*, the accountants receive 120,000 to 140,000, and each secretary is paid 70,000.

2. I know that some of these officials became very wealthy, and they did so working in the Casa dos Contos without having any other sources of income. If they did not obtain this wealth by illicit means, they would only have been able to live modestly. This was how former officials that I knew lived; these officials were honest and just lived simply. However, some of the current officials have extravagant country homes and tracts of palm trees, and carry a great deal of money around with them. Some of the means by which they grew wealthy I noted while I was a soldier, not when I became an official.

3. First, say a factor is about to occupy his position in Hormuz, or any other fortress. He will be paired with an accountant who will conduct his audit. When he gets to his post, he orders many things—bolts of cloth, jewels, and money, which is deducted from his salary. When his time in office comes to an end and he prepares to pay his bill, the accountant leaves off auditing some other poor official who has been waiting for two years and who has nothing to give or offer. The accountant then completes the account of the wealthy factor in four days, without sending an inquiry outside because he finds all of his account to be in order. If anyone has any doubts, he resolves them and closes the accounts. The money he has sent he places in a folder, while he redeems the old paper debt he has received. His salary is then paid in full.

4. In another example, an accountant promises a viceroy that he will give an official so many thousand pardaus, and the viceroy immediately issues a grant of that sum. When all is said and done and the account is totaled, the viceroy's account is found to have a debt of some five or six thousand pardaus, which it should not have. Right away the debt is collected, and the man's estate is sold. Later, when the account is reexamined and the man says it contains errors, the debt is owed by the royal treasury and is never paid. Others then enjoy the comforts of the man's house and lands, which were sold. Your Graces should know how harmful acts of this sort are, always reopening the accounts. In this way, the factors in the forts arrive with a lot

of money in hand. Today they get two thousand, tomorrow one thousand, and the next day five hundred. They go around paving the way as they wish and closing accounts with debts on paper, without bothering to audit them conscientiously.

5. Another person might say that reopening old accounts causes greater damage to the viceroy when he ignores the salvation of his soul and honor. All the money that remains from these accounts should be handled by the executor in accordance with standing instructions. However, the viceroy collects the debts and he replaces these with old paper, which he purchased at a quarter of their value, as I explained in the chapter on such deceptions. In this manner a great part of the king's wealth is consumed, and everyone else can hardly carry away all the wealth they have made in this process.

6. And there is more. When a factor who served in a poor factory arrives, he presents his accounts. He then turns in his papers and has empty hands. He is assigned to the newest and least knowledgeable accountant. Since he arrived empty-handed, his papers are thrown on the stack of dead files. They examine them as they do the others, and the accountant has a thousand questions and there is no one to clear them up. In this fashion, the poor martyr will pass ten years with no justice. It would have been better if he had given the accountant what he spent in two or three years, and in one month he would have been on his way.

7. Another painful misdeed that the king should punish occurs when a new accountant has an account in his hands, then another arrives from outside, and the accountant expects a greater profit; he discards the first and throws the poor man out, and then grabs the other account. In no time at all, he is done with that one. This happens everywhere, and great oppression occurs and many injustices are committed because frequently people pay what they do not owe and others do not pay what they should.

8. One more thing that I nearly forgot, very worthy of being punished. That is that the manager of the accounting house appoints accountants who are his toadies, and together they share the big accounts as well as the most lucrative ones with the biggest profits. The others never finish theirs, as I have stated above. The manager is guilty of another hundred thousand injustices for which he is never punished. Those responsible are mixed up in all this, and they want money any way they can get it. I think that only God knows how to fix this. If anyone around here could fix it, it would be

an independently minded manager, a truthful and just man, so virtuous that he would not pay attention to the opinions of accountants involved in these matters. Such a man would see and understand everything going on around him; he would award the poor quickly and punish those accountants who delay paying them. If the king awarded honors and gifts to those who served him truthfully and with justice, he would find such men. He should not award such posts to those who plead for them, but rather to those whom the king asks to serve. Not doing this causes a lot of chaos.

9. Nobleman: You have outlined these problems very well. Sometimes I went to the accounting house and saw that it was in a shambles, with few accountants, and I wanted to straighten it out. This is of no small importance and has not escaped the king's as well as others' attention.

10. Soldier: I wanted to mention many things but my conscience held me back. If those who can fix the problem do nothing, then the matter weighs heavily on my mind, and I cannot have that so I started now. Your Graces should be listening carefully because you will find this to be of great interest and it will be necessary to tell the king everything.

11. The accounting house gives a factor a bill and he leaves with a debt of twelve or fifteen thousand cruzados, which the poor factor knows he does not have, and he cries and begs for justice, which he does not get. His debts are collected, and his estate is sold and divided. The suffering man then dies in poverty, dispossessed of his estate. Then many years later his heirs arrive to reexamine the account, and they find the original error. They ask for a revision, and it is granted. They pass a certificate petitioning the king for their payment, which never existed nor will exist.

12. From these examples there are several that I could tell at length. The officials excuse themselves by saying they did not know anything more about it. The regulations forgive them since no penalty is involved. From my viewpoint, if an accountant finds a debt that has not been audited thoroughly and inspected repeatedly, the [responsible] accountant and the inspector should pay the difference out of their own pockets. From my experience with the accounting house and the evil way things are done in India, they will always want to create a debt or some fraud for the viceroys' benefit, as they enjoy doing this, or these officials will divide the spoils among themselves.

13. When the viceroys set their guns down and turn to the king's treasury, they like to get their hands into everything. Some, for that reason, pamper the accountants in a way that no one else can. They have no scruples as to where their money comes from, whether from a good or a bad source. They bring charges against others' estates where nothing is owed. What is worse is that sometimes the owners are deceased and their widows and children are forced to make needless payments, or the accountants take the estates because the heirs do not know how to defend themselves. Only their deceased husbands could have responded to the charges laid against the estate.

14. There is more! A factor was presented with a bill for a large sum. Since he had abundant funds, he bargained with the accountant to make it appear that he owed nothing. The accountant closed the account and gave him a certificate saying he owed nothing. He left without paying the debt, but not before this golden opportunity filled the pockets of the accountant and other officials. Some time later, the accounts were audited, and the error was discovered. The king was owed a great deal of money. The factor's estate and personal goods were confiscated. The accountants responsible for this were dismissed and had to live on what the man had given them. I could go on and on about such cases, giving Your Excellency as many examples as you wish, but I will stop because I grow tired.

15. Crown Official: Oh, do not stop; please tell me more!

16. Soldier: Why hear of such ill doings? Does Your Excellency know how many of these there are? During my day, I heard a number of people complaining that the closed accounts produced many papers going back many years, and these dealt with other officials, statements had been changed, and everything else. Yet these were paid right away. It is possible that this happens with the account for a deceased factor from which he was ready to collect. If his heirs want to close the account and collect, the papers of old debts will reduce the total, which could involve a lot of money.

17. Crown Official: I heard many things, of which I was unaware, and I will be obligated to attend to them, but this information about the accounts has to be the most important. It is an urgent issue that requires attention. I promise you that of all the things you have told me, this will be the first item that I bring to His Majesty's attention. I am very surprised that the governors do not write us about this or get to the bottom of all this themselves.

18. Soldier: There are others who reveal more of this to them, and because of this, they forget about those who may tell the king. The governors have these people in their pockets. There are now more royal tax supervisors than captains of war. From the little that I understand, these accountants are the ones who weave the webs and devise these frauds, yet they are the ones the governors praise to the king. They tell the king the accountants have increased his wealth more and more.

19. Gentlemen, I sincerely want to put a stop to these claims of increased wealth, since they deceive the king daily. I would like you to ask for a secret inquiry regarding them. In the same year that they claim there is increased wealth, you will discover that Portuguese Asia had more needs and miseries than ever. You will discover that, during that year, they asked the people for loans and failed to pay the merchants for rice, wheat, pitch, wood — in short, everything purchased for the fleets. If what is taken by force from subjects to give to the king they call "increased wealth," then I call it "theft." The ministers should stand before God to give detailed explanations of why they failed to inform the king of these actions.

20. What more can I tell you? I would like to conclude with this: The captains, factors, and other officials leave with their accounts in debt. These are certified right away and certificates are sent to Portugal stating that there are 50, 60, or 100,000 pardaus to collect. Then the various parties all call for justice, show their innocence, and are absolved of any debt. There in Portugal, they hope we have a bit of gold, and everything disappears in smoke.

21. Well gentlemen, I want to tell you how it really is. Few of these officials, including some of the viceroys themselves, have told the king the truth. I say that he should not believe these many letters he receives from them, but instead pay attention to other letters he receives from ordinary people. These people do not have an agenda; they write with love for their country and out of fear of their king. They are not asking for anything. What truths can someone tell if he does not fear his king or God?

22. The king should conduct an experiment. After one of these viceroys whom I have been discussing (not one of the uncorrupted ones) returns to Portugal, the king should order that one of the reports he sent to him from India be returned there by way of an upright and dependable priest, and that an inquiry be made about these things by honorable people who are above suspicion. He will discover the biggest lies in the world, and then he

will know the truth. Then he should severely punish the person who wrote those letters in order to make an example of him. Furthermore, he should not have so much faith in what they say that he believes nothing else. If someone from outside this circle writes to the king saying something different, he should tell the letter writer what the viceroys state in their letters.

23. If not, Your Graces, then look at how many times the city council of Goa has written to the king complaining that the viceroys failed to respect its rights and privileges. In response, the king writes only to the viceroys. What will the viceroy do, the viceroy who caused the problem with the city? What reforms will he implement? What justice will result? Do Your Graces know where this comes from? It comes from His Highness not examining the issues of India with sufficient time to get to the bottom of them. Normally, everything waits until January or February when the ships are ready to leave. Since time is short, the king and his advisors do little more than respond to what they receive. This puts the ball back into the viceroy's court, and he always does whatever he wants.

24. For this to change, there should be a separate council here in Portugal just for Indian affairs. The men on this council should be virtuous and passionate about serving the common good. All the correspondence from India should be reviewed by this council and, after informing the king, the council itself should respond to each letter. In this manner, when the ships leave, everything will receive a careful response. The city of Goa will have its complaints addressed, rather than being ignored by the viceroys, and individuals will be relieved from the injustices they encounter. Gentlemen, in a state so distant from the king where the viceroys and ministers of justice and treasury are unrestrained, it is an injustice when someone complains about a viceroy's actions and is told, "The viceroy is there and he will see that justice is done." If he is the person committing these injustices, how will he remedy them? As a loyal Portuguese, I cannot but feel this way and speak about it.

25. It is certain that some of the viceroys in India are the greatest enemies of the king's treasury and soul. You should not be misled by acts of virtue. I do not know what India possesses or what planet rules it that it alters people's good thoughts and wishes, which is astonishing. I do not need a better example of this than Your Excellency who is here; you who governed that state by emergency appointment. You had been such a good friend to the

soldiers, so passionate in seeing justice done, so vexed by the irregularities caused by the viceroys, that you frequently stated in your conversations that you were not handing out favors. You alone spoke about how they governed using their servants and relatives, how they did not allow the ministers to enforce justice, and how they took things from the warehouses and fleets without paying.

26. A viceroy should say what he did while governing. I am going to speak the truth, and Your Excellency can order me killed for that. I am sixty years old and have nothing to lose. During your time in office, I never saw justice done, nor was a soldier paid anything, nor a merchant paid for what was taken. Everything was sold for cash in the public squares: crying and wailing with no one to turn to!

27. This brings me to an example of something I wanted to mention. It happened to a nobleman. He was the captain of a fort, and another honorable but poor married nobleman lived there as well. One day the captain was talking with his wife, and he said to her, "For certain, I do not know a governor or viceroy who has such a bad moral sense that he will not give food to that nobleman." These complaints were made in public. It so happened that winter that the governor died, and this captain replaced him. Once in power, the captain's wife reminded him he had complained about the viceroy not giving food to the nobleman and asked him to remedy the problem now that he had power. He responded to her with these words, "Listen here, my lady, at that time I spoke as so-and-so, but now I have to act like the governor of India." Saying this, he then gave the man nothing. May God protect you both from those who protest the acts of the viceroys, yet when placed in that position, do much worse.

28. Nobleman: Will you not forgive me for these realities as I am present?

29. Soldier: No, sir, the world is in this state because people have not spoken about them. Do you know what really shocks me and what the kings need to account for to God? It is about all that you have said and yet they have not punished you or any of the other governors or viceroys. If you, sir, when you took over as governor, if you had feared that the king would punish you, would you not have governed more prudently? Of course you would have! But since you knew that everything would be ignored, and the worst that would happen was that you would be confined to your country estate, you paid no attention. You did not fear the king or God. You do not

want me to speak any more; it will make me go crazy walking the streets seeking justice for those who are guilty of doing these things.

30. Crown Official: Oh! Would it only please God to let me see a few of these crazy people. Do you know why the world is lost? It is because everyone is so calculating; they take care of themselves more than anyone else. They give nothing more than what they must.

31. Soldier: Do Your Graces know what I fear? I have to tell you this fact and please accept it, Your Graces, as boldness on my part, whatever the consequences. Officials here in Portugal and there in India do not care one bit about Portuguese India. It seems they would be pleased to see its end and wash their hands of the place. I say this because of the neglect shown here in providing Portuguese India with its needs; this is the conclusion we have reached there in India.

32. What does it mean when one year the cities, the nobles, the religious orders, and individuals write to tell you that Portuguese India is lost, that help is needed, that the viceroy is negligent and lacks interest in the welfare of all? That same year when we awaited a new viceroy accompanied by many ships, a great deal of money, artillerymen, soldiers, and supplies; instead, you gave us another year with the same viceroy about whom you had received so many complaints. The help we got in India was four ships with no people and none of the supplies we requested. Is that not your way of saying that you will send nothing or that you did not read our letters to you? If you did read them, you forgot all the complaints and requests in them.

33. For certain, if there were a Christian king whom the men could serve, they would have done so already rather than exhausting themselves with Portuguese India. However, over there we have only enemies everywhere, and they want to slit our throats. They know the goings-on of the viceroys as well as we do, the complaints written about them, when the ships arrive from Portugal, the men and arms that they bring, and how little those here give to India and how upset those there are at being considered important. Our enemies no longer have any regard for us. If they did not have their hands bound, you should know, sirs that the game would be over. However, thanks be to God, they have been struck with fear of the great Mughal emperor who wants to take their kingdoms. We should give prayers for his long life. If he should die and these barbarians see beyond their fears, I am

afraid they will unleash all their powers against us and conquer us. The era of Viceroy Dom Luís de Ataíde is over, and with it went his military might and invincibility. Look how it is now, without artillery, without weapons, with no ships, and even with no soldiers or leaders because all is lost!

34. Crown Official: God save me! Are we lacking all this? What do the viceroys do?

35. Soldier: It is funny that Your Excellency would ask me that question, because I have already told you many times! Let me ask you, How is it that the king does not ask what is in India, what provisions are in his warehouses, what is the state of his fleets, and how his appointed captains behave? The viceroys deal with what they wish; what is noteworthy is that they ignore their greatest duties. They reap the harvest belonging to others. That is how things are going from bad to worse.

36. Crown Official: Tell me about this, as I do not understand.

37. Soldier: Yes, I would be happy to do that. Your Graces need to pay attention to what I am saying. In the early years in India, when the name of the Portuguese was held in lofty splendor above the stars, the viceroys who ruled had no time for anything except spreading the holy Catholic faith, enlarging the king's wealth, enriching the state and its subjects, selecting captains, organizing and provisioning the fleets, seeking out the Turks at Suez, punishing and subjugating the rulers of Malabar, fighting those in the neighboring kingdoms, keeping the soldiers contented, practicing with their swords and guns, visiting the hospitals, and many other similar activities.[104]

38. Nowadays they do not do any of these things. The game has changed. The fleets patrol only as a formality and are thrown together without foresight or organization. Soldiers go around clamoring for assistance. Houses where they should be practicing swordsmanship instead are dancing schools, where young girls are instructed. Practicing with weapons is abandoned and has become a disreputable skill. There are no artillerymen in all of India who can hit the top of a hill, but rather they hit the bottom of it. Rather than hospital visits, now there are visits to the main accounting house and the High Court. Governors have become aldermen and captains have become priests. Everything is like this.

---

104. Dom João de Castro led an expedition up the Red Sea that resulted in a skirmish with the Ottomans in Suez in 1541.

39. Crown Official: Who are you calling priests and aldermen? Tell us this because I want to understand.

40. Soldier: Your Excellency knows very well, but I will tell you. The viceroys made themselves priests because nowadays the Franciscans and the Dominicans cannot select members except those whom the viceroy wishes. In this way, anyone he wants can be placed under religious jurisdiction. It would be a great deed if you could stop this. You will then see whether they silence your mouth and fail to pay your regular salaries! They do not see how God did not allow a king to enter a religious office, and how some were punished for doing that.

41. If you want examples, look how King Jeroboam, who wanted to assume the office of a priest, was warned by a man of God not to do that, since it greatly offended the Lord. He said that one from the generation of David would cruelly kill the priests of that altar and burn their bones there. So that Jeroboam would know that this was a prophecy not made in vain, the man of God said the altar would split in two. That exact thing happened in front of everybody, as the prophet had predicted. When the king lifted up his hand to order the prophet apprehended, his arm was paralyzed.[105] Uzziah the king of Jerusalem, because he also wanted to assume the priesthood, was confronted by the High Priest Azariah and the other priests. Then Heaven sent a powerful earthquake, and a mountain fell inside the city, and a ray of sunlight hit the king's face. He developed leprosy and was forced to isolate himself from his people.[106]

42. So what can I tell Your Graces? Even all this is but a small amount. Even up to the pope's holdings, and the differences between the Dominicans and the Augustinians, there have been viceroys who wanted to become involved. I am afraid this will provoke some great punishment. If nothing happens here, it will be there, where punishment is very different and

---

105. See 1 Kings 13:1–6 and 2 Kings 23:13–16. Jeroboam I ruled Israel from approximately 930 to 909 BCE. "A son named Josiah will be born to the House of David. On you [i.e., the altar] he will sacrifice the priests of the high places who make offerings here and human bones will be burned on you." King Jeroboam then asked the man of God to pray for him and ask God to restore the use of his hand, which he did, and his hand was restored.

106. King Azariah or Uzziah ruled Judea from 783 to 742 BCE. This passage from 2 Kings 15:3 and 2 Chronicles 26:4–5.

repentance is worthless. It is the theological doctrine that if Our Lord God punished every sin in this world, it would take away from us, according to the Christian belief, the Resurrection and Last Day of Judgment. One thing is clear: if here on earth we paid for all our sins, there would be no payment in the afterlife. Therefore, some sins are punished here and now in order to show God's providence and power, and cause others to fear him, while the punishment for many other sins awaits the next life, because that is where one gets one's due. Everything that I have said so far I submit for correction by the Holy Mother Church, because soldiers have no leave to be discussing such things.

43. This is when the viceroys become prelates. They say that they now also become aldermen. When the cities make their selections, which are [supposed to be] free, the viceroys have become so involved that only those aldermen and orphan judges, which they chose, will be elected. Once a viceroy was on board a galley, about to leave Goa during the very day that the town council was making such a decision. They took the list of candidates out to him on the galley, and he did not like it. He put the names he wanted on the list, and the aldermen had no say in the matter.

44. Do Your Graces know why it is this way? It is so they will have aldermen in their pockets to do whatever they ask and give them whatever they request, which they do and which is completely contrary to serving the king and his subjects. But I should tell you that the city council is equally guilty in these irregularities. Its elections and documents are so discredited by the king and the viceroys, as is the wording of their propositions, that no one takes any notice of them. Most aldermen are selected by their friends and by votes that they solicited, and some of them knew neither their mothers nor their fathers. They came from Portugal holding lowly trades; this makes them interested in obtaining such positions. They care nothing for the common good because they are only thinking of themselves.

45. Crown Official: This is new to me. Are they interested in becoming aldermen?

46. Soldier: That is a good question that Your Excellency has put to me! What things are there these days that people do not want to have? Your Excellency should know that I have heard people say that one year as an alderman yields five hundred dobras in income. Now you can see why it is so desired. This is how it is done: whenever there is a vacancy, their names

are always listed. There was a time in Goa when the government of the city of Goa was in the hands of no more than five or six men. No one who had a higher status or those in the know ever got those positions because their names were not listed.

47. What I have said about the town council I can say about the misericórdia. It would be a miracle if they sought out the most virtuous men for these positions. Instead, they find their closest friends and relatives. I heard someone tell a citizen who is my relative, a good, honorable, and wise man who was a brother of the misericórdia many years ago, that in the past they always listed the very best local people on the elections slate. None of them was ever left off the list. This was because the elections list was drafted in good conscience, and they never listed those who asked to be on the board, but only those they selected. These were never relatives or friends.

48. Now that I am discussing this subject, I wanted to be certain to mention one thing about the misericóridia. There was a time when the nobles who were brothers of the misericórdia, who ruled that organization in India, spent all their time altering the statutes or replacing them with others that were unreasonable, which is shocking. For certain, the king needs to remember that, in his role as protector of all the chapters of the misericórdia in his kingdom, he should order an inquiry into these things, especially the nature of the elections. They have broken all the rules established by the chapter in Lisbon, which is the head chapter. No brother may select new members, because if he did, it would prejudice all of them. It would determine the outcome of the election beforehand. If everyone knew the election was forced and the outcome was rigged, they would solicit what they wanted. All this causes chaos and is not a service to God.

49. Excuse me, Your Graces, as I have gotten off the subject of selection of aldermen for the town council, which I was discussing, and the great harm caused by the viceroys' interference in this process. Many things result from their interference, things about which I will not speak because they are shameful. They do not maintain the rights awarded to them by the king, because he who does not follow those from God will do anything! These misdeeds are clear indications that everything is collapsing. From the mouth of God comes the threat that ruination will strike the entire kingdom when it is estranged from him. What greater alienation can exist but that between the viceroy or governor and God? Look at the punishments he

inflicted on the people of Israel for this separation. The Holy Bible is full of examples of his punishments, as well as the rewards he made to kings and governors who ruled following his laws. He made their kingdoms flourish and destroyed their enemies.

50. Look at the example of Josaphat, the king of Jerusalem, pious and passionate in his love of the Lord. The Moabites came to destroy him with the Ammonites and the Arabs. The good king had no means of defense, so he and his people turned to God to defend them. The Lord wished to repay his love, so he caused hatred and division among Josaphat's enemies when they surrounded Ein Gedi and came together at the site of the battle next to the Dead Sea. His enemies slaughtered each other, and when Josaphat reached the desert of Theceforoua, he saw a landscape with no one alive. He and his people went among the dead and plundered their valuables, taking great riches from them, and then burned their bodies. Because God had shown them such mercy at that place, they named it "the Valley of Blessing," because the time to show gratitude for his mercy is immediately rather than later. In that way, the next time you need help, he will come to your aid.[107]

51. I see another warning in India, where I fear there will be grave punishments. The viceroys and governors are more attached to the honors and rewards of their positions than to their obligations and duties. May it please God to not allow this curse to spread to Portugal as well. This is something that injures the Lord and for which he will immediately punish the guilty. Look at what Saint Paul asks, "You wish to be rewarded and collect the blessings but refuse to work?" This cannot be, since when a viceroy and his ministers are called to serve, the first thing that they should consider is their obligations. These are great and weigh so heavily upon them that many would rather live in poverty than be so honored by so many duties.

52. From the pen of Otanes, the Persian, we have the story of how, at the death of Cambises, seven of the lords debated whether it would be better to have the seven rule collectively or have one ruler.[108] Otanes favored many ruling at once. The others thought only one should rule, and they needed

---

107. See 2 Chronicles 20. The valley is called "Berakah," or "blessing."
108. Son of Cyrus, was king of Persia and ruled from 529 to 522 BCE.

to make a selection. After some thought about the duties of the office, Otanes said that he did not want to be considered for the position, leaving just six from which to make the selection. Darius was chosen, and Otanes was free of any of the duties that the position demanded.

53. Livy notes that when Consul Minucius was in his camp surrounded by the Sabines and the Aequi, Lucius Quinctius Cincinnatus was elected dictator in Rome to bring peace.[109] Going with his troops, he surrounded his enemies in their camps just as they had done to the consul Minucius. In the end, he defeated them and placed them under his yoke. Returning to Rome, he was received in triumph, but within fourteen days, he resigned the dictatorship, even though he could have held on to it for six months. He returned to his work because the duties of the position affronted his dignity. This is what happens to other leaders who seek out positions (but not to those who are sought out to fill them): they cultivate their possibilities, and they may bribe to obtain these positions because they want the rewards more than the honors. They pay little attention to the required duties.

54. The Romans sent that virtuous Fabricius as ambassador to King Pyrrhus to redeem the captives he was holding after the Battle of Heraclea in Campania.[110] Consul Valerius had been in charge.[111] King Pyrrhus wanted Fabricius to stay with him and offered to make him a ruler of one-third of his lands, but Fabricius declined the offer. He felt it was too demanding, and he said he would rather die of hunger in poverty than assume such a post. Those Roman leaders who were received in triumph, in special circumstances, received ovations and other similar things—first they completed

---

109. Livy (59 BCE to 17 CE) was Titus Livius Lucius, a famed Roman historian; Minucius Esquiline's Augurnus was Roman consul in 458 BCE. The Sabines and the Aequi lived in central Italy. Cincinnatus (519–430 BCE) was a Roman consul and was twice elected dictator, once in 458 and later in 439 BCE. Both times, he resigned as soon as the crisis was resolved.

110. Gaius Fabricius Luscinus was a consul of Rome in 282 and 278. King Pyrrhus of Epirus lived from 318 to 272 BCE. The Battle of Heraclea (280 BCE) marked a great victory for the Greeks and loss for the Romans. Campania is south of Rome and contains the city of Naples.

111. Publius Valerius Laevinius, consul of Rome and commander of the Roman troops at Heraclea.

the duties of their offices. This is what brought them such honors. (Many did not obtain this. They failed to obtain numerous and great benefits because they did not live up to their obligations.) Let us turn to those who even sacrificed their lives for their obligations.

55. Livy also notes that Consul Marcus Regulus was held captive in Carthage, having been captured and disheartened by Hasdrubal and his troops, who killed thirty thousand Romans and captured another five thousand.[112] Later, Consuls M. Aemilius Paullus and Falvius Nobilior had such great victories against the Carthaginians that they were obliged to ask the Roman Senate for peace.[113] For those negotiations, the Carthaginians selected as their ambassador the captive Marcus Regulus. He had to first swear that he would return to Carthage after the negotiations were completed. When he presented himself before the Senate with his mission, the senators had differing opinions. At the end, Regulus himself was asked to give his opinion. In a very grave and eloquent speech, he encouraged everyone to continue the war and not make peace with the Carthaginians, because it was his opinion that they would never be true friends of the Romans. Given their current state, he felt it would be easy to subjugate and destroy Carthage. His status as their captive should not, he asserted, be an impediment to continuing the war against Carthage, which was for the greater good for all.

56. To add another word here, I wanted to be sure to censure the viceroys in the great mistake they all commit by making peace with the ruler of Calicut. It is well known that, as long as there are Muslims in his kingdom, he cannot be our ally. It has been our repeated experience that whenever they wish to break peace treaties by robbing our subjects, challenging Portuguese India, and tarnishing the viceroys, they do so. When diplomatic negotiations come to a halt, our ships should cruise along their shores and burn four of their thatched houses and a couple of their dugout canoes. We show them what damage we can do, and we negotiate peace with them. This tactic would not last longer than the Muslims wanted it to.

---

112. Marcus Atilius Regulus (307–250 BCE) was a Roman statesman and general. Hasdrubal Barca (245–207 BCE) was a Carthaginian general during the Second Punic War and brother of Hannibal. Couto refers to the Battle of Cannae (216 BCE), one of the major battles of the Second Punic War.

113. Consuls of Rome in 255 BCE.

57. As it is so poorly understood here in this kingdom and because it is clear that this causes such damage, the king should order that peace treaties should never again be signed with the ruler of Calicut. There should be a serious penalty for doing so. Instead, Portuguese India should wage total war against him. If the viceroys so wished, within four years they could incite the nobility of Malabar to rise up against the Muslims; we could put them all to the sword. If you told me we made these treaties as a crafty strategy, or out of necessity in order to save our resources, then that would be fine. However, Portuguese India does not have any need of this ruler. The cargos on the ships from Cochin or Quilon and the rivers of Kanara provide sufficient pepper.[114] Much more could come from Malacca.

58. In order to conserve resources, nothing is done. Whether there is peace or not, the ships have to go to Malabar, and this costs a lot. This is so well known: we should not make peace nor wage more warfare than to cruise down their coast, capture their ports, block their provisions, and keep them from using their smaller boats, which they use for raids. Only in this way, without fighting them on land or risking any troops, will we take over Malabar in four or five years. Really, I am amazed that people do not understand this or that we do not, for once, wage a good war so that the people of Malabar can have a durable and long-lasting peace. However, we do not know how to conduct a proper war with them. Our fleets go there to visit cities and to take relatives of the viceroys to be the chief captains of Malabar. They do not wage war and do not make peace.

59. Tell me, Your Graces, why does no viceroy have the backbone to do as I suggest? Sending a fleet to Malabar costs sixty thousand pardaus? Why not take twenty thousand and go to Cannanore, contact the nobility or even the ruler himself, and give him the money to have him issue a secret order to burn all the pirate ships in those rivers?[115] He could easily do this. For more money, the ruler and his nobles will hand over the children and wives of the pirates. This way, by burning the ships, it would not be necessary to send a fleet, but only a couple of fast ships to match a few of theirs.

60. If you were to tell me that the soldiers would be without a place for military practice if we did this, I would tell you there is Sri Lanka, Malacca,

---

114. Kanara is the coastal region just south of Goa.
115. By "pirate," I assume Couto means the Muslim merchants.

and many other places to secure. By doing as I have suggested, the viceroys could invest all the resources they wished and not spend royal money on the fleets. Do we not have Surat, Bharuch, and another three hundred places that are more lucrative for the king and the soldiers? What does it mean, "peace in Malabar this year" or "peace in the next year"? Ever since we have been in India, such peace has not been honored.

61. The Romans would have none of this, which Marcus Regulus understood, as I was saying earlier. Making peace with Carthage would have been such an insult and caused such damage that he urged the Senate toward war, even though he understood the risk to his life. He would rather have sacrificed his life than discredit his country. The Portuguese care little for such concerns, and the viceroys even less. They retire in wealth to their estates and ignore the attacks and insults made to Portuguese India. If and when all is lost in India, even those most guilty of milking it dry will boast that it did not happen in their day. They will boast about that to the one in charge when this happens (may God forbid it). In that way, they will trust that we will believe his actions have caused this. In the event this should happen, and I greatly fear it will occur under the rule of a good, just, and honest viceroy who is less greedy than the others, it will be those people who are responsible for the loss of Portuguese India, kicking the legs out from underneath it.

62. Going back to Marcus Regulus: after he persuaded the Senate not to accept a peace treaty, he asked for leave to return to his captivity. Everyone was stunned, and they tried to make him change his mind. However, he did not, saying that rather than going free, it was more important to him to complete his duties as ambassador and remain faithful to his oath. Saying goodbye to them, he returned to Carthage, where he was tortured and put to death because they knew he had obstructed the peace treaty.

63. So I have now arrived at the point where I have to say how poorly the viceroys and governors make their rulings and follow the oaths of office, to which they swear here in Portugal. I shake my head every time when I think about the oath they take at the hands of the king. They swear they have not requested the position themselves, nor had someone else do so for them. They swear they did not solicit the position, nor give a bribe for it, nor speak about it in any manner. They are so wise, knowing that the majority of them

did go to great pains to acquire, bribe, then bribe again, and perform even additional acts, which for the honor of some I will remain silent.

64. They also swear they will be just and follow the king's orders, yet their actions make a mockery of these things. They wonder if one day someone will ask for an explanation, but no one does. Arriving in India at their entrance to Goa, they swear on the crucifix and the Bible that they will respect the privileges of the city of Goa. Yet they fail to do so at every turn. Instead, they act without any scruples, even to gain very minor things. The viceroys believe they can do little unless they trample the laws and ordinances of the king, and sometimes they do so out of excessive pride.

65. The king is guilty in this because in his instructions to the viceroys and governors he says at the end, "And above all else, do what you think best serves me." The viceroys and governors do not understand this, even though, to put it another way, they use their misinterpretation of this statement to cloak their irregular actions and desires. They turn everything upside down and disregard all the instructions, laws, privileges, and provisions they wish.

66. Returning to the subject of the duties of office, which I was discussing, we read about Stenius, who was the governor of Mamertines.[116] He made all his people follow the side of Mario. When they were defeated by the forces of Pompey, Pompey decided to kill them all. Stenius then stood up and said, "It was not right all should suffer because of the guilt of one man. I was responsible for the people supporting Mario, and since I alone was responsible, I alone should be punished." In awe of his strength of character, Pompey forgave him as well as all the Mamertines, because he saw to what lengths their leader would go to fulfill his duties.

67. Titus Vespasianus, the eleventh emperor of Rome, took the duties of his office seriously.[117] One evening he recalled that he had not done a good deed that day, and he had distanced himself from his duties. He began to cry out loudly, saying that he had wasted the day and that kings and governors should consider as wasted any day in which they failed to do some-

---

116. Inhabitants of Messina in Sicily.

117. Titus Flavius Caesar Vespasianus Augustus (9–79 CE), ruled Rome the last ten years of his life.

thing good in fulfilling the duties of their positions. Every time Pericles was appointed in charge of the army, he said to himself, "Pericles, you are to direct and govern free men, Greeks and Athenians." In order to avoid making mistakes in office, Chrysippus turned down the office of ruler of his country, saying, "If I perform poorly, it will offend God, and if I do it well, it will offend the people."[118]

68. Now Your Graces can see what danger there is when the viceroys interfere with such confidence, as if they were going to a wedding! Because of this, each one should take care and reflect upon his actions and realize that sooner or later he will have to pay for the evil things he has done and all the oaths he has broken so easily. At this point, I believe I have accomplished my duties. For that reason, I ask your permission to leave since it is already evening time, and listening to me must have really tired you.

69. Crown Official: I believe that man of the Danube when he spoke before the Roman Senate was not as forthright and lofty as you have been in defense of the Estado da Índia.[119] I have heard such things from you that are strange and marvelous or, to put it more accurately, so base and ugly that I do not know how God has not reacted with great punishments.

70. Nobleman: I who governed that state could reply and show that, scattered among your many truthful statements, in some cases you have been overly emotional.

71. Soldier: For this I will delay my departure a bit because I would like Your Excellency to show me in what way, because I intend to defend the truth of my statements and my virtue.

72. Nobleman: It seems that you were very passionate when you said that the king was mistaken in the written instructions he gave us, where he says at the end that, above all else, we should do what best serves him. The men that the king selects for such a dignified position, and to whom he entrusts a large territory—it is not right to tie their hands. You have to see it from their perspectives. These cases are bigger than the laws, and sometimes things can happen that make it necessary to ignore all the instructions and regulations. I can tell you that it has been many years now since the Council of State here decided to allow the viceroy to rule without question, even

---

118. Chrysippus of Soli (279–206 BCE), Greek Stoic philosopher.
119. This is probably a reference to Julius Caesar but it is not stated.

though the captains may have other opinions. The viceroys, more than anyone else, have the duty to know what is going on and to be informed.

73. Soldier: Does Your Excellency wish to stir the pot and have me repeat what I have been saying? About this, I tell you that I can shout three hundred times. Is it possible that they never discussed leaving everything in the hands of the viceroys, since there are dignified religious figures and captains on the Council? If this were the case, what captain would want to give his opinion in council if, in spite of the voting, the Council then proceeded to follow the advice of the viceroy? For certain, such leaders would be discredited and would complain to the king. I believe that such an idea has never entered the imagination; it is an idea that would be of the greatest detriment to everyone in the world. If the viceroys were chained by the Council of India, then it is certain that many times they would go over the Council members' heads and do as they desired. Would following everything the viceroy thinks and desires not result in total chaos, and a list of disorders which would be infinite?

74. Certainly, most of them deal with their individual needs, and they have little concern that Portuguese India will be turned upside down. When someone asks them for an explanation, they give numerous accounts and say they have followed their understanding. Would I want their pleasures to cause some disaster that destroys a fleet, and which is dealt with afterward by cutting off a head? What consolation would that be for a poor widow or helpless orphan when they learn their husband or father was killed? I ask Your Graces that you present it so that in the Council the viceroys should not only listen to wise and experienced captains but also to merchants and, if needed, even to old soldiers. Four eyes see more than two, and a hundred more than twenty. Furthermore, in a state like Portuguese Asia, scattered from India to the Moluccas and Sofala, neither the viceroy nor the captains can possibly know what is going on in every corner of their territory. This is why it is very necessary to seek out experienced men who know what is happening to inform them.

75. They should not say that if someone is a commoner, he should not be on the Council. There are gentlemen in India whose grandparents were every bit as honorable as those of the nobility. If they were not honored, it was because they fell out of favor or some other reasons. Does their worth diminish if God gave them reasoning as good and superior as that of the

nobles, and they changed more than the nobles did? Are we as a people so miserable or so small-minded that we strive to destroy one another? Unlike others, who are happy to reward and honor their citizens, we do not do so. We read those writers, both Greek and Roman, where great leaders were raised up from humble beginnings, because all of them greatly valued virtues and bravery.

76. But we do not act this way. Few are born this way, which is the subject of that line from our great poet Luís de Camões in his *Lusíads*, "He who does not know the craft does not appreciate it."[120] He who practices virtue values it. We do not appreciate it, and this destroys those favored by it. Since I have been greatly delayed and the night is coming, I ask Your Graces to give me leave. Should you require more from me, I am ready to provide it another day.

77. Crown Official: I want many things from you, things that are necessary for me to understand for my responsibilities. For that reason, I ask that you return tomorrow afternoon, because I have a lot of information to obtain from you. You can also give me your papers, and I will strive to see that a decision is made matching your achievements.

78. Soldier: I will do as asked, and I will tell you what I know because I would like to take advantage of that opportunity.

79. Nobleman: I, too, will be here, because I enjoy listening to you in spite of the fact that you discuss many things that, in all honesty, make me feel ashamed.

80. Soldier: Your Excellency's ancestry and duty make you favor the truth, even if it turns against you. I can tell Your Excellency that the viceroys of India are like those who are infatuated with some vice or gambling, or obsessed with lust. They do not recognize the error of their ways until they are separated from it.

81. Your Graces, we will see each other tomorrow.

---

120. The greatest poet of early modern Portugal, Camões lived from 1524 to 1580 and was a friend of Couto's. *The Lusiads* is his epic work of the Portuguese voyages of exploration, first published in 1572.

THE SECOND PART

THE NEXT DAY, the soldier went to the home of the crown official, where he also found the nobleman, and the following dialog took place among them:

SCENE I
Irregularities in Making Appointments

1. Nobleman: Well look who is here! We were just talking about you.

2. Soldier: Isn't that like the old saying, "Speak of the Devil and he shall appear"?

3. Nobleman: We cannot say that about you. He who knows how to do everything so well, you also know the correct time to arrive. Sit down and join our conversation; it is good that you are here.

4. Crown Official: Speaking for myself, I find your presence to be irreplaceable. You have told me about things that I never heard from anyone else, and you did so with such truth and impartiality in all that you said. Now that we are alone and behind closed doors, I would really like it if you would tell me your opinion about something that kept me tossing and turning all last night. What solution is there for the king regarding people asking for these positions? I see men come from India with charges made against them, and many times these are absurd. This is quite contrary to serving God and the king, since the journey here to request offices is a very long and risky one.

5. Soldier: Of course, sir, Your Grace has reminded me of something that I forgot but had studied closely. I wanted to be the first to talk about it here in Portugal. If all of you understood it, noted it, and saw it, how would it be possible for His Majesty to not also examine it and help his subjects? What pleasure could anyone have to serve him, such as my having served twenty

years and, after I left that post, serving there another twenty? I thought I would be able to collect the fruits of my labor, only to find myself trapped in a web because of a legal error in my letter of appointment. It is the scribe who is guilty, yet they rule that my letter is invalid. I have had to return to Portugal, not only to correct the error, but also to ask for a new appointment, since the ruling excluded me from the old one.

6. How is that possible, sir? Do you think that it is so easy to return from India to Portugal, that it costs so little? You should know that many men make this journey before they are taken away to the hospitals to die and leave their wives and children dependent on the charity of the misericórdia. They come here to apply for their payments even though the voyage is very long and risky and costs a great deal. Food for one man and his servant and a modest little cabin in which to sleep cost eight hundred pardaus. For all of this, the ministers do not have to give an account to God? In the one hundred years we have been in India, they have not addressed this? The laws of this kingdom, which also govern all its dependent states, were drafted long before the colonies were ever occupied. The cases here are more complex than the laws, and it is my solution to have a judge examine them to see if they are correctly or incorrectly applied. On the other hand, I could have greater financial resources that I could give, but I cannot do that because I am poor.

7. Crown Official: All of this is known and has been discussed here. There are some occasions when a solution is discussed. Some feel that the business of appointing people to positions should be taken out of the hands of the high justices and given to the viceroy and archbishop. This would avoid the irregularities that take place now.

8. Soldier: Help me, help me! Who will come to my aid since I see myself lost? Does Your Excellency not know the Italian expression "out of the frying pan and into the fire"? This business is like that for sure. I can now understand that here in Portugal they will never understand how the administration works in India. Regardless of the material covered about this yesterday, I will return to this subject matter because it is very important. I will describe possible solutions to the oppression faced by the king's subjects.

9. Be careful that you do not make matters worse by taking this power away from the judges and giving it to the viceroys and archbishops, because I do not know a worse perdition for men. Many times the viceroys do not

allow these judges to act in a just manner in awarding posts and positions. When two nobles are contesting a position and one of them is a relative, the viceroy pesters, solicits, and even bribes the judge. What can they do when the viceroy holds all the cards? At a minimum, the process will be hurried along. I can affirm that this is the greatest of all the underhanded dealings of the viceroys in India.

10. Crown Official: This would be if the viceroy were the only one in charge. When the archbishop is also there, the viceroy would not be able to do anything.

11. Soldier: It seems that many times Your Excellency wants to challenge me regarding the irregularities of the viceroys. Even if the pope were there to witness it, I want to give you a complete explanation so that you will not fall into this trap. An opening exists for a fortress, and two captains want it. The viceroy delivers a letter already drawn up by a judge, delivering the fortress to one of them. The viceroy then explains his reasons to the archbishop, and then they vote. The viceroy favors one and the archbishop the other. What is the solution? It is then necessary to bring in one or two scholars trained in the law to break any tie in the vote, and the decision is postponed until the next day. The viceroy summons the scholar or scholars — these should be together — to his private chambers where they will meet. This is where the die is cast. The viceroy gives many reasons why the one should obtain the position, or he makes many promises to persuade them to support his man, and they give in. The next day, together with the archbishop, all of them discuss the matter and then vote. It is three against the archbishop. What can the archbishop do except resign himself and sign the order that he knows the viceroy wants?

12. Now, if the king removes from the hands of the judges the power to make appointments because he fears they act unjustly and receive bribes, and he places this power in the hands of the viceroys, thinking that the process will not be corrupted, then he is mistaken. This will be a gold mine for them. What ten should receive, one will get if this edict is put in place. Men will negotiate with or without justice and will open their wallets, since that is what is done everywhere these days. It is your mistake to trust any viceroy at all once he arrives in India. Even if they are not corrupt when they depart from Portugal, they are marred and twisted there. The business of handling pearls and richly embroidered cloth from the Orient is very dangerous.

13. Crown Official: I do not know how to respond to that. What solutions for these things await the king? He wants justice for his subjects, not hardship.

14. Soldier: There are some solutions. The ones I can offer now are these. The king should order that no letters of appointment be written in Portugal after the decisions have been made for all appointments. The results of these decisions should be sent to India more than once by way of several sailings of the ships.[1] The letters of appointment should be written there in India so there will not be any legal errors and corrections will not be necessary. Each man will take a certificate with him, signed by the secretary, stating what he was awarded. With this certificate, he will obtain his letter of appointment. By doing this, the king does two good things. First, he avoids the current confusions, damages, and hardships. Second, this will increase the income to the royal treasury in India, which needs all possible additional income. However, if this is not workable or you do not want to do without payment here in Portugal, at the time the certificate is written and included in the correspondence, those appointed can take them to the chancellery in Portugal and pay their fees there. The payment will be noted in writing and, once in India, the officials will receive their titles of offices. However, a better solution is for the money to be paid in India, which is also one of the king's territories. Either way, it is his money.

15. Another possible solution would be for His Majesty to create a judge in Portugal to oversee the letters of appointment in India. All the men would take their letters to him for inspection. Once he reviewed each and discovered any flaws in its wording, he would rewrite it to make it clear and uncontestable. He would then sign it at the bottom, and those in India could not argue that it contained errors.

16. Crown Official: This all seems very good but what if I see the letter of appointment and believe that the holder is a Jew, what then?[2]

17. Soldier: This does not happen very often. The king knows to whom

---

1. Because of the uncertainty of sending correspondence on such a long and dangerous voyage, many letters were sent several times to ensure that one would arrive.

2. This may be a reference to Garcia d'Orta (1501–1568), botanist and famed physician to the king and later to the viceroys of Goa, who was convicted after his death of being secretly Jewish. See note 2 in Pearson's foreword to this volume.

he awards positions, and these papers reflect his generosity before a judge. In India these things are very dangerous because, if someone wants to make such a charge of being Jewish, they will not be lacking in paid witnesses. I am sure Your Excellency recalls that phrase uttered by the great Afonso de Albuquerque when complaining about this.[3] He said, "You should know how rotten the people are in India; they spread it around that I was scum, but could they prove it to me?" He was such an honorable nobleman, such a good Christian, and so honest. No servant of his ever found him unprepared. In order to avoid this, His Majesty should order that all men who carry papers from this kingdom should have them inspected by this judge to ensure that, once they reach India, these certificates are flawless. Once a man occupies his post, he does not have to do anything but reap the fruits of his hard work.

18. The third remedy, which I think is the best both for the men concerned, as well as for the king's conscience, would be to create a Mesa da Consciência in India and have it composed of the most upright men, with the archbishop acting as its president. This council would exclusively deal with the business of posts. If some mistake should appear in the paperwork, the board would have the power to correct it. The king's intention is to reward his subjects with what their services have earned them. They should be able to enter their awarded posts and fortresses free of vexations, infamous scenes, and expenses, as I have already explained. By having this council, the king would avoid many disorders.

19. Crown Official: This is not a bad idea. I promise you that in the next session dealing with Indian affairs, I will forcefully outline these ideas because I am sure they will be accepted.

20. Nobleman: That would be good, but you should not do it, and here is why. Those of us on the Council of State do not ever like to do anything that appears to weaken the position of the viceroys, because they are our relatives and friends. It is our sin! By acting in this manner, we have greater intentions than serving the king and the common good.

21. Soldier: I am saddened to hear that from Your Excellency, since it

---

3. Second viceroy and one of Portuguese Asia's greatest leaders, Albuquerque was responsible for conquering many of the strategic outposts to control trade throughout the India Ocean.

Image of St. George at the entrance to the fort in Diu.
Photo by Timothy Coates.

would appear that all of you favor those who act unjustly and cause chaos. What Christian viceroy would not be pleased to have his conscience relieved and be unburdened from some of his many tasks, such as judging lives and ruling on other people's estates? He could then be free to ponder aspects of warfare, which is what he really should be doing as the captain general. There are ministers responsible for all the other things relating to income and justice. The viceroy wanting to get his hands into everything is why India is in its current state, as it was when I left it. Because Your Graces have given me permission, I plan to slowly explain how all this started and what caused India to enter into such decline.

22. Nobleman: We would really like to hear that. I understand that you are not going to skip over the subject lightly.

SCENE 2

The Importance of Truth, Valor, and Gold in Retaining Portuguese Asia

1. Soldier: Please, for the love of God, give me your utmost attention because the subject matter that I will be discussing is of great importance. The famous philosopher Seneca, as well as other philosophers and leaders, stated

that states are conquered with the same skills that will preserve them.[4] The Estado da Índia was conquered with truth, loyalty, generosity, valor, and strength. Now, looking at its current condition, is it not the opposite of these things? This is when I think about a very wise remark made by a king of Cochin when he witnessed that state beginning to decay; he said, "It will begin to decline when the Portuguese fail to have three things: truth, big swords, and gold coins."

2. Now, I would like to show Your Graces that the lack of these things has caused all the ills in India. The first of these is truth, and the truths with which this state was won by placing viceroys on board ships, caring for the use of arms, making war on enemies, expanding the royal estate, and enriching the state and the king's subjects. Just look at how India was at the time when these truths ruled, when Dom Francisco de Almeida, Afonso de Albuquerque, and all the other viceroys and governors ruled until the time of Jorge Cabral and even until Dom Constantino.[5] After that, truth was abandoned and lost. What happened to the viceroys and governors mirrored what happened to Hannibal. When he marched with his troops, carrying his weapon and sleeping outside on a hide of leather—which was his soft bed—he conquered all of Spain and Italy. He was even lord of Rome and would have been of the entire world if he had followed this true path. But later he lost it and retreated to the delights of Cápua, abandoning his weapons and losing all that he had gained.

3. So it was with the viceroys and governors of India. When they followed the path of truth, Portuguese India was prosperous and feared. Then truth was abandoned, and they put down their weapons and stopped going out on ships to stay home and enjoy the pleasures of Goa. When royal treasurers and magistrates of the High Court were sent, everything was turned upside down. We became cowards and lost all the respect our enemies had for us. We once lived on catching their spoils, but now they live by taking ours.

4. I do not want to omit something said by a Turkish captain about the troops that were attacking Diu when António de Silveira was in charge

---

4. Lucius Anneaus Seneca (4 BCE to 65 CE), Roman philosopher and statesman.

5. This work was completed in 1612, suggesting that Couto believes the Portuguese State of India began its decline in the 1560s; it is some of the viceroys and governors between 1561 and 1612 that he is describing in this work.

there.⁶ These soldiers put me to shame, as they have their share of glory. This Turk, after the battle was over, was speaking to Sultan king Mamude of Cambay, describing the amazing deeds and great acts of valor that he witnessed from the Portuguese.⁷ He spent a lot of time in praise and finished by saying, "I swear to you, powerful king, that, judging by what I saw these men do, they alone are worthy of having beards on their faces."

5. Now Your Graces can see to what depths Portuguese India has sunk. What the Turk found in us, which was so admirable and struck him with fear, we no longer hold dear. When the captains and the soldiers had long beards, they also were capable of being ashamed. I do not know if that is the case nowadays. For certain, I would like to have seen the days of King Dom Manuel and those old hands who conquered India with beards covering their chests, and with heavy vests down to their knees, and their shins covered with guards, and a breastplate.⁸ They wore shorts reaching the knees and a sash across the chest, tied with fuses to light guns.⁹ They had lances sheathed in iron that they held, or a bow slung over their backs. Standing next to them would be a soldier from that period, with a striped velvet cape, leather waistcoat and pants, silk stockings, hat with a gold ribbon, sword and dagger made of gold, a shaved or closely-cropped beard, and a front tuff of hair, puffed up high.¹⁰ It seems to me that the good king would turn over in his grave and demand explanations from his successors for how they have ignored Portuguese Asia to this extent. He would want things to return to what they were in his day so the Portuguese kings could keep the territory as theirs.

6. Tell me gentlemen, is there any place in the world other than India with as many borders, and where it is necessary to go around armed? Of course not! I am afraid that viceroys have not been paying attention to this,

---

6. A reference to the Battle of Diu in 1538. António de Silveira held his post with six hundred men against twenty thousand Turkish soldiers.

7. Mahmud Khan or Nasir-ud-Din Mahmud Shah III, who ruled Gujarat from 1537 to 1554.

8. King Dom Manuel I "The Fortunate" ruled Portugal from 1495 to 1521.

9. The original reads "a *crangia* across the chest," yet neither Rodrigues Lapa (hereafter RL) nor GM explain the term. Reis Brasil (hereafter RB) says it refers to a type of handkerchief or cloth, but I suspect it was a sash tied with fuses, or perhaps a belt.

10. "Topete," called a "quiff" or "forelock"; hair at the front of the head.

nor have they been living like exemplary soldiers, wanting to be leaders, so that others would want to be soldiers. This is the second thing that the king of Cochin identified as no longer coming from Portugal: large swords. He wanted to alert us that we would be leaving when our vigor and valor faded. He was almost alluding to that phrase said by our good King Dom João II, that a good Portuguese should bleed from wounds so deep they were made by the hilt of the sword.

7. So as time passed, some new things entered Portuguese Asia, such as long thin swords, new collars for shirts, and foreign clothing, and then everything was lost. War is not won because of inventions but rather with strong hearts. Nothing causes great empires to collapse more than changes in fashions and laws. If you do not believe me, look at the greatness of China and the famous Venetian Republic.[11] How could they maintain such strength for thousands of years? Is it not because they forbade any such changes?

8. The third thing that the king of Cochin said no longer came from Portugal was gold coins. These were used to purchase cargos of pepper and were held in such esteem by all the rulers in India that they made their treasures by holding onto them. Then foreign money started to arrive in India, and these coins started to disappear. I wonder if the king of Cochin meant "Portuguese as good as gold" because soldiers at that time, captains and viceroys, were all golden in their veracity, generosity, and fidelity; they were golden in their valor, skill, and strength. Really, all those golden things from those days we now see transformed into iron, and all those cherished traits are absent. This is what I fear is happening, because I see divine justice so angered against the Estado da Índia that its judgment has been sentenced with rigor for several years now. The principle is to punish general and public sins with general and public sinners. Are we not punished now by the hands of our enemies, people we previously dominated and subjugated? Even the weakest have raised their hands against the Estado da Índia. I fear Portuguese India will return to its former master if God does not provide help and divine mercy in light of the many virtuous people living there.

9. Crown Official: Everything that you say is completely true. How well we know that all would end if the Lord Our God had not laid his merciful

---

11. The Republic of Venice was an important empire throughout the eastern Mediterranean from 697 until 1797.

eyes on the sumptuous temples and so many devout and virtuous people, on so many innocents and, above all, on the piety, zeal, and Christianity of our kings. They sponsor all religious orders to receive the protection of God Our Lord. As frequent as greedy acts and sins might be, he allows his temples, where his holy name is praised night and day, to be transformed into abominable mosques of the vile Mohammed, and others are denigrated in their turn. God is merciful, and he sees this with the same gentleness and peace with which he dealt with the thieves on the cross.[12]

10. Soldier: I too trust in his divine grace; however, I also remember the large number of innocents, sainted religious figures, and beautiful temples that were in that unlucky Constantinople as well as throughout the Greek Empire, but God allowed us to see them and he knows why they were so judged.[13] On this earth there is nothing so sacred as the Church of the Holy Sepulcher, yet he allows this to be in the hands of the vile Muslims.[14] We should remember that he has done the same to so many other cities where he has been offended, where injustice prevailed, where they committed adultery, dishonored female orphans, heavily taxed the people, and where there was so much . . . everything that Your Excellency can imagine, could be seen at every turn.

11. God never allows sin to go without punishment. It is well known that he deals out punishment to all. When Adam sinned, he punished his descendants. At the end of that first era, God punished the world with a universal flood.[15] At the end of the second era, the punishment was lesser, since natural forces were weaker, so God only punished five cities.[16] At the end of the third era, he sent curses to Egypt because of its idolatry in worshiping Belphegor. He also killed twenty thousand men at the hands of the Levites by Moses's orders; God castigated them with a greater punishment.[17] At the end of the fourth era, God punished the Israelites with captivity, which

---

12. Luke 23, 32–43.
13. Constantinople was sacked and burned during the Fourth Crusade in 1204.
14. The site in Jerusalem where Jesus was buried.
15. Genesis: 6.
16. That is Sodom, Gomorrah, and three other cities, see Genesis 19:1–29.
17. During the Jews' exile in Egypt. Belphegor was an ancient God of the Moabites. See Numbers 25. In Christian tradition, he is a demon and one of the seven princes of Hell, associated with the sin of sloth.

Jeremiah had predicted nine years earlier.[18] At the end of the fifth era, the punishment was less, being largely the fear and affliction that Ammon placed in the Jewish people.[19] He did not punish them for Ammon's sin but because idolatry was practiced and promoted by the prophets of that era. Even though idolatry is a very great sin, during those times the natural forces were in decline, and God was content to punish them only with fear.

12. In the sixth era, which we are now in, since it is called the time of God's mercy, God waits for the sinner to convert.[20] However, he punishes the heretical Protestants and tyrants who kill saints, even though this punishment is not as severe as during the third era when he castigated Dathan and Abiram.[21]

13. In this time, God punished individual sinners, as we have seen in so many different Christian kingdoms—in Greece, in Hungary, and in others where they are oppressed by the Turks throughout the Germanic lands. He punished the town of Schallstadt in Freiburg of Breisgau for its sins. Schallstadt is about three leagues from Basel, and he burned it to the ground in an hour on April 10, a Wednesday during Holy Week.[22] France, Flanders, and England God punished with many continual wars, that still continue as well as with deadly epidemics that have struck them many times. The greatest punishment God inflicted on them was to abandon them.[23]

14. Wealthy Spain did not escape without such punishments, having been given to the Moors because of its sins. Nor did our Portugal escape these punishments. As we understand it, because of its injustices God sent earthquakes, epidemics, and famines, and most recently has punished us with

---

18. That is, the Babylonian captivity.

19. Amon was a king of Jerusalem, killed in 641 BCE. See 2 Kings 21:18 and 2 Chronicles 33.

20. That is, the time of Christ, the Christian era.

21. Two sons of Eliab who rose against Moses. See Numbers 16 and Psalm 106:17.

22. This reference is confusing. In the original, Couto says, "Schilstaun in Brisgoia," and his directions point to Schallstadt, just outside Freiburg in Breisgau (in modern Germany). However, the town of Schiltach (to the northeast of Freiburg in Rottweil) burned in an infamous fire on April 10, 1533, the Thursday of Holy Week. A local woman was blamed for it and burned at the stake as a witch. A woodcut depicting the execution made the fire well known throughout Europe. I am grateful to my colleague Jason Coy for this information.

23. Not stated but understood, I believe, is "abandoned them *to their Protestant heresy.*"

that African disaster where so many died in cruel captivity and many went to meet God.[24] Because of all this, we have lost our standing among the nations of the world.

15. Well, do you not think that God will punish the sins of India? You, sirs, surely know that he will, and I think he may have already started now with the lack of attention here to affairs in India, and to the limited fleets and supplies that are sent. Before so much evil entered that land, and the kings of Portugal ruled it with care, it seemed as if ships were born in the shipyard, money sprouted from the treasury, and from beaches sprang forth sailors, craftsmen, pilots, gunners, and men to repair the ships. All of these are lacking these days. God had moved the hearts of the kings to send such armadas, and so many supplies and people as well. We all know that in some years twenty ships left Portugal for India with four or five thousand men on board, and they all arrived safely. God in his mercy had seen the piety of these kings and the zeal of the viceroys and governors. As a result, everything was so prosperous that I remember walking down the streets of Goa and meeting more veteran captains and nobles who could become viceroys than there are people called "soldiers" today.

16. When the king here in Portugal wanted to appoint people to take charge of the administration in India in the event of a sudden death, there were so many who were qualified that the kings did not know who to select. Nowadays, if the king had to select four people for such emergency appointments, and Your Excellency can attest to this, I do not know whom he could select. The worst thing is that no one wants to sail unless he is made captain in charge. Since there are few fleets, many do not serve. They ask to remain in Goa in their large houses, spending a lot from their inheritances, which they sold here to support them there.

17. Finally, gentlemen, I have come to the conclusion that one of the worst punishments that God uses is to take away good, experienced people, as

---

24. A reference to the disaster at Ksar el-Kebir in northern Morocco, a battle fought in 1578 in which King Dom Sebastian died and many Portuguese nobles either died or were taken for ransom. Two years later in 1580, King Dom Philip II of Spain successfully asserted his rights to the Portuguese throne, and Portugal was ruled by the Spanish Habsburgs until 1640.

was done by majestic Athena, the mother of sciences. Rome was never so prosperous as when it was ruled by experienced, wise, and impartial men. When these were lacking and greed entered the picture, all was lost.

18. Crown Official: All that you say is very true. However, the generosity, faith, and charity of the kings of Portugal are so great toward their people and vassals, for that reason alone God should protect what cost them so much to attain. But God's judgment and punishment await those who offend him, and some pay this little heed. God is good and he will resolve this for us, as it should be, because he cares more about us than we do about ourselves. Now that this is all outlined, you have shown yourself to be a true Portuguese by the pain these deceptions give you. I understand your suffering, and I want to see that you are rewarded in the manner that your services merit. You have made an impression on me. Give me your papers if you have them, and the first time I find the king has a free moment I will present them to him. I will explain all the reasons why he should reward you for the zeal you have shown in his service. I am sure you will be well rewarded.

19. Soldier: I kiss Your Excellency's hand for such kindness. I only want your attention to my poverty, age, and years of service. Let these determine my reward. The papers are here. The wounds that I received are here in this arm from swords and another in the legs, and both wounds maimed me. Wounds from arrows and other weapons I have all over, and I was burned five times. Although all this is stated in my papers and explained, my story is clearer and more real to see the scars on my body.

20. Nobleman: I am a good witness to all these things, and your friend in no small way. Many times I saw you get off a ship and enter an enemy's territory, and I wanted to grant you many rewards but my time in office slipped away. However, now you are here and in front of someone who will look favorably upon your petition, giving you the justice you deserve. Your honor and deeds will be rewarded.

21. Soldier: That is what I believe for sure, and that certainty brought me to this house, without looking for patrons. Because I was so lucky to find such a good one as Your Excellency, by your hand I know I cannot but be well rewarded.

22. Crown Official: Let us place this aside. But tell me, what do you request in your petition?

Cannon at the fort in Diu.
Photo by Timothy Coates.

SCENE 3

Confusion in Making Appointments

1. Soldier: Nowadays there is nothing left in India to request. Everything has already been awarded for the next three hundred years, and I am too old to wait that long.[25] Give me whatever you wish, and I will return to India with my letter of appointment in hand. If I die, I die in a monk's habit, and

---

25. Couto provides another reminder that positions in the bureaucracy were awarded for three-year periods, and it became common for the crown to appoint far too many people to the same position. Thus, they were required to wait long periods before they could occupy the posts.

you shall see there is nothing for me to do. Now that we are speaking about this, I cannot help but be surprised about the great depravities there are in appointments made in India. We know that King Dom João III, who is remembered so gloriously, carried a book in his pocket where he noted all the positions and his appointments.[26] Whenever he made an appointment, he selected the most worthy individual, and he did not appoint anyone to a position he could not occupy immediately.

2. By doing things in this manner, men were pleased to serve the king and they would put their lives on the line—even to the point that there was once a nobleman who was ready to return to Portugal when a letter arrived for him from the king, appointing him captain of Hormuz or Sofala, where he could immediately assume his post. This manner of rewarding service is how it should be done. However, nowadays appointments are so entangled that I confess to Your Graces that men do not wish to serve. If they do, it is because they have no other alternative.

3. This occurred because positions were in the past awarded to those who earned them through their deeds. Nowadays they are awarded to those who have the most influence—these are the people who are favored; perhaps they also use other means. There are many people in India who never served the king nor even set foot on a ship, yet they are awarded better positions than men such as myself, who have grown old serving the king with broken arms and legs. This is what really grieves men like me. If there were another Christian king there whom they could serve, as I have already said, you should know that they would do so. Secondly, the men are disgusted, and there is no other way of putting it; it is necessary to cease this form of deception and allow none of these men to leave for India. They should seek their awards here.

4. Crown Official: You are quite correct, and all of us are guilty of these things. Let us leave the past alone, as we cannot change it, and instead look to the future. I would like you to tell me what would make those who serve happy. How can we prevent the undeserving from using deceit to obtain what they do not merit?

5. Soldier: There are many solutions, but chief among these is for the

---

26. João III ruled Portugal from 1521 to 1557, expanded and consolidated the Asian Empire, and retreated from the unprofitable cities in North Africa.

king to take charge of the appointments for several years to allow those who have been appointed correctly to serve and to block others from taking the posts. After handling these appointments, it would be clear who is being appointed, and these should be people who have served the king. In this manner, the men will be able to wait to occupy their posts. In addition, it is paramount that the king should not allow the viceroys to appoint people for positions of factor or lower, as doing so gives each viceroy more than thirty posts to fill. These appointments have become totally entangled, and a man has no hope of ever being able to occupy his post.

6. I am rather certain that no one here keeps a list of the fortresses and positions in India. Since there are no more than sixteen or seventeen fortresses, and every three years some ten or twelve appointments are made at each, putting aside those made in India; then there are additional positions in factories, judge of the customs house, secretaries, smaller captaincies, and treasury officials. These positions cannot total more than forty, but every three years more than fifty men arrive appointed to these posts. As a result, they can never occupy these posts. Additionally, there are those appointed out of sequence, as I said, which happens frequently.

7. In summary, when someone is appointed to a post, even if he is twenty years old, he will never enter that position until he reaches the age of sixty. So how can I hope to ever occupy a post? I am not so foolish. My honor brought me to this court to make the request; however, I have no expectation of ever occupying a position. I am here to fulfill my duty. When I die, I will take the letter of appointment with me to the grave so that the soldiers of my day will see that I did not shirk my duty, nor did I fail to be rewarded because of cowardice or because I was undeserving.

8. Crown Official: Now you should not say that! Many times we tried to stop people taking positions out of sequence, and I do not know why we were never able to do so. Everything that you say rings true and is well known here. However, not all of us want to stop these practices, because we have our own favorites. It is possible that in the future they will deal with the things you mention, but let us get back to our business. I would like to know what position would be a good fit for you, and you will have it right away. At your age, there is no time to waste. Examine what is available, and I will appoint you to it so that you can return to India on this season's ships.

9. Soldier: I do not think there is any suitable position that I can occupy immediately that will provide sufficient food for my table, except judge of

the High Court of Goa, chancellor, judge, or probate judge. Any of these would yield a tidy income. That way, even though I am old, I will not lack twenty thousand pardaus to marry. I do not know what these judicial positions offer, but people want them first, before captaincies of forts.

10. Crown Official: If these positions were your profession, you would be appointed to one. However, a person who serves in these positions must be educated and trained in secular and religious law.

11. Soldier: Oh good God, sir! I would be head and shoulders above some of those with legal educations who served in these positions. Some who only knew a couple of phrases in Latin were made High Court judges because people held them in high regard. The Latin they know, I too know. I will do more than some others have done. I will give judgments like some did: I will rule in favor of he who pays me more. I will not even look at Bartolus or Baldus, because that would mean the poor house and being tied to the poverty of following the law.[27] I want to have twenty thousand cruzados within three years.

12. Crown Official: God save me! Is it possible that the men His Highness sends to administer justice in India and who are paid handsome salaries enrich themselves in such a manner?

13. Soldier: That kind of justice makes me laugh, the type that I said they practice there. The people here have been hugely deceived. They do not understand what happens when a student of twenty-five years, all rosy-cheeked and good-natured, is placed in such a lascivious and enjoyable society, where pleasures rule. He has to rule justly rather than being driven by his desires. Can you see me at age seventy, with a white head of hair, being sent there in a position of authority? Instead, some lads are sent, barely able to grow beards, with more braids and curls than a mulatto's hair. They have long-flowing robes (worn by senators of antiquity), shoes with gold embroidery, trimmed capes, golden swords, horses decorated with gold and silver, and many footmen in front of them and pages following behind. This is after they have only been in India for a month! If you ran into them on the street, you would think they were ambassadors from France rather than High Court judges.

---

27. Bartolus of Saxoferrato (1313–1357) was one of the most famous law professors, jurists, and commentators on Roman law in his time. Baldus of Ubaldis (1327–1400) was his student and also a lawyer and jurist of note.

14. Who gave all this to them, if not those to whom they gave justice, the justice due to someone else? It is bad that it is so much like this; India was never so topsy-turvy as after some of these people started arriving. Until the time of Jorge Cabral, when there was only a head of Council, a chief judge, and a crown attorney, yet was it not a golden time? Times were better until the rule of Dom João de Castro, when there was only a chief judge. They ruled so efficiently and smoothly that someone who committed a crime was punished right away, but now, with so many judges, no one is punished.

15. Who was the fiend who deceived the king by filling a newly conquered land with staffs of office rather than lances? Portuguese India is surrounded by enemies, and it is always necessary to go around with a sword in hand, yet we have laws rather than armored suits and secretaries in place of soldiers. The truth is that we have many more of these than soldiers. Your Excellency should not think that I am off the mark because I am telling the truth, and I repeat that more people are normally present for vice-regal hearings than present on the ships. Plato said that, in the lands where there were many doctors, there were many illnesses. By the same token, we can say that where there are many judges, there are many misfortunes.

16. In those ancient societies, the serious legislators who governed them never used the judicial structure we use today, that is, "libel, defendant's response, replication, counter-replication, desist, conflict of interest," nor any of those other terms used in legal proceedings to keep a man from advancing. All of this was invented by human malice. Socrates never taught this to the Athenians, nor Solon to the Greeks, nor Pompilius to the Romans, nor Ptolemy to the Egyptians, nor Lycurgus to the Spartans, nor did anyone else who crafted laws for the good government of his society.[28] These were created to tie them to strife, frauds, promises, and claims.

17. It was because of this that well-known Lycurgus ordered that the laws he made when he reformed Spartan society should not be written nor posted in any form. Instead, they should be stamped on the spirits of the men. He did this because he was sure that the greatest part of happiness and good fortune of any well-structured society did not result from written laws but rather by preserving, applying, and retaining them with esteem

---

28. Numa Pompilius (753–673 BCE) was the second king of Rome. The Greco-Roman Ptolemy (90–168 CE) lived in Alexandria.

in the people's hearts. Those who followed this philosophy did not have to produce many volumes about nothing by which their citizens would suffer. Nowadays the piles of legal proceedings on the secretaries' desks are higher than the walls of these same cities.

18. What shocks me about all this more than anything else is that if ordinary judges or magistrates want to make an oral ruling on some minor issue, such as a wicked insult that one Indian gave another, they have their secretaries in front of them writing it all down and taking testimonies and proceeding in a judicial manner. When you look at this objectively, they are robbing the poor, but this cannot be proven.

19. The people of Locri passed a law such that whenever a man in their city drafted a new law or order he must fasten a rope across his chest and tie it to a gallows.[29] If the law or order harmed the people, he would be hanged. What a great law for Portuguese India to apply to those deceivers and liars who go to the viceroys with stories contrary to royal service and the common good! They deserve three hundred gallows. The worst thing is that the viceroys do not ignore them. Since these are profitable opportunities, they relish them. Those who do this always obtain what they deserve. I clearly said what I thought to the aldermen of Goa several times and suggested to them that they needed to maintain a public account from which nothing else was paid except for the execution of these harmful and disruptive people.

20. According to Cicero in the first *De Oratore*, laws are made to reward virtue and punish evil.[30] Nowadays in India, it is the reverse. Laws are rewards for those who commit evil and punishments for the good. He who performs some evil act, or lies in his testimony in court, is the one who matters and who is rewarded. The good are beaten down and disregarded; virtue is unknown. A philosopher said that he was unsure who to seek out, an evil rich man or a poor virtuous one. When he went to their homes, he always saw rich men among company and poor men alone.

21. Now Your Graces can see to what state our sins have brought us. Virtue is unknown. According to some philosophers, virtue is a perfect

---

29. Locri was a Greek town in Calabria, southern Italy.

30. Marcus Tullius Cicero (106–43 BCE), Roman philosopher and author of *De Oratore* (55 BCE), a moral and philosophical dialog.

reasoning that has its foundation in the understanding of the wise. Virtue has so much force that it repels vices, like that emitted by Our Lord God that shines on darkness and the blind. Just as light clarifies and exposes all things, evil hates light because it reveals its dishonor. Truth and light, according to Menander, were bitter to those who are evil.[31] They transformed them from their sweetness because the pleasure of judging was gone. For these people, truth and light were like those with pain in their eyes, like bats hate light.

22. Crown Official: This is serious material, and I like hearing about it. Are things going this way there? It would be good to have proof and for His Majesty to send new officials, those who are older and wealthy, who would honor their sons and grandsons by serving the king. These older men can serve in these positions. They will have sufficient salaries and favor to rule impartially.

23. Soldier: That would be a solution, but it would only be a patchwork answer. Some of these older men left Portugal wise and prudent, yet they have committed very grave injustices in India. I thought it a much better solution to examine their secretaries, since they are the source of this chaos and deception. I am sure that if one were caught, it would be sufficient to stop this malady among the rest. Lepers are separated from the population to stop the disease from spreading. In the same way, these deceptive people should be banished to St. Helena Island, where they would not be able to spread such great malaise.[32]

24. Al-Razi tell us in book 25 of his *The Large Comprehensive* that all fevers of the flesh, or those that are deadly, are for the greater part caught by close proximity to the ill.[33] This illness of which I speak is more contagious and fatal than all others because it kills the soul, which is more valuable than anything else. If this were true, which it is, we should note, as stated by Galen in his *Techne* and by Ibn Sina in his *Canon of Medicine*, that a healthy

---

31. Menander (341–290 BCE), Greek dramatist and author of over a hundred comedies.
32. St. Helena Island in the south Atlantic was an infrequent stopover for ships returning from India to Portugal.
33. The Persian Mohmammad ibn Zakariya al-Razi (854–925 CE) was one of the great physicians and medical authors of the Middle Ages.

condition can become ill.³⁴ In much shorter time in our case, it can corrupt. The poison spread by greed has no antidote, and it rots the heart.

25. When what Your Excellency says happens, when those High Court judges are sent, I advise that they bring a lot of backbone so they will not be easily corrupted. I saw some made of such weak moral fiber that one ruby or diamond made them fall all over themselves. The carpets, feather beds, pieces of silk, piles of fine plates from China, and other such things would make them fall on the floor. Those who are good never falter in spite of all the weight they might carry. There are those who are corrupted by a bribe of a horse, saddled and bridled. Sometimes they make the poor lose heart, taking their honor and goods. For this, there is no solution except to lift your eyes to Heaven and ask for justice from above. It will come when requested, since God does not ignore such matters. He will make the injustices vanish by using his heavy hand.

26. Xenophon tells us that the Persians did not have any figures or gods at their altars except a straight, thick, white staff that represented justice.³⁵ Its thickness represented how massive and strong justice needed to be. Its brightness represented the cleanliness and purity of justice. Its straightness represented that justice must not bend to a father or mother or for all the treasure of this world. From this example, you can imagine what would happen if such a practice were followed and justices used a straight rod as their insignia.

27. The best solution would be to return India to the way it was originally. If we did that, there would only be a chief judge, chancellor, and lower court judge. This would save more than twenty thousand cruzados. The High Court judges spend that each year from the royal treasury, and this solution would stop the irregularities of the men and correct these traps and frauds. Let them do their buying and selling in the main square with none of the

---

34. Galan (129–216 CE), Greek physician and philosopher who wrote many medical and philosophical works, including *Techne* on medicine. Abu Ali al-Husayan ibn Abd Allah ibn Sina (980 to 1037 CE), known in the West as Avicenna, was a great Persian medical authority.

35. GM notes that Xenophon (431–354 BCE) was a historian, military figure, and Greek philosopher known for his writings on the culture and history of Greece. He was in service to the Spartan king Agesilau II.

hindrances they have now. Their dealings and breaking of agreements may lead to their banishment if there is only one judge.

28. Nobleman: You have a good idea. It is possible that this plan would bring the people back to the good ways, avoiding fraud and so much disorder and the breaking of solemn oaths.

29. Soldier: Does Your Excellency know the origin of this word *preito*?[36] It comes from Castilian and is very old. In the good times, it meant "concord," as it appears in the laws of the *Forum Juzgo*, and from there you get *preitesia*, or *preito*, of the homage of the captains and viceroys at the hands of the king.[37] This homage was made at the time the king appointed these people as governors or captains. Nowadays the meaning of this word has changed. What was "concordance" is now "causes enemies and unrest." King Dom Pedro of Portugal understood this very well, as during his time the chaos from legal demands was corrupting the kingdom.[38] As stated in a handwritten chronicle, he ordered all jurists to find another profession because he wanted his people to be at peace.[39]

30. In such a public ceremony, King Matthias of Hungary ordered the expulsion of all jurists from his kingdom.[40] This is described in Vives's work, *De Corruptis Artibus*.[41] After that happened, there was peace in his kingdom. The Catholic queen Dona Isabel attempted the same deed in Salamanca, but her good zeal and spirit were checked by the advice of Catholic lawyers.[42] I do not know why they would block such an important Christian action, which would have been fruitful and resulted in peace.

36. A solemn oath.

37. Legal code of the Visigothic kings, a significant collection of Iberian law from the medieval period.

38. King Dom Pedro I (1320–1367), called "The Just" or "The Cruel."

39. RL and RM believe Couto is referring to *Crónica do Dom Pedro I* by Fernão Lopes, chapter 5, where the king ordered all lawyers to leave the kingdom. Lopes wrote this work between 1440 and 1450, but as it was not published until 1735, Couto must have read a manuscript copy, perhaps in the archives in India.

40. King Matthais Corvinus (1443–1490), called "The Just" and known for his wisdom; he introduced his country to the Renaissance and instituted a new legal code.

41. Juan Luis Vives, famous Spanish humanist, wrote this work in 1531.

42. Queen Isabel of Trastámara (1451–1504), Queen of Castile and León, known as "The Catholic."

31. Crown Official: It could be done this way, as kingdoms did in the past. But kingdoms cannot be ruled without laws, because this would cause great chaos.

32. Soldier: Laws are holy and good, but we use them poorly. We study them to twist their meanings into something very different from their intentions. Legal scholars in the past omitted much from their laws so they would not be suggestive to men. This is why Solon never spoke of the penalty for patricide. He did not want to suggest the possibility of such a great evil deed as a man killing his father. Nowadays, people only seem to seek out new ways of being evil and filling other's heads with new ways to find Hell. Some find their way there and choose to enter it.

33. Do Your Graces know to what extent it is this way? The evil ways of India have gotten to the point that there are men who buy petitions and legal orders from others. They go daily to the officials' audiences, and from secretary to secretary and judge to judge. They do this with such pleasure that I wonder if it does not make them happy. Nowadays, those who come to Goa will see a school formed of these secretaries, the little ones and the bigger ones, judicial inquirers, solicitors, and informers.

34. For certain, this causes a great deal of chaos in a land surrounded by enemies who want to drink our blood. There should be schools to teach using weapons, making fortified walls, and fighting like soldiers. We always show our enemies our arms in order to scare them, but instead they see what I have already described. Even then, the Brahmins who converted to Christianity learn this legal canon from us and then cheat and swindle us, since they know the law better than the lawyers.[43] This is what we went there to teach them.

35. Pirates at sea take our ships because no one is guarding them. The convoys go at the wrong times, and even then they lack sufficient soldiers. Back on land, the vice-regal audiences are stuffed with men flowing out into the streets. This has led me to want a governor who is so obedient to serve God and king that one day he would grant an audience and then round up all those attending it and send them to the ships to fight the Indian ships. I believe that if someone did this once, it would reduce cheating and idle-

---

43. Brahmins occupy the highest caste in Hindu society.

ness. The soldiers would leave on the ships and later be paid. There would be no lack of men for the galleys, so many judges would not be needed, nor would there be a need for so many books and legal cases.

36. I remember reading in the Holy Scriptures that the Pharisees carried pieces of parchment with the 613 commandments written on them.[44] They were sewn into the seams of their cloaks. These slips of parchment were called "mysterious fragments," or *custodia amoris*, since the Pharisees said they had the love of God with them. They took the metaphoric meaning, as *filacterion* signifies "the keeper of the love against poison." They believed that keeping the commandments meant having these slips of parchment on which they were written. Because of that, Jesus Christ our Lord reproached them for hypocrisy, saying that they did not do what they said; they extended and widened their nonsense, that is, their errors.[45]

37. In the same way, some of the trained jurists in India have become guardians of the laws contained in large books that you can see in their homes, just like the slips of parchment of the Pharisees. These laws are all clearly copied and have commentaries written on the sides. On the outside, the jurists are all piled up with laws, but only God knows how their hearts work. I still will argue that there are some honest and upright High Court judges, and there have always been people on the court who wanted to see justice done. There would be more if the viceroys did not interfere. There has also been one on that bench who wanted to see justice carried out. However, I heard someone say to one of them, an honorable and independent man, that one was not enough. The viceroy always has three loaded cannons seated at the court with which he can win or demolish any case.[46] Some men that I know resigned from the court because their consciences bothered them.

38. Crown Official: I never imagined that I would hear such things from a soldier. It seems as if an angel were speaking through you to tell us the matters of which we are unaware. I will write these up in a long account and present it to the king to investigate. But let us return to you. I want to see that you are rewarded, as you desire. Tell me word for word the scope

---

44. These are the 613 commandments of Judaism known as the *mitzvot*.
45. See Matthew 23.
46. That is, he always has three men in his pocket.

of your services, so that I will know more about you when your position is discussed.

39. Soldier: I went twice to the Straits of Mecca to await ships coming without our safe-conduct passes.[47] I was three years straight fighting in the war in Sri Lanka, and I took part in the siege of Kotta.[48] I served two years along the Malabar coast, where I helped capture many Indian ships, and I was wounded several times. I spent each winter in fortresses along the frontier and I did some other smaller actions cited in my papers. I spent a total of twelve years in continuous service for the king there. In this court, I spent five years serving in the royal chambers and another three on ships here in this kingdom.

40: Nobleman: You are surely worthy of a good award. I would like to hear from you, and I wanted to ask you why armed convoys no longer go to the Straits of Mecca as they did in our time?

41. Soldier: That question, Your Excellency, you should ask the secretary here. He will know if defending the king's territory is the reason. What I can say is that it was a great service to the kings of Portugal and a great asset to Portuguese Asia for those convoys to go to those straits. I ask Your Graces to listen to me discuss this a bit.

SCENE 4

The Red Sea Fleets; How to Select a Viceroy; the Three Traits of a Good Leader; and the Importance of Clemency

1. Soldier: Before we had fortresses in India, the first convoys sent by the kings of Portugal went with instructions for the captains in charge to visit the Straits of Mecca. This was to ensure that the Ottoman Emperor would know that our ships could block the commerce and pilgrimage to the

---

47. One of the chief methods used in Portuguese India to obtain income from taxes on trade was to issue passes (called *cartazes*) to ships carrying merchandise. They directed the ships to load and unload their goods in Portuguese-held ports, thus insuring payment of tax to the Portuguese. Ships that refused such passes were attacked, and those entering the Red Sea from the Indian Ocean were frequently difficult for the Portuguese to control.

48. Kotta was a kingdom in southern Sri Lanka, which the Portuguese occupied from 1594 to 1612.

Moat of the fort in Diu.
Photo by Timothy Coates.

heinous center of Mecca. At all times, our kings had as their primary intention to honor our Lord God. Another objective was to capture some of the ships from the Muslims. The Muslims used these to try to end our presence in India.[49] We could use these ships to further spread the holy word. For that reason, later on specific convoys were sent to those parts. One of these was headed by the great Afonso de Albuquerque, who started fighting in

---

49. Couto refers not only to the Red Sea and Hormuz but to the various battles over Diu in the 1500s.

both straits.⁵⁰ This continued in the kingdom of Hormuz for three years without stopping. He was able to provision his fleet with what he captured from Muslim ships.

2. Later, King Dom Manuel ordered that we establish ourselves in India. We put our feet on the ground and began to construct forts. In my opinion, the viceroys had no greater income from any source than from the seizure of goods at the Straits of Mecca, where our galleons went every year. Later, King Dom João ordered his governors to continue this patrol at the entrance to the Red Sea.⁵¹ This was done as much to insult and challenge Islam as for the great income it provided Portuguese Asia. Until this beneficial practice was stopped, it paid for the fleets with confiscated properties, since Portuguese Asia had no other income.

3. In addition, there were many other good reasons to patrol the straits of Mecca. There were always galleons available for this, and soldiers were satisfied with the goods they seized. The Turkish galleys feared to leave the Red Sea, and the few times they did, our fleets captured them right away. Commerce with the great kingdom of Ethiopia and everything concerning that Christian kingdom went so well that every year our ships docked at their ports. We took bishops, patriarchs, and religious men to instruct them in the faith. Then later, everything stopped, due to the absence of our fleets.

4. The neighboring kings were astonished by the strength of our galleons and caravels,⁵² to the point that the Spanish never sent a fleet of ships to the Molucca Islands. When Emperor Charles V disputed the ownership of these islands with our kings, did our fleets not go there to assist, and did they not capture the city of Goa by force?⁵³ Were the forts in Hormuz, Malacca, Diu, Bassein, and other places not captured by our galleons? In some ways you could say that each galleon was a fort floating on the sea that cast a shadow over the entire world. When Francisco Barreto was governor

50. The Straits of the Red Sea (Bab al-Mendeb) and of Hormuz.

51. King Dom João III, the eldest son of Manuel I, ruled from 1521 to 1557.

52. Caravels are small three-masted ships with triangular and rectangular sails developed by the Portuguese.

53. Emperor Charles V (or I of Spain) was a Habsburg king ruling Spain from 1516 to 1556. The issue of ownership of the Molucca Islands was resolved between Spain and Portugal by the 1529 Treaty of Zaragosa, awarding the islands to Portugal.

of India, fourteen galleons were burned all at the same time, and within a year they were replaced with new ones.[54] These were handed over to the Viceroy Dom Constantino fully provisioned. I saw this myself along with some others.

5. All of this was done by seizing goods at the Straits of Mecca; the entire state of Portuguese India at that time did not have more than 600,000 xerafins in income. Nowadays it has 1,400,000 cruzados, but there is none of this, no fleet for the straits, and not a galleon available if it were needed. Our little cutters are only for coastal patrols.[55] If there were some emergency there, we have no one to help us except our shadows!

6. Crown Official: Oh, sweet Jesus! How is that possible? I read the letters the viceroys send His Highness and the certificates that come with them. They claim that Portuguese Asia has a certain number of galleons, galleys, cutters, and so many barrels of gunpowder and other provisions. Because of this, the king believes that Portuguese India is secure for many years.

7. Soldier: After the viceroys took better care of themselves than they attended to God or served the king, they began to use these schemes so they would be believed. What reason do they have to neglect the armadas and build galleons? Your Graces are deceived. The Roman Empire did not begin to decline until it began to sell judgeships. By that standard, Portuguese India is finished. Nowadays nothing is awarded for merit; everything is sold for money.

8. Do Your Graces know to what extent? Even the captaincies of the galleys, ships, and the docks are sold for the appropriate prices. I was told of a very young nobleman who was not old enough to be a captain of a cutter. He was given a galley for duty in Malabar in exchange for a slave and a silver saltbox shaped like an animal. A very low-caste man told me that he had a brother in service in a very lowly job who nevertheless said that in the summer he would serve as captain of a ship going to Malabar. When I asked the man who would give his brother that position, he said his brother would receive it from a close associate of the viceroy for the usual price of two hundred pardaus.

---

54. Barreto was viceroy of Portuguese India from 1555 to 1558 and was followed in office by Dom Constantino. See list of viceroys and governors on page xxxv.

55. The ships Couto refers to are foists, or small ships with one sail and several oars.

9. Now Your Graces can see what a terrible state Portuguese India is in. I ask for the love of God and king that you tell the king this so that he can attend to it because it will be the end of us. He should know who receives these positions, as I said. Not all those who serve the king do so satisfactorily. There is no reason to give a position to a tradesman or to his son when it should go to me. I am a very honorable gentleman, and for the past three hundred years my ancestors have served the kings with swords in their hands.

10. Crown Official: That what you say is very true, and I am amazed to see the many ways the Devil entraps these men!

11. Soldier: What does Your Excellency think? The Devil is a child, and he has a thousand ways to deceive men.[56] The worst part of it is that we all know that he is deceiving us, and we allow ourselves to indulge in that gluttony reflected in this black vice. It is certain that "greed" must be the name reserved for the most ugly demon in Hell, and also the most foolish. No, I have misspoken; the foolish ones are those who are deceived by something so base and harmful to the soul.

12. But one thing amazes me: to see the viceroys entangled with the king's treasury and that of his subjects, taking a position from one to award it to another, all without any restitution up to now. These deeds sit so lightly on their consciences that I am stunned. Here also we see the cunning ways of the Devil. Greed makes it easy to take a fortress away from one person as if it were nothing, and give it to another who has the influence and wherewithal to pay for it.

13. Well now, I will return to what I was saying. If I did not so firmly believe in the faith of Christ and in the commandments of his law, these deeds that I see men commit would make me speechless. These men easily call themselves "Christians," as if they were performing some great holy deed. God is in Heaven and is not asleep. The fear is that all of us will pay. Those of us in Portuguese India will begin to have a difficult time and not have any influence on his judgment. I am beginning to lose my train of thought because of the fear of this, and I am not saying what I mean. So I ask Your Graces to excuse me because I want to retire.

---

56. Acts 13:10.

14. Crown Official: You should sit down because I want to know some more from you. The first is what sort of man should a viceroy be; the next one that His Highness will appoint to India this year, and what things are needed there?

15. Soldier: Now that Your Excellency wants to know everything that I have to say, leaving nothing out, I cannot run away. However, this will take some time. If this is annoying, the blame will be yours for asking me. You can always ask me to get up and leave, whenever you are tired.

16. Crown Official: This I will never do to you because of my pleasure in listening to you, and the value I place in what you are saying. So discuss this material as thoroughly as you wish, because this is very important to me. I want to understand it well when the time comes for the king to make his selection.

17. Soldier: I will obey everything. Your Graces should pay attention because I will strive to make this brief.

18. When it is time to select a viceroy for the Estado da Índia, the process should follow that used by the emperors of China to appoint officials to their provinces. They have this custom: they only select a viceroy or governor to rule a province if he does not have any relatives there, not even very distant ones. In this manner, he can administer justice without any obstacles. Most of the disorders caused by the viceroys in India have relatives at their sources. Sometimes the viceroy awards a ship to a relative who does not deserve it, or sometimes he takes fortresses away to give them to kin.

19. There is something else. When the viceroy or governor appointed by the Chinese emperor arrives at his post, it is without pomp and circumstance. As soon as he presents his letter of appointment, he is waited upon and esteemed by all as if he were the emperor. The Chinese wait on him hand and foot. When his term is over, he leaves alone just like any other ordinary person. The first thing they do is conduct an inquest of his administration. If he committed an injustice or owed someone something, he is served the ultimate penalty. This is not done to our viceroys, for as soon as they are appointed, they gather an army of relatives and servants for which three Estados da India would not suffice. All of them are accommodated by hook or by crook, and the viceroys or governors act as I have described throughout this discourse during the years they govern Portuguese India.

20. When they return to Portugal, all the ships of the India fleet are not enough to carry the relatives, servants, and their possessions. About the injustices and insults committed in office, or the debts left behind, no one will ask. One of the greatest tyrannies that these men commit while ruling is that the king owes them nothing, because they were all paid beforehand. Yet, the poor widow, the crippled man, and the helpless orphan girl are not paid their pensions for virtually the entire time of the governors' rule. If one of them had a certificate that claimed that the king owed money to other parties, and he wanted to keep the account open to later claim that he had not paid, the viceroy was reimbursed.

21. Another thing, as stated in the laws of the land, when there are different opinions about who should be selected for a post, the person who is chosen should be someone who is most concerned with the people's welfare. It is the people who support him more so than the king's wishes. That is the person who should be appointed. This has been noted by many scholars. In the same way, no more and no less, the viceroy selected should be a man whom all are certain would serve the king and the welfare of the people in his appointed place more than himself. All of the appointments made beyond these limitations, made through solicitation or to please one party or another, are the ruination of Portuguese India. That is about the selection process. In regard to the characteristics of the man to be selected, they should be those three that the great captain Gonçalo Fernandes de Córdova said a good leader should possess: mercy, generosity, and prudence in speech.[57]

22. Of these three, I will discuss the first, which is that the leader should be merciful. He placed this first because it is the most necessary of the three. Aeneas had many praiseworthy virtues, but at no time did Virgil expand on these except in the case of mercy and piety, because these two contain all the other virtues.[58] Mercy even captivates one's enemies, as occurred with

---

57. According to GM, a "noble, political and military Spanish general who lived from 1453 to 1515 serving the kings of Spain."

58. Mythic Trojan hero Aeneas was the son of Prince Achises and the goddess Aphrodite. This is a reference to Virgil's most famous work, *The Aeneid*, written between 29 and 19 BCE.

Achaemenides, the Greek captain and companion of Ulysses.[59] He was lost on Sicily and hiding so that he would not be killed by the giant Polyphemus. The giant had slain his companions, and suddenly along came Aeneas in his galley. When the grieving Achaemenides became aware of Aeneas, he had the following conversation with himself:

> If I stay here in the wild, I will die of hunger. If I appear in the open, Polyphemus will kill me. If I go with Aeneas what will happen to me if he wants to extract his revenge for all the evil I, along with all the Greeks, have committed on Troy? What will I do? The son of Venus and Anchises should still be generous. No great captain should want to crush the oppressed nor vex the grieving.

Thus making up his mind, he left his hiding place and went up to Aeneas and told him of his misfortunes. Aeneas welcomed him and treated him humanely, like a companion. Because of this and similar deeds, Aeneas attained the title "compassionate."

23. On the other hand, when authors wanted to denigrate King Cinna, they called him "cruel."[60] His cruelty was why he was killed at the hands of his own soldiers. The Emperor Antoninus Pius, how did he acquire the great and heroic last name if not for his actions as a leader, esteemed by all?[61] Great Caesar did not do anything else to become king of the world except to cry over the decapitated head of Pompey, his worst enemy.[62] This was the reason why the great Fabius was crowned in Rome with a crown of leaves.[63] He then granted clemency to the captains, and after the wars were concluded, his soldiers returned safe and contented.

24. The great captain Miltiades became well known in the world because of his clemency and agreeable character.[64] They write that there was not a

---

59. Son of Adamastus of Ithaca in Greek and Roman mythology.

60. Lucius Cornelius Cinna was not a king but a Roman consul who ruled Rome from 87 to 84 BCE.

61. Anthoninus Pius was emperor of Rome from 138 to 161.

62. Pompey (106–44 BCE) was Caesar's friend and later his rival. He was beheaded by King Ptolemy XIII in Egypt, and his head was sent back to Rome.

63. Quintus Fabius Verrucosus Cunctator (280–203 BCE), Roman general and politician who five times ruled as consul and twice as dictator.

64. Leader of the Greek forces at the Battle of Marathon in 490 BCE.

man, no matter how lowly he might be, to whom he did not listen carefully and compassionately, as if he were one of the high and mighty in the land. This is the chief reason people will hold their prince in high esteem. King Philip of Macedonia was so endowed with this great trait that he refused to conquer a city by force, because it would put his soldiers at risk. This same thing the illustrious Scipio Africanus did, many times saying that he preferred saving one soldier to destroying one thousand enemies.

25. This is good lesson for the captains in India, who over matters of little importance place their soldiers in harm's way, as if they were sheep. They sit back all pleased with themselves as if they had achieved some great victory, while three or four hundred Portuguese are beheaded. What is really scandalous to me is that when they write the certificates for the soldiers who took part in these battles they fill them with praise: they destroyed and burned the enemy. Yet they do not state how many soldiers were lost. If someone is surprised, they respond that only some vagrants were killed, forgetting that these soldiers were the ones with whom we conquered Portuguese India and its fortresses.[65] On rare occasions some noblemen were killed during these battles, as I have said elsewhere.

26. Returning now to our subject matter, Pompey was worthy to be known as "great" because of his clemency. He returned from Africa to triumph even though he had not been a senator. Sulla was the first to call him "great" and the one who most hindered him.[66] Pompey turned to him and said, "Sulla, don't you know that many more love the sun when it rises rather than when it sets?" By this he meant that someone who is growing in virtue should be held in the same regard as someone who has it already. When Sulla realized Pompey's gentle compassion, he began to cry out, "Glorious victor!" However, Servilius the senator did not want to award Pompey that title without receiving a bribe from him, and Pompey responded that he would not pay, since purchased honors become vituperative.[67]

---

65. Vagrants and criminals were routinely sent overseas to solve the never-ending manpower shortages in the military.

66. Lucius Cornelius Sulla Felix (138–78 BCE), Roman general and politician who twice served as consul.

67. Publius Servilius Vatia Isauricus, a friend of Julius Caesar's and later consul of Rome in 48 BCE.

27. Oh! I just wonder how these ideas would be welcomed here and in the Estado da Índia when so few captains remember this about Pompey? Nowadays we see more honors purchased than earned and more fortresses that are grabbed rather than deserved. I might say the same thing about the government. Do Your Graces know the source of all this? It stems from the little importance given to the appointments in India, as I discussed earlier. This did not happen to Pompey, who was willing to turn down a title rather than risk being accused of buying it.

28. The consul Marcus Fabius was awarded the title of "great victor" by the Senate for his victory over the Etruscans of Veii, but he rejected it.[68] In the battle, his kinsmen the consuls Manlio Fabius and Quincio Fabius were killed. He felt he did not merit an award because so many of his kin had died.[69] It is not good that the captains of Portuguese India enter Goa triumphantly, full of themselves with feathers and gold swords, after they left their comrades in arms headless on the beaches of Calicut and elsewhere. This is very scandalous and should be investigated.

29. However, returning to our subject of clemency and the captains, since this trait is needed above all others, Plutarch in his *Life of Romulus* lists three virtues by which kingdoms and empires grow.[70] These are clemency, moderation, and truth. He placed clemency first because it is paramount. This is why Marcus Claudius Marcellus constructed a temple to virtue in front of another dedicated to honor.[71] He wanted to show that it was impossible to enter the shrine to honor without first passing through that dedicated to virtue, by which he meant clemency. This is, if a leader has a perfect degree of clemency, he will have all the other virtues, since they are interwoven. However, if someone has less than an absolute degree of a virtue, that virtue stands alone. It is not possible to be just without also being temperate, strong, and prudent. This is the same in the virtues of theology. It is not possible to have a perfect degree of faith without also having hope and charity.

---

68. Marcus Fabius Vibulanus, twice consul of Rome in 483 and 480 BCE.
69. The Battle of Cremera was conducted by the Fabii clan against Veii.
70. Recorded in Plutarch's *Parallel Lives*, written in the late first century.
71. Three-time consul of the Roman Republic, military leader during the Second Punic War who lived from 268 to 208 BCE.

Tombstones in a church floor in Bassein.
Photo by Timothy Coates.

30. This virtue of clemency of which I speak the Greeks called *philathropia*, which means, "love of mankind." These same Greeks, when they wanted to praise their gods and kings, called them *meilichoi*, which is the same as calling them "mild and loving." This made the kings resplendent, because men want love to motivate them in all things. Because this virtue was so needed, God ordered that kings be anointed with oil, signifying meekness and humanity. Oil has the ability to soften, and God wanted kings to be kind to their subjects. Regarding all this, I have said enough.

31. Crown Official: You said everything that a scholar would have, but do not stop. Continue with this subject matter because it is very instructive.

SCENE 5
The Importance of Generosity

1. Soldier: The second trait that a leader should have is generosity. This is so important for a leader that without it everything else will amount to nothing. The captain who is miserly yet wants to conquer regions is like someone looking for gold in a silver mine. If jurists were to describe the traits required for those in the legal profession, they would say a closed mouth, an open purse, and feet firmly planted on the ground. For a captain, these traits are even more important, as he is set to conquer regions rather than just three or four people in a courtroom: the judge, the secretary, lawyer, examiner, and solicitor.

2. Until now, there has been no case of a miserly captain conquering enemies. Yet daily we see generous captains conquering strong forts and subjugating wild, uncivilized nations. Generosity is nothing more than the moderate use of riches. Wealth should be awarded sufficiently that it may be spread around so that it is not lacking, yet not so generously that a captain could be called "prodigal." What is needed is a midpoint between these two extremes to show when, how much, and to whom wealth should be given. On the other hand, greed is an unruly desire, an insatiable covetousness. It is an illness that spreads throughout the body. It grows daily and makes men weak. According to the Platonists, in order to be wealthy, it is necessary to break the bonds of greed and not allow treasures and riches to accumulate.

3. We have seen many kings lose their kingdoms to greed and lack of generosity, while others have acquired new realms using it. King Achius of Lydia was so miserly with his soldiers that they were no longer able to tolerate him, and they killed him and threw him into the Pactolus River. They said doing so created golden sands, and that that is where his thirst was quenched.[72] Croesus died for the same reason at the hands of the Parthi-

---

[72]. It may be that Couto has here confused two stories from antiquity. The story he recounts is that of King Midas of Phrygia who was given the power to transform all he touched into gold. Midas eventually wanted to rid himself of this power, and to do so he washed his hands in the Pactolus River. The river took the power from him and turned the sands along its shores to gold. See *The Works of Francis Rabelais*, 2:17n9.

ans.⁷³ Lepidus was one of the members of the triumvirate, and he took charge of Sicily after defeating Captain Sextus Pompey.⁷⁴ What caused his reign to be so brief, if not being miserly?⁷⁵ While chasing him with his army, Octavius was joined by Lepidus's troops, who deserted Lepidus because of his greed. Lepidus was defeated and sent to Rome with no other title given to him than *Pontifex Maximus*.

4. While this infernal curse of greed was absent, Rome ruled the world. After Commodus Antoninus succeeded his father to become Emperor of Rome, he began to sell judicial appointments.⁷⁶ He surrendered the soul of the empire to greed, and Rome began to decline from its glory. This also happened in Portuguese Asia. While governed by untainted men, men who obeyed the laws of God and king, and friends who sought honor, they always managed to keep their enemies underfoot. They were sustained by capturing loot that supplied our fleets. After this infernal curse came among them, everything started to unravel. Our enemies lost their respect for us, and they sustain themselves nowadays on what they pillage from us.

5. We will not spend time discussing the miserly but will leave them to their own despair. We will turn to generous leaders who are famous because of this trait. We read of the great Bacchus, who was the first to show generosity to soldiers. In addition to their usual salaries, he gave them gifts of cash, crowns, weapons, statues, trophies, and other similar things. These made his soldiers so contented that they happily followed him over impregnable mountains in the Orient, filled with wild beasts and fierce uncivilized peoples, to make him the lord of India, the first foreigner to conquer it by force.⁷⁷

---

73. Croesus (595–547 BCE) was the last king of Lydia, famed for his wealth. Accounts disagree about his death, but many believe he died on a funeral pyre set by the invading Persians. Parthians were from northeast Persia.

74. Marcus Aemilius Lepidus (30BCE to 33 CE) was a member of the Second Triumvirate of Rome with Octavian and Mark Anthony. Sextus Pompey (67–35 BCE), a Roman general.

75. Pliny the Elder (23–79CE), Roman historian, author, and naturalist.

76. Emperor Marcus Aurelius Commodus Antoninus Augustus (161–192 CE) was a particularly sadistic emperor of Rome.

77. According to legend, Bacchus set out across Asia to teach people how to cultivate grapes and make wine.

6. For Alexander the Great, nothing else made him famous throughout the world except his generosity. According to Curtius, he distributed thirty thousand gold talents and many different lands that his enemy Darius had offered him as a dowry for his daughter.[78] This seemed odd to Alexander's friend Parmenion.[79] Alexander responded by saying, "If I were you, I would have accepted this offer, but I am Alexander and I desire honor more than money. I remembered that I was a king and not a merchant."

7. At this point I could refrain from speaking ill of some viceroys and governors of Portuguese India, who stopped ruling to become merchants, allowed their obligations to fall by the wayside, and ignored the fleets and everything else. They satisfied their desires and engaged in trade with the king's money. They neglected to send out important fleets, and when they did send them, they went at the wrong time, as I have already said, because the governors had been withholding the funds. There is one thing that I do not want to omit, and it is something of great importance for the king and something by which he is deceived daily. This is how the viceroys and governors obtain money for themselves. They pretend that there are pressing needs required in Portuguese India. They pretend to take some of their own money and loan it to officials on the fleets. They then obtain certificates stating that they loaned the king so many thousand pardaus, without the king knowing that this is false. He says that no one comes from Portugal with anything to loan. Oh sir, tell the king these truths so that he will know what is happening and punish those who deceive him. It is as bad to deceive him as it is to cheat him.

8. Leaving this aside, we can return to the subject of generosity of leaders. The great Pompey conquered Pontus, Armenia, Syria, Cilicia, greater Mesopotamia, Phoenicia, Palestine, Judea, and Arabia, and many other nations with this virtue.[80] He established Roman fortified outposts in thirty-nine cities and left nine hundred other cities without them. He built a thousand

---

78. Quintus Curtius Rufus, Roman historian from the first century CE, who wrote a ten-volume history of Alexander the Great. Only eight volumes survived, and these are incomplete.

79. Macedonian general.

80. Pontus and Cilicia were two regions in Anatolia, northeast and southeast respectively.

towers and captured nine hundred ships from different pirates. All of this is as Plutarch says, as well that the third time Pompey was victorious in Asia, he captured all these places. The tribute that he brought from these provinces amounted to 300,400,000, and he also brought urns filled with gold and silver weighing twenty thousand talents for the public treasury.[81] This was in addition to what he distributed among the soldiers, which was at least 1,500 *drachmas*. From what Appian says, the tribute collected amounted to 8,500,000 in gold.[82] He also deposited 12,000,000 into the treasury, not counting the twenty thousand elephants and four thousand horses he gave to the soldiers.[83] This would appear to be insufficient to conquer all these provinces, but what really conquered them was his generosity. The good treatment he showed his troops and his many gifts to them doubled their strength, and each one fought two or three of the enemy.

9. Appian also stated that Pompey had twenty-five *legatus* in his army, while none of the other leaders had more than ten.[84] His generosity made all his men want to follow him. In regard to the army, the Senate never made any relative a captain in charge, as Cicero says in his *Letters to Atticus*, because it wanted to avoid excesses, and it did not want the relatives to get what belonged to the soldiers. This was the reason Cleon, when he began to govern his state, dismissed all his relatives and friends, as they do when someone dies.[85] He understood that it was impossible to effectively rule a kingdom with relatives in the midst of everything. That is the truth, because there is no quicker way to the ruination of a kingdom than having a handful of people with special rights and the deference given to family members.

10. Here I would like to discuss one additional point about relatives and servants of the governors and viceroys of Portuguese India. They are the

---

81. The original figure here is "500 of 200 million" which does not make any sense and appears to be an error. RL says Plutarch stated that the tribute for Rome was 200 million and that Pompey added an additional 100,400,000 sestertii. I have altered the text here to agree with that figure.

82. Appian of Alexandria (95–165 CE), Roman historian of Greek background.

83. Regarding the elephants, the original reads "infants," or princes, but both RL and GM believe this to be an error. The number seems impossible for princes and is difficult to believe for elephants.

84. *Legatus:* Roman general.

85. Athenian statesman (d. 422 BCE), leader of Athens during the Peloponnesian War.

ones who undermine and destroy these officials. I would just like to add what I know about this matter. I can clearly state one thing: when relatives are pulling the governor's strings in Portuguese India, it will decline. This will happen just as it did in the Roman Empire after it abandoned the rule that relatives of the consul could not enter into the army, as I stated earlier.

11. Returning to Pompey (if for the sake of curiosity he could only hear this), the legatus of whom I spoke were second in command after the consuls. Vegetius, in the second book of his *Concerning Military Matters*, writes that Pompey distributed 1,500 drachmas to each foot soldier, 3,000 talents to each soldier on horseback, and twice that to each centurion; each legatus received 1,000 talents, and *prefects*, who ranked just under legati, received the same sum.[86] He said that Pompey distributed 420,000 *libras* of silver just to his foot soldiers and those on horseback. Each libra was worth ten *escudos*, which equals 4,800,000 gold escudos. This sum does not include what he gave the centurions, foreign troops, ambassadors, spies, and other various expenses. Appian calculated that he spent 9,600,000 escudos, and all of this came from the ancient kingdom of Lydia.

12. I have mentioned these detailed accounts because I noticed something about them that is contrary to our current customs. Neither Appian nor Livy, who wrote about the great actions and generosity of Pompey, mention what Pompey kept for himself. This is because it was understood that leaders at the time sought honors more than profit; however, with the governors and viceroys of Portuguese India, it is the opposite. Let the profit come forth; honors can go to whoever wants them! Those leaders of antiquity desired to enrich their subjects; nowadays, viceroys want to impoverish them. This has reached the point that the thirty thousand cruzados the king gives the viceroy to distribute to his subjects he instead pockets himself in imaginary awards to people who never existed.

13. Plutarch tells us that Ptolemy II Philadelphus responded to some of his critics, who said he gave away too much, by saying that he did not want to be known as wealthy, but rather as someone who made others rich.[87]

---

86. Publius Flavius Vegetius Renatus, author of the standard and highly influential text on Roman military, *De Re Militari* or *Concerning Military Matters*, probably written in the fifth century CE. A *praefectus castorum* was a camp commander and third in line of command.

87. Pharaoh who lived from 309 to 246 BCE.

Alexander the Great was accustomed to saying that a good king or leader gives gifts and awards to his friends, while favors and good deeds keep enemies on his side. According to Plutarch, Dionysius of Syracuse entered the house of his son, the prince, and saw, when he looked around, many objects made of gold and inlayed with precious stones that he had given his son. In a very passionate voice, Dionysius said:

> It is certain that you would make a better merchant than prince of Sicily, since it is your nature to hoard treasure rather than give it in awards and gifts. This is what you should do if you want to inherit this kingdom from me, because I can attest that great and mighty kingdoms are not sustained by hoarding, but by giving and sharing.

14. Did Caesar not become king of Rome because of his generosity? It was so great that it lifted the spirits of his friends and dampened those of his enemies. Because of his magnanimous nature, he paid generously by the fistful, saying that it would shortchange people to do otherwise.

15. Woe to me if I were to suggest that the viceroys of India commit sins by being so different from Caesar in all that they do! Caesar gave money by the fistful, while poor soldiers in India cannot pry five pardaus from the viceroy's hands. If Dionysius of Syracuse were to see what is happening in Portuguese India, he would have better justification to call these viceroys "merchants" rather than "leaders." They walk around with notebooks in their pockets, detailing receipts and expenses just like merchants with their account books.

16. Returning to Caesar, about whom by the way I do not want to omit anything, since Your Graces have given me such great leeway; in book 2 of *Civil Wars*, Appian states that after conquering the empire Caesar gave each soldier 5,000 Attican drachmas.[88] Each captain of cavalry received four times that (Varro and Vegetius tell us each squadron of cavalry was thirty men on horseback), and men in the cavalry received 10,000; all the people received a *mina*, an Attican coin.[89] Suetonius Tranquillus, the ancient writer, stated these gifts in *sestertii*, of which he gave 400 to each person.[90]

---

88. Attica refers to the area around Athens, Greece.
89. Marcus Terentius Varro (116–27 BCE), Roman scholar and author of many works, only two of which survive.
90. Gaius Seutonius Tranquillus (70–126 CE), Roman historian and biographer.

Appian says that was the number of minas from Attica. By his calculations, each soldier got 5,000 drachmas and the cavalry twice that. Suetonius also says that Caesar gave the cavalry 24,000 *nummi*, which was 6,000 drachmas. When he made these payments, there were twenty thousand men in Rome.

17. Aulo Hircio in his *Da Guerra Africana* said that there were twenty thousand veterans, and each was given 5,000 drachmas, thus agreeing with the figure from Appian.[91] This totaled some 10,000,000 in gold, and adding the amounts given to centurions, cavalry, tribunes, residents of Rome and other Italian cities, it becomes an infinite sum. When Appian described his triumphal celebration, which lasted four days, he stated that the money minted for this surpassed 65,000 talents and 2,800 golden crowns that weighed more than 20,000 libras. According to Appian, 39,000,000 in gold talents were minted for this occasion, and 10,000 libras were worth 1,000,000.

18. I have listed these examples to show how generosity and greatness conquered the world. These leaders won by granting gifts more than by fighting. It was with this alone that Philip, Alexander the Great's father, rose to greatness—by opening his palms. Many times he said there was no fortress so strong that he could not conquer it if a donkey laden with gold could climb to it. With this trait alone, Nicias won the favor of the people and rose to power as lord of all—by being generous.[92] This was a prudent action for a leader. By giving, he achieved the title of "generous prince" and received the love and goodwill of his citizens.

19. When both of them were magistrates of public buildings, Marcus Bibulus said that Caesar was sponsored by Castor and he by Pollux.[93] The temple they were building to honor these two gods was only known as that of Castor. All the magnificent buildings that Caesar and Bibulus had completed were all attributed to Caesar and none to Bibulus. This is what hap-

---

91. Aulo Hircio (90–43 BCE), legate under Caesar, consul of the Roman Republic. He wrote *The Commentaries of Julius Caesar*, of which *Da Guerra Africana* (*On the African War*) is book 5.

92. Athenian general and politician (470–413 BCE), leader during the Peloponnesian War and rival of Cleon.

93. Marcus Calpurnius Bibulus (102–48 BCE), Roman politician and consul with Caesar in 59 BCE, known as a staunch opponent of Caesar. Castor and Pollux are twin brothers in Greek and Roman mythology who became known as the Gemini.

pens when people are friendly and generous; they are always remembered. The miserly and deceptive, such as Bibulus, are forgotten.

20. Did not Themistocles, the captain of the Athenians, become famous because of his generosity, wanting nothing for himself and giving everything to his soldiers? At one point after a victorious battle, where he crushed a barbarian army, he was walking along the seashore and saw many of their corpses. They were wearing bracelets and other gold jewelry and precious stones. Without paying any attention to them, he said to some soldiers, "Take all these things, soldiers; you are not Themistocles." Who would ever see some of the viceroys whom I have known pass by a catch such as that! They have to enrich themselves, demand their fifth of all spoils, keep a sharp eye on something if they are lacking it, and even demand their pound of flesh from the soldiers. These people have nothing in common with Themistocles.

21. You see, sirs, what strength generosity has that when Alexander the Great was conquering Asia. When he began to attack Hyrcania and the Marcos people,[94] Thalestria, the queen of the Amazons, came to see him because of his fame. Some call her Minoteia and she came with 300,000 men at arms.[95] They traveled twenty days just to see such a generous leader of whom they had heard so much. Marcus Junianus says that she became pregnant because she wanted to have a child with such a great leader.[96] The same thing happened with the queen of Sheba, who came from such a distant place to see the greatness of King Solomon, to whom she brought many gifts.[97]

22. Concluding with the subject of generosity, I will cite only one more example. Famous people from antiquity used to have trumpets sound loudly whenever they were about to eat so that the poor could come forth and receive their servings. Sharing with the poor demonstrated their greatness. This, I have to say, sirs, has ended in India. The captains have changed

---

94. Hyrcania is the region of ancient Iran at the southern end of the Caspian Sea. It was captured by Alexander the Great in 330 BCE.

95. Other sources say she came to his camp with an honor guard of 300 (not 300,000) warriors.

96. Roman historian of the second century CE.

97. According to 1 Kings 10 and 2 Chronicles 9, "She gave the king 120 talents of gold, large quantities of spices, and precious stones. Never again were so many spices brought in as those the Queen of Sheba gave to King Solomon."

Tombstones in a church floor in Bassein.
Photo by Timothy Coates.

this practice to one where they eat in silence with their houses locked up since they have no reason to share with poor soldiers. That which, in the past, was honorable and great, that sheltered and sustained the soldiers, has been replaced with disgrace! This is the current state of things! I fear that Portuguese India will not continue for long.

23. Nobleman: You speak the truth; a pity it is this way. I also have their same fear.

24. Crown Official: This really reflects poorly on the captains and the viceroys when you make these contrasts with figures from antiquity. I do not know how they justify this or what they call it.

25. Soldier: It is "having" and "keeping." I do not know if this plague came from here and went to India, since everyone arrives there with this phrase on his lips: "However much you have, that is what you are worth." I have grown tired. I ask Your Graces to give me leave.

26. Crown Official: But you have not done us the favor of finishing your discourse and concluding with the third part, which remains for you to deliver.

27. Soldier: Well, if you insist, I will give up the idea of leaving. Since you have asked me to continue, please give me your attention.

SCENE 6

The Importance of Prudent Speech

1. Soldier: The third trait that a good captain needs is prudent speech, which is a truth stated by Plutarch. What a beautiful thing it is to hear kind and prudent words from a viceroy or captain! Such beautiful words once uttered cannot be withdrawn. Because of that, the philosopher said many times, people regret speaking, but they are never sorry to remain silent. Good words are a form of generosity because through them a captain can give, although they may not be recognized and the intent can be denied. However, someone will be grateful and appreciative for what has been said. Words are a testimony of the heart. A twisted, distraught, and miserly heart does not know how to give, nor does it know how to speak.

2. It is only natural for a soldier to want to be honored and valued by his captain. He takes the greatest risks and wants to be seen in the thick of battle when he knows that deeds and appreciative words will follow. The nature of a captain is to give, because he knows he gains much more than he receives. He attains fame and glory. The soldier gets what is his and is owed nothing more. Praise from the captain is so precious a treasure that all the gold in the world cannot equal it. There is no trumpet or drum that can lift the spirits of a soldier as well-chosen words from his captain. Many times these words are the ladders that allow them to scale towering walls, the arms with which they conquer forts and the cannons with which they destroy powerful armies. Well-chosen words burrow under impregnable bastions and destroy armor and breastplates; they make dangers easy and burdens light. They make soldiers full when there is nothing to eat and rested when there is no sleep; these are what make the weak strong and the strong bold. These words make the mountains flat, the dark night happy, and the sad day sweet. Above all else, such words make an ugly death beautiful. This is how critical prudent words are from the captain, as critical as firearms. Prudent words conquer enemies and lift the spirits of the victorious.

3. In no other aspect does a captain reflect his prudence more than with his speech. In war, a lack of funds is not as important as disorderly speech. The proverbs tell us that the right word softens anger, just as scripture tells us that drinking tepid water will rid the stomach of its contents. This is what the right word does to anger. At this point, Plutarch said that bridles control horses and prudent words govern anger and passion.

4. Diogenes says that just as a man's face is a mirror his inner soul is reflected in his words.[98] It is possible to know by its sound if a glass is broken or not. In the same way, it is possible to know the character of a leader by the sound of his words. When he was asked about the character of Argaeus, son of Perdiccas, it was because of this that Socrates said, "I never heard him speak."[99] A man's words are the true sound by which he demonstrates his prudence. From the mouth of man comes good or bad. He can have as many good traits as he wishes, but without prudent speech everything is darkened and tarnished.

5. Pytheas, the grand duke of Athens, according to Plutarch, was an honored prince, a much feared and brave captain. However, all these traits were blotted out by his indiscrete words. For leaders, more attention is paid to what they say than what they do. Every once in a while, a captain takes part in a battle, but he never puts his life on the line. In spite of this, to him go the honors and glory of victory. Even though the soldiers are physically engaged and use firearms, the captain uses good and prudent words and directs them. If an army is not led by a leader with prudent speech, we could call it an army without a captain. This is what Caesar called the army of Marcus Petreius and Lucius Afranius that was in Spain fighting for Pompey.[100] According to Suetonius Tranquillus, after Pompey took over the Roman monarchy, he went to the city of Dyrrhachium.[101] Caesar was determined to seek him out but decided not to because it was winter. He decided to go to Spain, and he said to his troops, "Let us capture the army with no captain and then we will seek out the captain with no army." He said this because Pompey's captains, Petreius and Afranius, were not of prudent speech, but Pompey was. As a result, conquering Pompey was more doubtful than defeating great armies in Spain with leaders unworthy of the title "captain."

---

98. Diogenes of Sinope (412–323 BCE), famed Greek philosopher.
99. Kings of Macedonia, Perdiccas (700–678 BCE) and his son, Argaeus (678–640 BCE).
100. Marcus Petreius (d. 46 BCE) was a Roman politician and legatus. Lucius Afranius was a Roman legatus, killed fighting Caesar's troops at the Battle of Thapsus in 46 BCE.
101. Durrës (in modern Albania); a siege took place there between their forces in 48 BCE, and Caesar withdrew.

6. The famous authors of antiquity, both Greek and Roman, did not extol the deeds of famous leaders as much as their speech. They understood that deeds are understood through words. They wrote about Darius, saying that one day while eating he was discussing Alexander the Great with his underlings. A captain by the name of Menon, who was not prudent in his speech, eagerly disparaged Alexander. Darius would have none of that, and with anger in his voice he told him, "Shut up, Menon; I did not ask you to join me in order to dishonor Alexander with your tongue, but to defeat him with your sword." Here you can see the difference between the prudent speech of Darius, who would not even speak ill of his enemy, and that of his captain.

7. Regarding this same Alexander, it is written that he overheard certain soldiers maligning him, and he said in a very prudent manner, "Great captains may not hear very well, but they do good things." He then gave them a reward. When Scipio Africanus was competing with Claudius for control of Rome, Claudius in a manner lacking prudence was listing his merits, and among these he said, "Oh, esteemed and noble senators of Rome (and at that point he named them all), who knows your names as I do?"[102] He said, "Is it not for love that you cannot deny me the position?" However, Scipio responded with prudence by saying to the senators, "What Claudius says is true; he knows all of your names. However, I always worked for all and you all know me." With that comment, he was elevated to the position of dignity for which he aspired.[103]

8. Tiberius Caesar was told by malicious people that some in Rome were maligning him.[104] He responded in a very prudent manner by saying that, in a free city, people could speak freely. Emperor Carlos V is famous throughout the world, and I think it was for his prudent speech.[105] Neither a friend nor a subject left his presence discontented, nor was any enemy scandalized. He showed his prudent speech in many ways. Above all other occasions, it

---

102. It is not clear to which member of the Claudius family this refers, possibly Appius Claudius Pulcher, named consul in 212 BCE.
103. Elected consul in 205 BCE.
104. Second emperor of Rome; he lived from 42 BCE to 37 CE.
105. Charles V, Holy Roman emperor and king of Spain.

Façade of Nossa Senhora da Saude Church in
Sancoale, Goa. This Jesuit church was built in 1566
and destroyed by a fire in 1834.
Photo by Timothy Coates.

was the lofty and very Christian words that he said when he defeated the German Protestants, which he viewed from beyond the Albis Mountains: "I came, I saw, and God was victorious."[106] In doing this, he imitated the first Caesar, but one spoke as a heathen and the other as a Christian.

9. To conclude with this subject, the man selected to rule Portuguese India needs to have the three qualities already mentioned: clemency, gener-

---

106. This may be a reference to the Battle of Kappel in 1531, a Catholic victory in the Wars of the Reformation in Europe. The nearby Albis Mountains are a chain located south of Zurich.

osity, and prudence. These are the three muses, which the poets call Aglaea, Pasithea, and Thalia.[107] These represent happiness, graciousness, and joyous beauty. There is nothing happier than clemency, nothing more gracious than giving, and nothing more beautiful than well-chosen words. Because Your Graces must be tired, and the time has come, please allow me to leave. For certain, I had no intention to develop this discourse as much as I have. I got carried away and forgot the time.

10. Crown Official: Your speaking made me forget the time as well, and I could listen to you until tomorrow. You have said things to me that I never anticipated hearing from a soldier. You are able to explain everything so well that we need to see each other tomorrow. It is a service to the king for you to tell us what is needed in Portuguese India for its defense. We also need to know which is better to conquer first, Sri Lanka or Aceh, because opinions differ.

11. Soldier: I am not sure that I have the knowledge about all that, but as Your Excellency tells me this is for the king's service, I will comply. As they say, I will bend over backward to do my best. Tonight I will review these ideas to have clearer explanations.

12. Nobleman: You have really captivated me and troubled me. You have been discussing very important and weighty issues. God willing, tomorrow I will return here because I want to hear what you have to say. I want to be informed about these issues when they are discussed in Council.

13. Soldier: I would really appreciate that; because Your Excellency is so knowledgeable about Portuguese India, you can inform me about many things. For now, may God be with Your Graces.

---

107. Muses of ancient Greece, daughters of Zeus and Mnemosyne. Aglaea was brilliant and shining, the wife of Hephaestus; Pasithea was the wife of Hypnos and represented relaxation; Thalia was joyous and caused flowers to bloom.

THIRD PART

T HE FOLLOWING DAY in the afternoon, the soldier went to the home of the court official since he had been invited to return. He found him speaking with the same nobleman about the matters they had discussed the previous day. They praised the openness with which the soldier had spoken and his vast experience with all aspects of Portuguese India. As he entered, the nobleman addressed him as follows:

SCENE I

Supplies for Portuguese Asia; Attending to Those Absent; Vice-regal Correspondence and Orders

1. Nobleman: You should be proud, soldier, since this past night we both were unable to sleep because we were thinking about all the things you said. These really need to be written down, which is what we were doing, this official and myself. By telling us all this, you have done us all a great favor.

2. Soldier: It is no small thing to deprive Your Excellency of your sleep when you do not lose your responsibility to govern Portuguese India, having the weight of that position upon you. For certain, I do not know a governor who even enjoys what he eats, nor one who has time to relax, with all the vexations and troubles that go with the position. Many times I thought that the governor had lost his common sense, or he thought very little of everything. I saw governors when they received news that the Moluccas were in trouble, that Malacca was under siege, or that in Malabar someone had taken a gold mine belonging to one of the king's subjects. Other bad news might arrive that the captain in charge of Malabar raided the enemy's river, losing two hundred men in causalities, or that one hundred had been lost in some other disaster, or that someone captured a ship coming from China laden with gold. To all of these, the viceroy acted as if nothing had happened.

3. Those sayings of the old women are little gems, especially that one, "Where no one governs, there is no pain," which is very true. These people who govern are not in charge of Portuguese India, and it pains them little. They want to get rich, and everything else is neither here nor there. They come here all upright and proud, while the poor people in Portuguese India are crushed and downtrodden. It is the captains in charge of the fleets who amaze me. They pull themselves together and, with scarred faces, having lost some ships, they enter Goa's harbor with so much celebratory cannon fire that even the deaf can hear it.[1] When they leave their ships for land, they are dressed in such elegant finery with feathers that you would think they had defeated some global menace. In the certificates, as I said before, it is all praises, what they did, what they destroyed, and what they spent. Now Your Graces can see if what I say about these people having little invested in what they do is true. I am sure Your Graces have no wish but to challenge me, to make me all hot under the collar.

4. Crown Official: You speak the truth. I have those certificates. The worst part is that there are two nobles who have submitted their certificates and both were captains of the fleets. When they speak to me in private, one tells me a thousand insults about the other: that he does not know how to be a captain, he lost ships, he failed to guard the convoys, his soldiers lost their respect for him, the people in Malabar killed so many of his men, and he did not really spend anything. When the other one speaks, the deeds he reports are even worse. I listen to all this with great patience and say nothing.

5. Soldier: Now Your Excellency understands what I have said. So what decision will you make?

6. Crown Official: God brought these people to my door, and they are as troublesome to me as listening to my wife. I have to tell you that I found them so tiresome that I gave them everything they wanted so I did not have to see or hear them anymore.

7. Soldier: By doing this, these troubles will put you in Hell. By my word,

---

[1]. This is a confusing passage in the original, where it says, "não há quem se ouça" or "no one hears it." Clearly he is talking about a loud entrance that everyone would hear. I think Couto omitted a word and it should read "não há quem se *não* ouça" or "there was no one who did not hear it." Again, this demonstrates Couto's fondness for double negatives.

this is really good! Here I am with my legs and arms all scarred, with musket wounds and sword cuts that I received in royal service, and, because I have not caused any trouble, I await receiving a position. That is good justice! Posts and forts are awarded to those with the greatest service or to those who cause the greatest annoyance. If that is the case, I will advise the soldiers to forget guarding their certificates and to forget avoiding any risks, but instead take lessons in the school of being bothersome, as being tedious is what calls the shots in this kingdom. If by chance you say you are keeping an eye on India and all should be lost there, and you send cannoneers to fire the cannons and men for the artillery, galleons, money, soldiers, and everything else they require, then you can throw me in jail as a troublemaker! I really do not understand this. He who speaks the truth gets the leftovers, while he who tells lies is rewarded for being a troublemaker! Give me an order stating that, so I can take it to India in my pocket, and the men will know how to phrase their requests.

8. Your Excellency has caused me a great deal of confusion by telling me all this. I did not know anything about this, but somehow I sensed it in my heart. Two soldiers who came with me to make their requests have presented themselves in your home, and at the homes of other crown officials. One of them said exactly as he wished and dictated orders and said things that made the body tremble. This soldier called you and your colleagues this and that, various names, saying that soldiers never got anything from you without paying something and making other similar statements, which I heard. Several times he said, "Listen here you, either these men will give you something so they do not have to listen to you, or you should [prepare to go unheard and] enter an asylum as a lunatic."

9. So it happened that this fellow was awarded what he desired, and he says they did so because of his manner of speaking. Meanwhile, the second fellow who is prudent and calm, mild-mannered, a good man and very much a gentleman, has been conducting his business in a very honorable and patient manner, not causing any troubles. He is still waiting to receive his post, even though he has twice the service record of the first fellow. What should I think? A couple of times, someone told him, "In these things you have to be unpleasant. You have to scream and speak up, because around here they give more to someone who talks a lot than to someone who fought a lot."

10. Now you see with what pleasure these men seek those who have the obligation to do them justice, yet they so clearly see these injustices! Now it pains me that I am not of the right age to enter a religious order, as the world has really deceived me and I hope for little good from it.

11. I want to share a story with you of what happened to me while I was in the expedition that went to the Gulf of Cambay. When we left the ships in Goa, I was speaking with a rich merchant, who was a heathen, and another heathen came up and entered the conversation. When I asked the merchant who that man was, he said, "This man is a great fighter. When the Turks surrounded Muscat, he fought bravely." When I asked him what he had done, he said, "When the Turks were walking around robbing people, this man was on top of a very high hill continuing the struggle there, waving his arms and insulting the Turks." That story really amused me, and I retold it many times as a good anecdote.

12. I can say that many of the nobles and soldiers that have been quickly rewarded here fought like that heathen on top of the distant hill, waving their arms and cursing loudly at the enemy. Meanwhile, I went around with my sword unsheathed, covered in blood, fighting among the enemy, receiving many wounds, but as of yet I have not received any reward. That is the way of the world; better to fight with one's mouth and forget hand-to-hand combat.

13. Crown Official: This is a really funny story, and I appreciate that you brought it so appropriately to our conversation. You really get right to the point. Many men in India fought in the manner you describe, and they come here and slay me with what they have to say. It looks like the Turks and I face the same danger from them.

14. Soldier: Your Excellency should relax as they have not killed any Turks, nor will they harm you. They are happy coming here imagining that they fought bravely and then believing it. They then ask to be rewarded for what they imagine rather than for what they really did.

15. Crown Official: What can I tell you? I say it is my fault. They give me a bundle of papers, which I would not read even if it meant being awarded a noble title. These papers express the opinions of old and experienced soldiers. God save me, but I award them with what they request rather than what they deserve. From now on, I have learned what this costs.

16. Soldier: It is the king who pays, as do I because you award these positions in a disorderly manner to undeserving people. However, my requests are denied even though I am much more deserving. But for now, let us leave this aside and return to the first subject that we decided to discuss today. That is, we were to discuss what was needed to provide Portuguese India for its defense. I really want this to be completely understood here, even though I have not been appointed to any post, nor have any others. The collective good outweighs individual need.

17. Crown Official: This is the Christian answer and I am pleased to hear it from you. Many others were only interested in what they would receive and forgot about anything else.

18. Soldier: I am not sure if Your Graces understand this as well. You know the current state of Portuguese India. When we know that the fleet is about to leave for Lisbon, we leave everything else aside and complete the dispatches so as not to miss the chance to send them. We ask for a huge armada and that many veteran captains knowledgeable about warfare be sent to India, as well as many cannoneers, artillery men, and a great deal of money. Then my hopes are dashed when I see four ships return, laden with provisions, awarding more to you, and your underlings are the ones appointed to positions. There are many laws against the poor residents, and there is nothing from the king, nor is there anything to provision the state.

19. Crown Official: What would you do? People here are aware of all this because that is what the viceroys tell us. We put a lot of faith in their letters, as they have an obligation to tell the king the truth and find solutions for problems.

20. Soldier: There it is as it always is! A viceroy writes that it is not a good thing for men to be going around in sedan chairs.[2] They should not have Portuguese as pageboys, and there should be no responses for those who are absent. Old debts should not be collected, and that there should not be any chests free of taxes except those from India. This means there is more fraud than ever and three hundred other laughable things. If good, honest, free, God-fearing men, men who are loyal to their king, write that you should

---

2. Sedan chairs were a comfortable (but somewhat extravagant) method of transportation in Goa using slaves. See the illustration on the cover of the book.

send assistance to India, that all will be lost there, you make a joke of it. You think they are mistaken. On the other hand, to those who harm people you provide so much that it is astonishing.

21. Tell me sir, what principle is there in this kingdom to ignore those who are absent? Those who serve should be attended to first, those who remain in service in India rather than those who left it at a time when men were greatly needed. Does not someone who now serves his king deserve more than one who left royal service? Everyone can come to this kingdom and petition for an award. If not many have the means to do this, it is because they would right away lose rights to their back pay. The taxes on imported goods in their personal chests, which they pay here in this kingdom and which are demanded in India—who can pay for this if they do not receive their earned salary? They should receive four quarterly payments each year, but they only receive two. How can a soldier survive on twenty pardaus a year? This places them in danger of committing theft or running away to work for the Muslims, as many have done.[3]

22. Acts of justice such as these do not make a king poor but rather enrich him. Paying those who serve him their due amasses great treasures of mercy from God. This will ensure that the king's kingdoms remain at peace and in harmony, and it will increase his income. Now I would like to know what harm is caused by a married man going around in a sedan chair trailed by his servants? What if he is not feeling well or his horse is sick?

23. Crown Official: All that you say is the truth, but what do you think the king should do if they write him from India that their income is sufficient for all their needs? As to why we appoint men here for positions there and not deal with those who are away, it is because those who are here will return to India where they are needed.

24. Soldier: This is justice! You give appointments to those who are here so they will return to India and those already there serving the king can just wait! To act justly, those who are not here should be awarded first because they are extending their service. If the men saw this happen, they would not journey here, and you would not award those here more than they merit simply because they will return.

---

3. Many Portuguese soldiers left Portuguese-controlled areas to work for nearby Muslim rulers, especially the Mughal emperors in Delhi.

25. Crown Official: I agree with that. This business of ignoring those who are absent should not be a closed book, then we will be able to ensure that many of them are rewarded each year and all get rewarded. In regard to what you say about riding around in the sedan chairs, it is a bad habit and it seems that effeminate men use them. Because of this, noblemen do not have horses to accompany the viceroy when horses are needed. They seem to be living the soft and easy life, which is not fitting for a soldier.

26. Soldier: This is all very good. I am the one who fails to understand this. For these sinful men, the innocent married men must pay. It is all well and good that those others should not go around in the sedan chairs and are required to have horses, and those who do not accompany the viceroy are punished. For these noblemen, no other punishment is needed except losing their appointed positions and not receiving any new ones. Any other punishment is a joke for them. Once they are aware they might lose these positions, I give you my word that they will fall in line, since the wisdom of this action will force them to abandon their sinful ways.

27. Furthermore, sirs, did you know they made this law about the sedan chairs only after life in India became so easy and rich for the viceroy's servants? I have seen these people sell permission for businessmen to use sedan chairs. Some told me that it would cost them twenty or thirty pardaus. Since these men pay for everything from the accounts of fools, they pay very well. They pay especially well for what gives them pleasure. I know of some who bought belts made of gold chains and necklaces of precious stones for which they spent ten to twelve thousand cruzados for their lady friends. After this, they broke their ties and fled with great sums of other's money. Even though I advised some friends against this, I do not know what gift they have to obtain the money of others, but when those who first loaned it to them scramble after them for repayment, they even bribe them to get it back. I am certain that all the money made in India is through deception. God allows the Devil to entrap men this way, as well as by other means.

28. Now, leaving this aside, slapping enormous fines on those who parade around in sedan chairs, but not fining those who refuse to serve the king, will not work! Truthfully, I tell you that I wish I were insane so that I could boldly speak about this. I saw two young lads who served two seasons as ships captains, and now they only want galleys to command. If they get these, then the next season they will only be happy as captains of the fleets.

If they spend one season in the north, then the next they will only want Malabar. Each person only thinks about his own needs and not those of the king, whom he serves. They are more deserving of irons or jails than service on the fleets!

29. If a viceroy had the backbone to apprehend one of those who refused royal service and throw him in irons into a ship, I guarantee the others would gather around him. I do not think that even this would solve the problem. I believe that such a person arriving here in Portugal would not only be awarded a fortress, but be given a special allowance for the chain he brought with him. Leave me so that I can vent my anger against all those who award these positions, so that I can struggle against them.

30. Crown Official: The king is fully aware about those who refuse royal service. He has heard about this several times and is well informed about everything.

31. Soldier: I know nothing about this. If royal edicts were sent, the viceroys made them disappear because they were never enforced. This is how God punishes them for this sin because, just as they fail to comply with the king's orders, others ignore the viceroy's orders and standing instructions. This is the source of the lack of credibility and disrespect for the law. Many times in India I saw such instructions announced only to be disregarded after three days. It seems like a children's game or nonsense.

32. A viceroy issues a decree regarding pages. It says that captains in Hormuz, Sofala, and Malacca can have four pages. Captains of other fortresses can have two, and all other nobles can have one. People paid attention to this for six days. Another viceroy issues another decree forbidding the use of adorned saddle blankets. What nonsense! Another viceroy orders that African slaves cannot hold little umbrellas and walk in front of horses but must instead let them get wet with the winter rains. There is nothing more to do than make the announcement and stop. For certain, this order was given just so that people would know who the viceroy was, because he wanted to have his name announced in the public squares: "Listen to the decree ordered by viceroy so-and-so." I told the criers, "I already know; tell him to issue an edict against the people of Malabar, who each year take twenty or thirty of our ships."

33. One time I was on horseback, going around Goa accompanying a distinguished nobleman. We came across a drummer playing as if in the

middle of a battle, and the noble's horse began to get nervous. The nobleman was aware of this, and he went to the drummer and told him to stop, asking him who he worked for and where he was headed. He answered that he worked for the governor, and he was making a public announcement. Then the nobleman told him, "Tell him to think about this: the sailors of Malabar rule the seas and he parades around here splitting our heads open with his drum. He should order than no one from Malabar set sail; that is what is important. This other stuff you go around announcing is stupid, unimportant nonsense, which should be ignored."

34. Crown Official: This is not a bad story. What you say is correct, except the suggestion to pass a law against the pirates because they would never obey it.

35. Soldier: They could care less about that.

36. Crown Official: Tell me sir, why would that viceroy limit the number of pages?

37. Soldier: To fire a shot at those nobles without positions who have been given the privilege to have four. Do you know what that caused? One of these men who had four added four more to have eight, and no one questioned him.

38. Crown Official: What harm does it cause for a nobleman to have many pages?

39. Soldier: It is actually a service to God and the king, since two hundred boys arrive each year on the ships, and if they did not have anyone to shelter them as these nobles do, they would die without any help. They are then raised in these homes, and later they become soldiers and honorable members of society. When their patrons go to a fort, they go with them; they do well and many become rich. In this way, one-third of the honorable residents living in these forts were once children such as these. This is the damage this decree causes; by removing it, some want to do something good.

40. Nobleman: You have explained this very well. In India, the majority of the residents were servants of the captains where they lived. After their three years of service, each one leaves the foursome married and rich.[4] The viceroy who wanted to defend this, did he state his motivation?

---

4. That is, he leaves the group of four pages.

Front and reverse of a Portuguese *bazaruco*.
From cirani@en.wikipediamedia commons

41. Soldier: This did a lot of harm to those who govern India because favoritism shown to former pages caused several great injustices. I heard there was a viceroy who received greater pleasure from satisfying his desires than from his obligations, and it required little to put the entire state on the line, just because of his desires. You ask me where this comes from, and I can tell you that it comes from being in that place where it is allowed to display one's power, even against God, if I can say that, because harm to God results from injustice.

42. Crown Official: This subject matter is very important, and you should explain it thoroughly because I am really eager to hear what you say.

43. Soldier: Since it is so, please listen to me Your Graces.

SCENE 2

Fraudulent Actions of the Viceroys; the Importance of Attending to Little Things; the Cowardice of Soldiers Nowadays; and the Needs of Portuguese Asia

1. Soldier: This is how it starts. A viceroy wants to do one of those underhanded things that I have been discussing, and an independent-minded High Court justice as well as a religious figure say that he cannot do it. Then, the Devil enters and says to him, "Go ahead, you can do anything." The viceroy takes it so poorly when they tell him he cannot do something that it is as if they are trying to take the government out of his hands. "How is it that I cannot do this," he asks, "if I can do anything the king can do?" Insofar as he has here included what others have told him, he has stated

correctly. The king cannot commit injustices. If this misunderstanding were not corrected, all would be lost.

2. If the viceroy wants to mint counterfeit money, I can call his action that since it harms the people. Copper costs forty xerafins per quintal, he mints *bazarucos* based on a rate of sixty or seventy xerafins. Then the Muslims come from the other side of the river, because they are always watching what we do.[5] When they see the excessive profits made this way, they mint many bazarucos inland and introduce them slowly into Goa. This nets them a little gold because they make their coins smaller.

3. Then come the merchants selling cows, and the bakers, shopkeepers, green grocers, and all the others. They either refuse to accept the money or, if a xerafin is worth 300 réis, they demand 360. If the price for rice, fish, and meat rises by a bazaruco, then the baker makes the loaf of bread lighter and likewise with everything else. The poor complain and suffer. Then they come forth with the solution, which is to devalue the money. Three bazarucos are now worth two, which is a great theft. The people suffer while the viceroy's servant who minted his copper gains five or six thousand cruzados. If you go to the viceroy in person and tell him he cannot mint those coins, he laughs at you and makes a joke of everyone.

4. Crown Official: What are these honorable nobles thinking? Do they go there only to allow us to lose Portuguese India? Why do they not pay attention to this, and why does the king not punish them?

5. Soldier: I have already said that some of that sort are there. I do not want to keep repeating myself. It would be better to stop playing this game.

6. Nobleman: We all want to do the right thing, but it is not possible to attend to everything as much as you would have us do. What are we to do? If we go there to fix things and return without any money, people will ignore us. Regarding the punishments that you say should be instituted for those who excuse themselves from royal service, this cannot be done, for the king is in need of men.

7. Soldier: I have already refuted this. Men who flee service, avoid boarding the ships, and refuse to aid the forts—of these there is no shortage. But I want to address this point. Why not just ignore them and not provide them with rewards? Why not send a list of these people each year, people

---

5. The city and region of Goa in 1612 was quite small and bordered by rivers.

whom we can call "vagrants," so that when positions are being awarded, they get none? What greater punishment would you like to see, other than having them come here and then return with no awarded post? Would others not then be ashamed to refuse royal service?

8. I give you my word that if you did this, it would reform everything there so completely that everyone would be astonished. If everyone saw that people received so much without going to Lisbon, as much as those who continue to serve on the fleets, they would do well to continue serving. You, sir, now award those who, in your words, bother you. They would do well to live as they wish, and not have the troubles I had throughout my life. I never left service except during the three months of winter, and even then I had more to do than when I was with the fleets. I struggled against hunger, which is an enemy against which strength and weapons are useless. While on the fleets, I always had a plate of rice and little salted mackerels; these are the gifts by which we serve the king there.[6]

9. It is certain that a life serving on a cutter is a life of penitence for one's sins. I am not sure if it is not a harder life than that of the hermit monks who sleep on the ground in caves, warm and sheltered from inclement weather.[7] They eat cooked greens with a piece of hard bread and are sustained by their spiritual strength. They live more than a hundred years. If they do not drink wine, they have fountains of sweet water to console them. However, we soldiers for the entire year or all our lives sleep on the deck of a cutter in the open air, exposed to the sun and rain. The ration of rice that we eat is filled with stones and dirt. The water that we drink comes from barrels and stinks so much it can make you ill. Now see if this is not sufficient penitence for my sins! We suffer so completely because we have no other choice.

10. In well-ordered societies everything works toward the good, and people strive to fix little things as well as very big ones. If a little thing gets into your eye and you do not remove it, it will bother you a lot. That is the way of little things in the eye of our society; if you fail to attend to them, they

---

6. Indian mackerel found in the waters of the Indian Ocean around south and southeast Asia.

7. It is unclear whether Couto means hermit monks in general or members of the Order of St. Augustine, an order of hermits.

will continue to make you uncomfortable. "Great harm can come from little things," the old women say.

11. If a small stone gets in your shoe, it makes you limp. Do you think that these nothings, these little things of allowing these men to go around and live as they wish, are of little importance? You should know, sir, that this is everything. If society does not attend to a soldier who has nothing, where does it come from, all that gold, velvet, all those Portuguese pages? Is there not so much that it is astonishing? The young nobles who come from Portugal without a cruzado, who want a house for thirty to rent for a month, a horse adorned in silver, and beautiful saddle blankets—where does this come from?[8] To enter their homes is like walking into a wasteland or an enchanted house. There are four chairs in the front rooms, in the bedroom a little cot where they sleep, and as for the remaining rooms, you could practice swordsmanship or play ball. So, what is this? Why not remove this speck from your eye? Why not remove it? In order to afford all this, these people have to seek out every illicit scheme that they can, deceiving the young lady, the widow, and dishonoring the married woman. This is the beginning of the ruination of our society.

12. When Portuguese India was in its prime, no such young noblemen had a house or a horse. Some five or six of them got together and lived with an older nobleman who had either already completed his position at a fort or who was just about to obtain one. They had only one page and one servant to carry an umbrella. In this manner, they lived a quiet and reserved life, very praiseworthy for its modesty at the time. It would have been extremely rare for one of these men to be involved in some vile act, nor did they marry, as they do nowadays, for four cruzados and then spend it all. Soldiers would also band together in groups of five or six in a local house, which they would rent for two pardaus monthly, where they all got along and shared two capes and two suits, and they would go out during the day. They ate food given to them by an older nobleman, or they would pawn a musket to get rice and oil to feed themselves. They did not engage in vile acts, nor would you find them parading around the streets. When the fleets were ready, they would have been embarrassed to remain in the city.

---

8. I assume Couto means thirty pardaus, but the text specify a unit of currency.

13. I will tell you a witty little story about this very subject, told to me by a lady of the evening. One night a soldier knocked on her door while the viceroy was at sea with the fleet. She asked who it was, and he responded "a man of peace." To this she quickly replied, "I really believe that, because someone who remains in Goa while the viceroy is at war must be a man of peace." In this way, men at the time did acts for God, and when they embarked on the ships rarely returned without significant plunder and many small ships that they had captured. Nowadays, it is exactly the opposite. No one gets on the ships, people walk around Goa all winter, and when summer arrives and the fleets need to be staffed, they quickly hide. As soon as they are aware that the sails are set, they reappear in Goa and there is no viceroy to question what they are doing. (When the fleet is formed, it is because the Moluccas, Malacca, and Sri Lanka are in need of assistance.) Some of the men who sail on the ships remain in the forts in Kanara, while those in Goa hide in holes like spies. Something good rarely occurs with the fleets: no one fights and no one comes to the aid of the soldiers in the forts.

14. You should know that the viceroys notice that there are many missing from the rolls, and after the fleets have left, these men are seen walking around the streets of Goa all brilliant and glorious. Yet the viceroy does not hang four to instill fear in the others. I am sure that some care little if the soldiers come or go, because they only operate these fleets as a kind of exercise. They write to Portugal saying that they organized so many fleets, that brought them so many victories, in spite of whatever happened, and they obtain very little for the crown from all this. Please pay attention to this, sirs.

15. Crown Official: God will attend to this in his time, as will the king in his, if we are not deceived by our intentions. However, returning to the issue of what is required in India, which is why we are together today, you should tell us the most important things to bring to the king's attention.

16. Soldier: Your Excellency has spoken correctly. Let us drop these absurdities of which we were speaking. The first thing is the extravagant clothing the soldiers are wearing. They should be ordered to dress like soldiers and not ruffians. Issue a law stating that viceroys should look like captains-general, which they are. Everyone takes pleasure in looking like a soldier, marching in a company, wearing cotton breeches that go half-way

down the leg, a short sword, if decorated in silver, worn on a leather belt with iron.[9] They should not be dressed in velvet breeches, gilded swords, with so many gold braids, appearing ready for a court dance.[10] They wear so much gold and silver that I wonder where it comes from.

17. This is the speck in the eye, sirs, that I told you about. If you ignore it, you can sometimes lose both your eyes. By not removing that stone in your shoe, you can damage your foot.

18. Certainly, gentlemen, you would enjoy seeing a soldier from my day, with a black jerkin, cotton or fiber drawers, doublets made the of the same materials, a military doublet of worked leather, a cap from Milan, and a short sword with a belt made of tapir leather.[11] You would enjoy even more seeing them fight. You both seem to be such refined gentlemen, you would lose to these fellows. Nowadays, everything is the opposite, although some of the soldiers today are very skilled. I am afraid that today's soldiers are all dressed up and are only concerned with acquiring new finery. When they meet those from Malabar, they struggle to save their clothes, which cost them so dearly.

19. We were discussing the other thing that should be regarded and that receives so little attention: the viceroys need to follow the provisions and standing orders from the king. This is the source of all good and all evil. The king should order that all men who are Jews or foreigners embark on the ships for Lisbon because their presence damages the Estado da Índia. Such a provision should be announced that they must leave on the ships. Do this to give them sufficient time, because they will have to conclude their business. Since they are involved in local affairs and enjoy the pleasures offered by India, as I have said, they make secret deals, and provisions are passed allowing them to wait for another year. Then they undermine the provisions for the following year, and year after year passes without remedy. They remain in Portuguese India, contrary to the king's wishes, and are detriments to the population.

---

9. Breeches are men's pants that end above the knee.
10. In the original, the *passapé* or *passé-pied*, a French court dance popular at the time.
11. Jerkin: a sleeveless coat that goes below the waist, half way to knees. Doublets: snug fitting long-sleeve jackets, waist length. Tapirs are four-legged mammals similar to pigs, originally from South and Central America as well as South-East Asia.

20. The king issues another provision stating, "So-and-so will serve as treasury superintendent, and someone else will be the secretary, and so-and-so the learned gentleman will be the chief judge, another will be the judge, and a third will be the crown attorney," and so on. This provision is then delivered to the viceroys, who stash it in their desks and ignore it. They then award the positions to whomever they wish. The others are unaware of what the king has ordered. In conclusion, sirs, if we were to list all these things, it would be endless, because the power the viceroys have assumed is infinite. Let us change the subject as this involves many people.

21. Nobleman: In spite of the fact that you are a court official and deal with these matters, you do not know any more about them. It is this way, but many times such men as these viceroys deceive the king. The ministers here in Portugal also give whatever they want to whomever they wish, because those men are loyal to them and are therefore rewarded.

22. Soldier: Is this good? Be it as it may, the king ordered it, and it should be done as he has mandated. Do as he ordered, obey his wishes, write him back, and he will tell you what he wants. Who told you that there were no viceroys who deceived the king? Because of that, these viceroys ceased to be received by their king and obey him. The king can do as he wishes without anyone asking him for an explanation.

23. You should know, sirs, that there was a viceroy whom the king wrote, telling him that he wanted a certain person put in a position because he deserved it due to previous service. The more the king insisted, the worse it became. The viceroy wanted to give the position to one of his men, and the king wanted his man in that position. The viceroy took the position away from the king's man, and the viceroy's man served in that post. The worst of it was that the man who lost the position was advised that he was at risk of being killed if he went to Portugal. He entered a monastery and then left on a ship where he hid, being afraid.

24. Crown Official: And this incident passed with no punishment?

25. Soldier: Those punishments are laughable. The viceroy's heirs received his salary, and, regarding the disobedience, he ended up right as rain. When the king strictly punishes those who disobey his provisions, things will get on the right track and there will not be so much chaos.

A man wearing a doublet, jerkin, and breeches.
From an original chalk drawing done by
C. Arthur Brooks, used here with his permission.

SCENE 3

To Conquer Sri Lanka or Aceh? The Importance of
Conquering the Silver Mines of Mutapa

1. Crown Official: Let us leave these sad subjects. I am afraid there are no solutions from them. Let us deal with the subject matter of yesterday: which would be better to conquer first, Sri Lanka or Aceh? Many think that Sri Lanka is more important, because it is closer to Goa and the island is both large and very fertile. It is capable of providing for all the Portuguese scattered throughout India. I have always heard that, in the past, kings wrote in their instructions that if events in India turned hostile; the best thing to

do would be to gather all the Portuguese and take them to Sri Lanka. From there, they could focus their attention on India and recapture it. Others said that Aceh is more important for the security of the entire region, including our forts in Malacca, the Moluccas, and trade with China and Japan. One fort in its port would ensure everything. Now we would like to hear your opinion about this.

2. Soldier: This subject is beyond the scope of a poor simple soldier such as myself. I can tell you about my gun and warfare, but these are subjects for knowledgeable leaders. However, even though I know little about this, if Your Graces insist, I will tell you what I know and what I heard from old hands.

3. In the first place I can tell you that, when the valiant captain and viceroy Dom Francisco de Almeida ruled Portuguese India, the king directed him to establish a number of forts. The viceroy responded that India would be better defended by many galleons, fleets, all well stocked, and by clever warfare. Forts, he said, were like sheep pens. India would be more prosperous with as few of them as possible and would also have fewer places to defend. I agree with this even today, because many forts have no function except to create expenses, be poorly provisioned, and stand in harm's way. If one of these were captured, the word would spread around the globe that one of the king's outposts was lost.

4. If you told me that five or six of these forts were needed for some good reasons that existed previously, and they now functioned to provide posts for deserving men, that would all be well and good. However, how can the specific demands of one place merit risking such a great thing as the honor of all of Portuguese Asia? These places become very expensive. Each year, these forts spend four thousand pardaus each (which is paid by the state because they produce nothing). Give the money to those you wish to reward and they will be content, and the state will have no responsibilities for them or any of the sudden attacks on the outposts. If they paid tribute, which is four *fardos* of rice, and if you bought a fifth fardo, this would supply a fleet at the entrance of the enemy's harbor. They would fear this more than the forts, which have no soldiers or ammunition.

5. The most important forts, which provide all the might and income of Portuguese Asia and which I already discussed, had so much wealth they could support themselves and grow. Yet they are now in such miserable

condition they have just about totally collapsed. If this is the case, how do you expect to sustain other forts that provide you with no income whatsoever, but rather cost you money? If you told me there are some, such as Mombasa, Muscat, Mozambique, and Sofala, that are necessary to keep the Turks from entering these areas and to defend the gold and silver mines, this I would concede. However, these need to be as well provisioned as Hormuz and Diu, not so much for what they pay, but for their importance. They operate with a free will, are not organized, and ignore the needs of the king. I am speaking in this manner with Your Excellency because I do so to everyone who is responsible for allowing this state of affairs to continue.

6. Crown Official: We are all responsible. Those of us here are responsible for not knowing how things are there and for not advising the king of these things. The viceroys are responsible for not paying attention to such an important matter for which they are responsible. Dom Jorge de Castro was responsible for such an act. At the age of ninety, and with many years of service in India, he surrendered the fortress at Chalé, yet he was not as guilty as were others whom we appointed here.[12]

7. Soldier: It would take three entire lives to tell you what I have seen and what goes on there, and I forget some things here and there. However, I want to drop this and answer the question Your Graces asked me: Which is it more important to now conquer, Sri Lanka or Aceh? I say that both are important, but first, in order to take either, it is necessary to take the silver mines of Chicoua in the kingdom of Mutapa.[13] These are well known, so very rich and prosperous that they exceed all others in the world. I once saw some ore processed from there that Vasco Fernandes Homem brought, and many others brought some as well.[14] One ounce of it was given to me by a priest from the Church of São Domingos, and this was two-thirds silver and one-third stone.

12. Dom Jorge de Castro surrendered Chalé, or Chaliyam, at the mouth of the Baypore River near Calicut in 1571 at the insistence of his wife. Other sources say he was eighty and a hardened veteran of war in spite of his advanced years. See Edward McMurdo, *The History of Portugal*, 188.

13. Mutapa was a Shona kingdom in what is now Zimbabwe that flourished from 1430 to 1760.

14. Homem led an expedition of four hundred men into this region of Africa in 1574.

8. This wealth, this happiness, is within your reach, and no one can obtain it without passing through the entrance you control; you fail to obtain it because you are ignoring it. Why? It is certain that it could not be greater, and when we can all see that the income of Portuguese Asia is insufficient to maintain such a large empire, clearly it is necessary to augment it with something else. This has to be mines, since a state without them will always be poor.

9. Look at the strength of Castile and how it defends and protects so many kingdoms, duchies, and counties. In Flanders alone, the Catholic kings have spent 40 million in gold fighting the rebels.[15] If they did not have mines in New Spain and elsewhere, how could they possibly bear the cost of such an effort?[16] Would the Roman Empire have been able to rise to such greatness if not for the wealth of Lydia, Arabia, Persia, and other provinces filled with mines? If you do not believe it, look at the incredible riches that I have already discussed, which Pompey deposited in the public treasury and the rivers of wealth he poured on his troops.

10. If someone doubts that these silver mines exist, it is because he does not have the experience that I have had. I was on Mozambique Island in the house of a relative of mine when Vasco Fernandes Homem returned from these silver mines and brought their ruler with him as a captive. They stayed in my relative's home, and I heard them discuss these mines many times. They explained how they did not excavate them, yet how the Africans removed the rock. This same lord, who was called Chaá, told me how they extracted the ore and cast the silver.[17]

11. However, leaving this aside, India just barely provides sufficient income to support itself. It is a miracle that it sustains the Portuguese presence

---

15. This is a reference to the eighty-year war between Spain and The Netherlands, lasting from 1568 to 1648.

16. New Spain was the name for Mexico, a great source of silver for the Spanish crown.

17. Recent scholarship has found that Mutapa produced a great deal of gold and that silver was produced only as a byproduct of gold mining. Part of the mining technique at Mutapa was to use fire to heat the rock face and then cold water to crack it, thus exposing the ore. This may have been the information Couto is suggesting here. See Bethwell Ogot, *Africa from the Sixteenth to the Eighteenth Century*, 327–29. The ruler of the kingdom of Mutapa from 1560 to 1589 was Negomo Chirisamhuru.

from Sofala to Mozambique without such treasures and with only what it produces. Even if it had greater resources, it still has many expenses. For these reasons, explain this to the king: if he wants to effectively rule India, it will be necessary to conquer these mines. Doing so will not only allow what we have planned here, but it will enrich Portugal and Spain.

12. Crown Official: This is high-stakes business. I do not know why we have not put our shoulders to the wheel and applied ourselves to complete something so very great and needed. If this had been the business of the kings of Spain, it would all be completed and they would be the rulers.

13. Soldier: Our kings also did this. They were inclined toward finding these mines, and made efforts to find them, but it seems that mines were all reserved for the Spanish. It pleases God that none were left for our country!

14. Crown Official: That is very bad! Is not the king of Castile also Portuguese like us?[18] Why do you say this?

15. Soldier: I see our king is a young lad, not married and without heirs.[19] If it remains this way, outsiders will move in, and I only see the old hatred between the Castilians and us.[20]

16. Nobleman: When this happens, I do not fear anything. This feeling is only from the common people; among nobles it is very different. Who is more accomplished than the Spanish? Who is better mannered? Who is fairer? Who is more prudent? Who is more of anything that you might wish? No, I do not fear any of this.

17. Crown Official: Let us not dispute what is in the hands of God but rather return to the subject at hand. Tell us, sir, what is needed to conquer these mines?

18. Soldier: Less than what was needed to conquer the mines of Peru and New Spain. Only two ships are required to leave from this kingdom, with

18. King Dom Philip II of Spain was the son of Charles V and Queen Isabel. She was Portuguese and the daughter of King Dom Manuel I of Portugal.

19. King Dom Sebastian, who ruled Portugal from 1557 to 1578 died unwed and childless at the age of twenty-four on the battlefield of Ksar el-kebir in Morocco. Here Couto is setting the time period of this work, around 1570.

20. The Spanish, or more specifically the Castilians, were the historical enemies of the Portuguese. The Castilians repeatedly attempted to conquer and annex Portugal beginning in the period 1383–1385, then again in 1475–1479, 1580–1581, 1640–1666, 1776–1777, and 1801.

three hundred men on each, sent directly to Mozambique, carrying cloth from Covilhã and Portalegre, and some wine.[21] Everything else can be sent from Goa.

19. Crown Official: What would that be?

20. Soldier: I will tell Your Graces. The year before, from this kingdom send 80,000 cruzados on the annual fleet to Goa. Send 20,000 on each ship so that they will purchase a thousand bales of cloth of the type that the Africans like to obtain in trade. These will be worth 60,000 cruzados. That will leave 20,000 cruzados for expenses, which I will explain shortly. These thousand bales of cloth you sell in Sena and Tete at a rate no lower than 200 gold cruzados per *corja*. That will yield 100,000 gold cruzados, which will be more than enough to pay the six hundred men their salaries and feed and shelter them. Paying them four payments each year will cost 24,000 cruzados. That figure subtracted from the 100,000 cruzados leaves 76,000.

21. From this figure, you will need to spend 60,000 for another thousand bales of cloth. That leaves 16,000 cruzados to be sent each year to India to buy raison wine, flour, jams, dried plums, almonds, and other similar foods for the sick. Since the men have bread and wine and there are plenty of chickens and meat available, only a few will get sick or die. What kills people there is hunger or lances thrown by the natives.

22. The 20,000 cruzados remaining from the first transaction can be sent to India to buy cloth to cover expenses. Some fraction of that, or half, should go to the coast around Malindi to purchase *pate* cloth, which is made from silk and cotton. This is worn by the kings and lords, and it is very valuable as a gift in the kingdom of Mutapa to be given to the lords of that kingdom. This will still leave a lot of money to pay the workers and craftsmen and for the materials to build a fort at the mines. These expenses will not be very great since things there do not cost very much.

23. So here it is, with a sum of 80,000 cruzados, you can pay the expenses for 600 soldiers for as many years as you wish. These soldiers in groups of 100 to 150 can take breaks by boarding the ships from Lisbon. Once the mines are well known and fortified, then anyone from Portuguese India who wants to trade can use his own ships to do so, bringing clothes, flour, wine, and jams. The area will become so prosperous and abundant that

---

21. Covilhã and Portalegre are two cities in the interior of Portugal.

towns filled with Portuguese and local Christians will spring up and make it into another New Spain. From there, it will be possible to make it through the heartland of black Africa to reach Angola, which would then link the Atlantic with the Indian Ocean. I believe it is less than two hundred leagues to make this connection.[22]

24. In the fort of Mozambique I saw a letter written by Governor Francisco Barreto to the king in which he addressed this subject of the conquest of the kingdom of Mutapa.[23] He said that he went to the coast of Malindi to conduct some business. While in the kingdom of Atondo, he said that some elderly Muslims told him that it was fifteen or twenty days' journey from there to the other sea.[24] The king responded by saying that he should get to the bottom of this, because it was of greater importance to him than the mines.

25. Here we have listed the benefits of conquering these mines in this manner: the state of Portuguese Asia will become so prosperous that it will be able to conquer whatever it wishes, and its subjects will be as wealthy as those of New Spain. The Roman Catholic Church will become wealthy with so much land under its control, and the African people will convert to the faith of Christ and smoothly submit to the yoke. Since they have no laws, they will not reject those taught to them.[25]

26. The land is so fertile that wheat will grow, as will barley, beans, and other legumes. Herds of cattle will grow fat and produce more and bigger calves than anywhere else in the world. What more is there to desire or to hope for? You can plant all the fruits of the world, and they will produce more than anywhere else. You can cultivate beautiful grape vines because

---

22. Two hundred leagues would be 800 to 1200 kilometers. In reality, the distance from Harare, Zimbabwe, to Luanda, Angola, is 2,100 kilometers, or about twice Couto's estimate.

23. Viceroy of Portuguese India, he later led an expedition to Mutapa to conquer the gold mines, where he died in 1573.

24. RB says Atondo was a kingdom near Malindi on the east coast of Africa. "The other sea" would have been the Atlantic Ocean, which would have been much more than fifteen or twenty days' journey from Malindi. It is more likely they meant Lake Victoria.

25. This statement is a reminder that missionary efforts were an important motivator of early modern Portuguese interactions globally.

the grapes in Sofala are wonderful. I ate several bunches of them, which were growing wild, and they are like those in Portugal. I ate melons that were like those from Abrantes.[26]

27. The vegetables are excellent and olives trees will grow well there. The soldiers with Nuno Velho Pereira, who were shipwrecked at the Cape of Good Hope, and who crossed this entire region of southern Africa, found wild olive trees with fruit just like olives.[27] It must be easy to hunt pigs, deer, rabbits, and everything else, because the land produces so much. As soon as we become the lords of the silver mines, we would also become the masters of the gold mines in Botonga, Maçapá, and all the others.[28] There is an abundance of wool and cotton to make cloth and piece goods. They have everything that Europe has, and they have things of which Europeans know nothing. Because of this, Europeans pay little attention to such a huge opportunity.

28. I wanted to ask Your Graces one more thing. Here in this kingdom, would they normally agree to conquer African kingdoms if they believed that we should abandon India, because it is ruinous for Portugal to keep it? If we conquered kingdoms in Africa, would it not be for greater fame and fortune?

29. Nobleman: You have spoken well. I can tell you that there have been many debates here in this kingdom regarding this question, with many written opinions for the one side or the other. Maintaining India is not such a crystal-clear objective. For one side or the other, there are doubts, honest differences, and very valid and urgent reasons to do either one thing or the other. However, because maintaining our presence in India would be very expensive, no firm decision has been made.

30. Soldier: Well, my word sirs! I do not know what could cause abandoning an empire. I trust there is not another superior in the world in terms of greatness, jurisdiction, and beautiful cities, as well as in terms of wealth and Christianity. Even if it were only for this reason, the kings should spend

---

26. Historically, Portugal has produced a great deal of grapes and wines. Grapes grow throughout the country and virtually every region produces wine. Abrantes is a town in the center of the country.

27. Pereira was governor of Mozambique from 1583 to 1586, later of Malacca.

28. Botonga was in the Kingdom of Sofala, Maçapá was part of Mutapa.

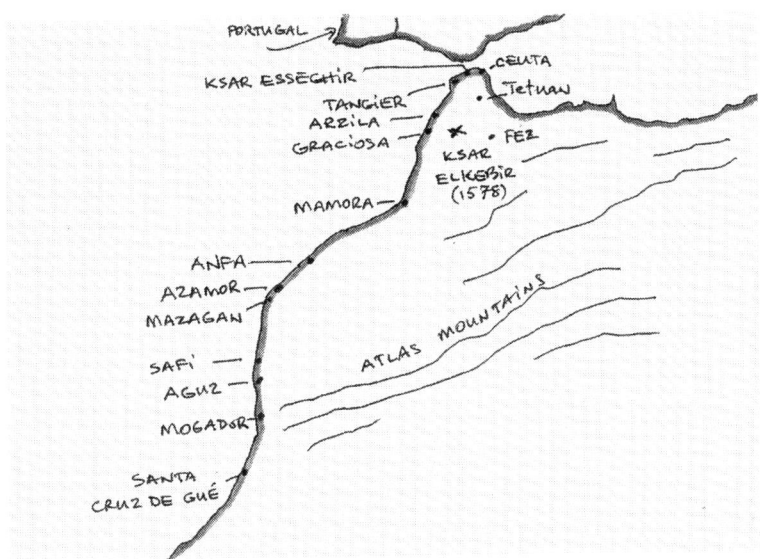

MAP 5. North Africa, showing places mentioned in the text.
Map drawn by Timothy Coates.

their entire fortunes retaining it. It could be for this reason that God has maintained the kingdom of Portugal for many years, and favored it with all the many conquests of its kings. God has placed the king and his subjects at the top of the wheel of fortune. His subjects have shown great piety in these conquests, as well as performing marvelous deeds in Portuguese Asia, guarding and defending Christianity.

31. It seems to me, sirs, that, being here, you are very far removed from this reality. In all of the Estado da Índia from Sofala to Japan there are more than 2 million Christians, not counting the large numbers who are baptized daily. This is what you want to abandon? For certain, God will forsake those who consider such an idea. Given that I am a poor, simple soldier, I will need to speak about this is some length. I trust in God that he will purify my speech as he did for the Prophet, allowing him to roar and shout about his honor.[29] In the same way, I will list the reasons stated by those who

---

29. This reference is unclear but it might be to 1 Samuel 3:19, "The Lord was with Samuel as he grew up and he let none of Samuel's words fall to the ground."

support conquering Africa and abandoning India. If Your Graces would like to hear them, I will add my own, but if not, you can ask me to leave and I will gladly do so.

32. Crown Official: I will not order such a thing, for sure. Rather, I would ask you, in service to the king, to tell us all that you know about these issues, speaking with the same candor that you have employed up to now.

33. Soldier: Now, Your Graces, pay attention so as not to interrupt me.

Portuguese Outposts in Morocco

CURRENT MOROCCAN NAME	PORTUGUESE NAME OF CITY	HELD BY THE PORTUGUESE
Ceuta	Ceuta	1415–1668
Ksar Essehgir	Ksar Essehgir	1458–1550
Tangier	Tangier	1471–1662
Asila	Arzila	1471–1550
Larache	Graciosa	1489
Mehdia	São João de Mamora	1515
Casablanca	Anfa	1515–1755
Azamour	Azamor	1515–1541
El-Jadida	Mazagan	1485–1769
Safi	Safi	1488–1541
Souira Guedime	Aguz	1506–1525
Essouira	Mogador	1506–1525
Agadir	Santa Cruz de Gué	1505–1541

SCENE 4

The Wealth and Riches of Africa versus India

1. Soldier: I will begin, gentlemen, with the reasons people give that it is better to conquer Africa than India. These people say that a kingdom must have two things to be prosperous. The first of these is food—abundant crops and livestock sufficient to feed the people so that they are not oppressed and overworked as they would be if they had to import these things.

The second is mines of gold and silver, as well as other metals, to maintain the peace and provide the wherewithal for conducting warfare. The African kingdoms have these things in great quantities. The kingdoms of Fez and Morocco have so much bread, barley, vegetables, and cattle, both fat and young, all in great quantities, that they could share these with their neighbors.[30] They also have everything else that people require, such as linen, cotton, honey, wax, sugar, many different types of fruit, most of which grow without cultivation. They also have the gold mines of Tivar, from which, people say, much of its production goes to Morocco.[31] These mines are very prosperous. Nor are such riches absent from the Atlas Mountains, but they are not excavated.[32] The gold that annually leaves from the factory at São Jorge da Mina is so great that it astonished the ambassadors in Malabar when Dom Vasco da Gama took some of it to India.[33] He showed a chest of it from a ship he had encountered that was carrying twenty thousand cruzados' worth of chains, bracelets, and other large pieces of jewelry. They say that the gold from São Jorge made Portugal wealthy and made the African conquests possible. King Dom João III gave the Emperor Carlos V ninety thousand gold cruzados in dobras as a dowry for his sister Dona Isabel.[34] This was all gold from São Jorge and not from trade with India. To make this treasure all the greater, he included the fabled golden apples from the orchard of the Hesperides from the African coast, and other similar things, which I will describe shortly.[35]

2. I will tell you gentlemen that I do not deny that the kingdoms of Africa have everything that people claim they do, and in sufficient quantities

---

30. Given that by the time Couto was writing, the Portuguese had had over 150 years of interaction with the kingdoms in Morocco (starting with the conquest of Ceuta in 1415), it is not surprising he would include this commentary.

31. The location of Tivar is unknown, but, generally speaking, gold produced largely in the upper Niger River region of modern Burkina Faso.

32. The Atlas Mountains, running through the middle of Morocco to modern Algeria and Tunisia, have peaks as high as Mount Toubkal at 13,665 feet. See map 5.

33. A reference to Vasco da Gama's initial arrival in India in 1498.

34. They were married in 1526.

35. In Greek mythology, the nymphs who guarded Hera's orchard and the tree that produced golden apples lived in the Atlas Mountains.

to support their people without needing anything from their neighbors. I think this is because they have more than enough bread and cattle and everything else they want—gold, mines—all they need to do is ask for it and they have it. Who would be able to conquer this, with what force, if the Romans were never able to rule Africa in spite of attempting to do so for many years and having powerful armies? Why did Scipio Africanus destroy Carthage if not because he could not rule it?[36] The Roman and Holy Roman Emperors of Germany, who are defenders of the Roman Church, why have they not attempted such a conquest while the Arabs rule over Africa? This was a huge Christian region with many bishoprics sending bishops to holy councils.

3. What force would these people have our kings use to conquer so many provinces and kingdoms? Who would they have us employ when our troops are so poorly trained in warfare that they do not know how to aim a musket, mount a horse, or throw a lance? In some emergencies, when they wanted to send three thousand troops to India, they had to empty the jails in Portugal, including people with death sentences![37] Sometimes, some of the few places that we held in Africa were surrounded by Arabs; it was only with great effort and trepidation that help was sent.[38]

4. Arzila was certainly at risk of being lost when the Conde do Redondo was there, since he lost the town and took his last refuge in the castle.[39] All would have been lost if God had not allowed Dom João de Meneses to arrive with a fleet. Tell me, what did it cost to send aid to Mazagão? Did they not capture the fort at Agadir? Did you not abandon Azamor and two or three other forts you had along the African coast? Even those you still maintain, are they not at risk? At Mamora, was not all the country's

---

36. A reference to the Battle of Zuma between Scipio Africanus and Hannibal. Scipio Africanus won but did not destroy Carthage.

37. Like most early modern European states, Portugal used its convict population as soldiers in times of emergency. Death sentences in Portugal were rare and were virtually never enforced.

38. Couto refers to a string of coastal outposts in modern Morocco, which were held by Portugal.

39. For all of these North African cities, see map 5. This battle in Arzila occurred in 1549.

strength and nobility lost?[40] These cities are all at the edge of the ocean, and help can climb off the ships at no risk.

5. What efforts would be needed if Portugal possessed cities and forts in the hinterland! For certain, they would not be able to send them aid. How much more would you have me say? With what force would these people have us conquer such a huge empire if we witnessed King Dom Afonso V, with the best that Portugal had to offer, become disorganized and lose the battle, going for help to the French?[41] Ten thousand, twenty thousand men going to Africa—what are they to do and who will provide for them? This is laughable.

6. They use as an example that we arrive at the ports of Morocco with our army. This is an unexpected attack; we arrive and then leave. Do you not recall, gentlemen, seeing those valiant captains Nuno Fernandes de Ataíde and Dom João de Meneses, with the flower of Portuguese nobility, routed and scattered? They were veterans with so much experience that I doubt anyone has had more from that time until now. Our kings of the past, when they first ordered the discovery of the sea route to India, did they not consider this? Well beforehand, they had charted the coastline of Africa and constructed and occupied forts where we now have them. Had it been better to conquer Africa than India, why would they have made such a questionable undertaking? Do we not know they had trusted leaders at that time with whom they discussed such a plan and who appraised the kingdom's strength against that of Africa? We also know that, after attempting to implement this plan many times, after they were no longer misled by the idea of capturing Africa, they turned to conquering India. Our Lord God showed us mercy many times, as we know.

7. I would ask those who malign the discovery of the route to India if this were not so much more beneficial than conquering Africa? The Catholic kings denigrated and dismissed the importance of the spices from India. Later, Emperor Carlos V had many disputes with our kings over the Moluccas, even though many times our kings were cousins, in-laws, or relatives. Those islands have nothing except cloves, nutmeg, and mace, and they are

---

40. Mehdya, Morocco, occupied by the Portuguese from 1515 to 1541.

41. In the struggles for succession to the throne of Castile, King Afonso V lost a battle in 1476 and sought help from the French.

very poor, so poor that these products from trees sustain them. To rule them, it was necessary for new ocean passages to be found by a trouble-making subject who acted against his king.⁴²

8. They did these things so deliberately, with so many wars and expenses, which they did to obtain a great empire in India. It is so wealthy that I cannot describe for you one part in one hundred. What greater riches could you want more than the profit from the fine, unique cloth from there, or the two fisheries that produce the beautiful, rich pearls from the Gulf of Mannar and the Island of Bahrain?⁴³ This is leaving aside the many other things there are in India. Who could exaggerate the mineral wealth of the island of Sri Lanka with its rubies, cat's eyes, sapphires, jacinths, *robazes*, amethysts, and all sorts of other stones?⁴⁴ Who does not know about the wealth from the fine diamond mines of Vijayanagara?⁴⁵ Every hour of every day they extract diamonds the size of small eggs from these mines. Many of these weigh sixty, seventy, or eighty *mangelins*.

9. What can I say of the precious and fine rubies from Burma, of which there were many of great value? Their kings wore them pierced with holes, hanging from their ears as earrings, and I can attest that even at night they glittered. The same could be said about the admirable and very expensive jewel that King Dom Manuel sent to His Holiness the Pope that impressed the College of Cardinals much more than the chest of gold from São Jorge da Mina.⁴⁶ They were not so bold as to put a price on the stone, estimating its value at 400,000 or 500,000 or 600,000 cruzados, and some put the price even higher. Then there is the unique piece of jewelry that King Dom Sebastian owned, which was admired by the princes and emperors of the world. Even the kings of Fez, Morocco, and Tetuan and the others did

---

42. Ferdinand Magellan, the Portuguese sailor who made the voyage for Spain to the Moluccas. Although he died on the way there, his expedition reached the islands in 1521. His relationship to the Portuguese king has never been explained satisfactorily.

43. The Gulf of Mannar is a shallow body of water separating India from Sri Lanka. For the references to Bahrain, see *The Commentaries of the Great Afonso de Albuquerque*, 114n1.

44. Jacinths are transparent red gemstones. The exact meaning of robazes is unknown.

45. Hindu kingdom inland from Goa.

46. Sent by a special ambassador, Tristan da Cunha, in 1513 to Pope Leo X.

not have sufficient money to buy one. This is not mentioning the private jewels, such as those of Dom Antão de Noronha, Francisco Barreto, or those brought from India by Dom António de Noronha, which are now in the possession of the Count of Cascais, his son-in-law. Stones like these, and others weighing seventy or eighty mangelins, were appraised at 70,000 or 80,000 pardaus each. As a result, there was no king or lord in Europe who could afford to buy them.

10. What can I tell you of the riches worn by your wives and daughters, and which the queens of Europe wear in necklaces, belts, bracelets, brooches, rings, sets of buttons, and decorations everywhere else that are beyond price?[47] Did these come to us from Africa or from India? Let us not forget the gold mines. Where else in the world do they produce one-fourth of what I said comes forth from Mutapa and other mines in Black Africa? These African mines send some 200,000 *miticals* of gold to India, which is more than 500,000 xerafins. This does not mention the two hundred *bahars* of ivory, which are worth around 80,000 pardaus. There is much of this for the world to admire: there are bars of thirty tusks, bars of twenty, bars of ten, and bars of five and six. By these figures, I estimate that from that part of the world each year they export three thousand tusks, which also means that around fifteen hundred elephants die annually.

11. From China I can ship bars of gold shaped like boats, two marcos around. Each of these is worth 280 pardaus and only eight hundred leave China each year. The merchants prefer to buy pieces of silk and damask, fine silks, taffetas in every color, and all sorts of silks, gold and silver in thread, porcelains, and many other types of merchandise for which there is a great demand.[48]

12. I have not spoken about the great wealth of the mines of Monancabo on the opposite shore from Malacca. It is common knowledge that each year ships with rowers visit Malacca and arrive with gold. Even after we entered India there were *chatins*, who are merchants, and they only deal in bars of gold, and each bar is four quintals. Above all the other great things, it is

---

47. Buttons were separate from blouses and shirts and more like cuff links or studs of today.

48. Damask is a firm shiny woven fabric, usually made with silk or cotton. Taffeta is a smooth fabric made from silk.

possible to point to one as the most admirable. It is from one of the islands east of Solor, where we have a fort and a Christian community guided by Dominican fathers.[49] This island was visited by chance by one or two Portuguese, and they saw such a huge quantity of gold that they were amazed. The firearms, waistcoats, shields, and spears were all made from the finest gold. It is presumed that these are the islands of Solomon. Whatever their name, they were discovered by Alvaro de Mendaña de Neira.[50]

13. I can tell you about the city of Basrur on the coast of Kanara, which even at the time we arrived had many chatins who dealt in gold *candis* shaped like pagodas. This is money as large as a white bean, and it is shaped like the pagodas where these heathens worship. Each of these is worth more than four hundred réis. A *candil* is fifteen *alqueires* of wheat from our country. This does not even mention the silver that comes from Japan each year on the great ship under contract.[51] Its cargo is calculated in bars and totals more than one million in gold. Nor have we discussed all the wealth that comes from Persia and all the kingdoms in the hinterlands of Asia to our fort at Hormuz. There they buy goods that arrive from India on ten or twelve ships loaded with spices, herbs, medicines, clothes, agarwood, sandalwood, camphor, porcelains, and many other expensive things, which are exchanged for larins, horses, carpets, damasks, brocades, and other fine ornaments.[52]

14. What more can I tell you gentlemen? The mind reels when we talk about the riches of the East. If that were not so, tell me, where did King Solomon send his fleets to look for gold and all the other precious materials used in the Temple?[53] Was it to India or to Africa? He had the regions of

---

49. Solor is an island near Timor in modern Indonesia.

50. He was the first European to arrive in this island group in 1568. Because of the large quantities of alluvial gold, he believed he had discovered the source of King Solomon's wealth and named the islands "the Solomon Islands." They are not close to Solor or Timor as Couto states, but rather to the east of Papua New Guinea in the southwest Pacific Ocean.

51. A reference to the ship that sailed each year from Macau to Nagasaki to trade Chinese silk for Japanese silver. The sailing was awarded to one merchant each year under a contract. See Charles R. Boxer, *The Great Ship from Amacon*, or, by the same author, *Fidalgos in the Far East*.

52. Agarwood is a naturally scented wood used for incense and perfume.

53. The First Temple, built in Jerusalem and destroyed ca. 587 BCE.

Africa next to him, much closer than India. He could have looked in Africa if these riches had been there. If we conquer those kingdoms, they will provide us with bread and cattle, as I have said. What India will provide, you know.

15. Let us look beyond the viceroys and governors and go to the captains of Hormuz. In three years they will rake in 200,000 or 300,000 pardaus. The captains of Sofala will make a little less; in Malacca they will make 100,000. Captains of Diu and Chaul will make 70,000 or 80,000, while those in Bassein and Damão make 30,000 or 40,000, as will those in Mombasa and Muscat. Each voyage to Japan will make 70,000 or 80,000 pardaus. All the other posts in India, all of them, will make the same amount. Show me where in Africa such a sum can be made in three years, ten years, or more that is equal to one of these smaller forts. If you tell me that the money from India is not used to any advantage and that here in Portugal there are few estates or homes funded by it, I will respond by saying these people take everything from the forts, as I have said. If the Devil takes it away from them because of their excesses, what fault of that is mine? They can be happy with less, make the best of the situation, and not stuff themselves to the point of making themselves sick.

16. Now we can examine these riches with more precision. Arrianus, the Greek author, estimated that the customs duties from Indian goods entering the Red Sea, when Egypt was part of the Roman Empire, yielded seven or eight million in gold.[54] He lists all the clothes, spices and herbs, precious stones, pearls, and all the other luxuries that came from the East. After the collapse of that empire, the area came under the power of the sultans. How else were they financed if not by the taxes on goods from India?

17. After we became the masters there and began to block the commerce flowing into the Red Sea, the effects were so successful that the Ottomans sent ambassadors to the pope, asking him to intercede with the kings of Portugal to make them stop interfering with their business and blocking the pilgrimage to the house of their prophet Muhammed.[55] If the Portuguese

---

54. Lucius Flavius Arrianus or Xenophon (86–160 CE), Greek, historian and philosopher during the Roman era. Obviously this is a lot of money, but it is unclear seven or eight million of what coin.

55. Muslims do not visit the actual site of Muhammad's home but instead make a pilgrimage to the Kaa'ba, an ancient shrine in Mecca and a series of sites in both Mecca and Medina.

kings refused to do this, they would destroy the Holy House in Jerusalem, the Holy Sepulcher, and all the other holy sites. The reigning sultan at the time then ordered that we be expelled from India by that overconfident fleet he sent, commanded by Amir Husain Al-Kurdi.[56] It was defeated in Diu by the valiant Captain Dom Francisco de Almeida.[57]

18. Once the Ottoman Sultans gained that empire, did they not strive to throw us out of India to free the way to rich commerce? When Lopo Vaz de Sampaio was governor, did they not threaten us with a powerful fleet of galleys that was exhausted before it left the Red Sea because of the differences among their captains? Afterward, did they not send more than seventy galleys, ships, and galleons to attack Diu, when Nuno da Cunha was governor, and all of these were defeated and more than half their sailors killed?[58] This victory came in spite of their having all the support of the kings of the Orient, which they unified to try to harm us. How many more times did they send other fleets to attack us, all of which lost? These expeditions cost them dearly and were motivated by their envy of the great wealth of India, which made these expenses seem minor.

19. Now some condemn this conquest of India; may it please God that the kings of Europe do not yet know about this, which is denigrated here. Some of these kings have attempted using great navigators to find a passage to India by sailing above Lapland, Gotland, and Norway. They attempt to sail along the Tartary Coast to discover the way to the Sea of Japan.[59] You attach so little value to something so many envy, a conquest worth its weight in gold! You are now repentant of having seized such a great land!

20. It is certain that those who do not agree with this need to examine the fact that this discovery was ordained by God and not by man. Who has the understanding that would allow for someone from the western edge of Europe to find where the sun first rises? This was done without knowing the way, not knowing where to sail, without an astrolabe, with no sailing

56. Sultan Al-Ashraf of Mamluke Egypt.
57. First battle of Diu in 1509.
58. Diu was attacked in 1531, 1538, and 1541.
59. Gotland is an island in the Baltic Sea. Tartary is an old name for central Russia. The maritime route Couto describes was attempted repeatedly and became the focus of the Great Northern Expeditions. The first complete maritime passage across the Arctic Ocean above northern Asia was made in 1878.

charts or any other nautical instruments that would be used later.⁶⁰ This is not widely understood by everyone. God was the pilot, and he guided the brave Dom Vasco da Gama on a path that today is well known and used, but that at the time caused great fear and alarm. With good reason, we can say that God brought us out of Egypt to the Promised Land. What a fortunate place it is, never having any diseases, free of starvation and cold, with sultry weather. Everything is so mild that there is nothing more to desire. Where else do you find such happiness? This Egypt where you are living, do you recall how many earthquakes it has had?⁶¹ It is still possible to see the ruins and devastation they caused. Look at the very cruel plagues that have struck this city and that just in Lisbon have killed sixty thousand people! How many periods of starvation and other miseries have the people endured?

21. India has the purest air in the world. Its crops and water from wells and rivers are the best and healthiest in the entire world. It produces enough bread, barley, all manner of grains and vegetables, and fat cattle to feed the world. It has all of the best things. We are the worst thing there, we who harm that wonderful place with our lies and falsehoods, frauds, our cheating, greed, injustices, and so many other vices that I will not list. Now we consider leaving India and turning to the interior of Africa. If we were to fail, what would become of all those men who had come to India? For certain, they would turn on each other here. As a last resort, we would try to recapture India, but who says God would give us a second chance at what he had saved for Vasco da Gama?

22. If you made a list of the gifts God gave the people of Israel when he led them from Egypt, and another list of what he gave us on our way to that Promised Land of India, we would find that what he gave us was greatly superior. He guided the Israelites during day, covering the sky with clouds to protect them against the harsh sunlight. At night, he provided bright stars, and water came from the heavens. This manna was precious, and he knew everything that was needed. With these gifts, he also gave another 300,000 favors. Which was the greater, a journey of a bit more than two hundred leagues covering forty years across rugged deserts on dangerous roads attacked by enemies? The Israelites were punished for their ingrati-

---

60. An astrolabe is a nautical instrument used to determine latitude.
61. By "this Egypt where you are living," Couto means Portugal.

tude toward God when they worshiped the golden calf instead. They were punished for that when, of the 600,000 who left Egypt (that was the number of men who could fight), only Joshua and Caleb entered the Promised Land.[62]

23. This was not the way for us, the Portuguese. Once God had decided to extend his holy law in those parts of India, and we were to be the actors of such a huge undertaking; this was a greater gift and blessing than all those given to the children of Israel. He opened the way for us across the ocean, some six thousand leagues and six months with no risk or danger. The three ships that left for India all returned to Portugal. How is it that you would now abandon a state that God reserved just for us to the enemies of your faith, who would obtain it through our weakness and cowardice? The heathens and Muslims would think that the God we adore does not have the power to allow us to remain there. They would think he abandoned us if we left such a large place that was the envy of so many kings and lords of the world.

24. Leaving aside for now the great wealth India has given us, wealth that is incomparable, what we can value most are the times that the Lord God gave us such great and memorable victories there. As a result of these, we came to be feared and were so proudly famed among all the nations of the world that others were envious. Many obtained great wealth and a lot of material goods from India; many wealthy men came from there. However, in none of the histories will they be recorded, in spite of their nobility. For those of more modest backgrounds, their deeds will be underlined, and because of them the wealthiest people in the world will be jealous.

25. A land that gave you so many things, such riches and honor—who believes it would be good to leave it? I think, for sure, gentlemen, that it would be an infernal enemy of everything that is good and honorable. Because of that, gentlemen, it is not necessary to discuss this, because it is against Divine Majesty, and we could be greatly punished for abandoning such a huge region that the Holy Roman Apostolic Catholic Church rules in those parts. If a captain abandons his fort to his enemies, even if there is no other solution, the king orders his head cut off, and then haughtily con-

---

62. Numbers 1; Exodus 36; Numbers 14.

fiscates all the captain's goods. What will happen to he who abandons many forts and such great stretches of land and such a large number of Christians? For certain, he would be punished for four generations.

26. I will not speak about this any more out of fear of Heaven, and therefore I bring this discourse to an end, as well as our conversation, since it is growing late. The other subjects will remain for other days, and now if Your Graces would be so kind as to excuse me, and allow me to leave.

APPENDIX

*Draft Letter of Matias de Albuquerque to
King Dom Philip III of Spain and Portugal*

THE FOLLOWING IS NOT part of the original work by Couto, but is a letter drafted by a viceroy to the king of Spain and Portugal, responding to charges of financial irregularities in the official audit completed at the end of his term of office. It thus provides an example of the type of inquiry Couto mentions often. Here we can hear another voice in the debate about corruption in Portuguese Asia: a viceroy explaining his actions. In his response, you will also see that the viceroy is in hot water, and these inquiries may not have been the general whitewash that Couto claimed.

Matias de Albuquerque ruled Portuguese Asia for two three-year terms, 1591 to 1597, exactly at the time Couto was writing his critique of graft and corruption. This letter is not signed (because it is a draft), but internal evidence suggests Albuquerque as the only possible author. It is dated ca. 1603. There may or may not have ever been a formal response sent to King Dom Philip III, since Matias died shortly after the draft was written. Historians have generally considered Matias to be an honest viceroy. However, as the letter makes clear, the accounting procedures he describes are confusing and complex and lend themselves to graft.

The original letter is held by the James Ford Bell Library of the University of Minnesota, and this translation is published here with their kind permission.

1. Sir, Bishop Dom Pedro de Castilho, viceroy of this Kingdom [of Portugal], directed me through his secretary Cristovão Soares to answer the issues raised in the book (already forwarded to me by Doctor Sebastião Barboza) referring to the income and grants during the six years that I served as viceroy of India. My poor health does not give me the strength to waste a lot of words answering the questions put to me. After I ruined my health and dedicated my life to serve the kings of this crown as the loyal subject

that I always was, I will obey Your Majesty's commands. These questions brought me some contentment because I will depart this life with only the good conscience of the many deeds I performed for the king, now in eternal glory, the father of Your Majesty.[1] It seems to me that this response will ensure that the greatness of these deeds will not be slandered or wrongly interpreted. I can only trust that time will confirm this, as well as the truth of this response.

2. You ask me, Your Majesty, why I exceeded the financial limits of the provision sent on the convoy of 1591 by the king, now in eternal glory, the father of Your Majesty, for the final five years I was in office. First, the enforcement of this provision was not part of my duty, since these things occurred before the receipt of this provision mandating that governors and viceroys of India are not to spend more than thirty thousand cruzados or forty thousand pardaus each year.

3. So that it will not appear that I am giving you the well-worn answers that other captains have already given to similar questions, I say for my part—or even if Your Majesty does not take my word for it and wishes to ask my enemies—I performed extraordinary services while I governed India. How was it possible that there were many great victories by land and by sea? How did I prepare the many ships for the conquest of the three kingdoms? It took a lot of money, artillery, munitions, and arms to conquer and destroy impregnable fortresses, and to defend our positions against great and powerful sieges. When I began my term, I found India restless and at war with nine enemy kings. I was able to leave it at peace to my successor, and Your Majesty's treasury was put in order and had no debts. The treasury was so greatly increased that its increase refutes the accusations made against me. These facts are further supported by the confessions of my enemies and the justices. The Estado da Índia never had as much income as it did in my time. When Your Majesty considers the extremely important and extraordinary services I performed, in addition to my great diligence, zeal, experience, and strength, was there any other effective strategy but to enliven and to encourage the captains and soldiers with grants and benefits? These were paid from my inheritance, left to me by my grandparents. If that sacrifice is not enough, I can only offer my head—many times split open, as

---

1. That is, King Philip II (I of Portugal), who died in 1598.

were other heads, by gunshot and cannons in service to Your Majesty and to your forefathers. In the six years that I governed India, I did not get rich but rather lost much of what I previously had. When I returned to Portugal and went to court to kiss Your Majesty's hand and spend the months there that I did, I had to sell some of my belongings to raise 100,000 réis.

4. I recall, among everything else sent to me in that book, there was a question regarding the entries for each of the six years. One entry was marked "ordinary expenses," and the other was "extraordinary." Later, both of these were totaled, exceeding the limits of the referenced provision. This accounting should not be made in this way because those expenses called "ordinary" cannot be counted as simple and absolute. They are actually wages and salaries, as can be seen in the entries in the books from India, as well as in the conclusion and summaries of these, where this matter is addressed. The payments made to people and to institutions ordered by law are listed as "ordinary expenses" from Your Majesty's treasury. Clearly, anyone who wishes to read the entries cannot fail to understand that these so-called "ordinary expenses" are, in reality, payments and salaries for soldiers and officials. The captain in charge of Malabar receives 1,000 pardaus, which in our money is 300,000 réis. The captain in charge of the north receives 500 pardaus, or 150,000 réis, while the captains of the ships receive 300 pardaus, which is around 90,000 réis.[2] The captains of the galleons and smaller ships receive 100 pardaus, which is 30,000 réis. This accounts for the greater part of what are called "ordinary expenses." It is obvious these salaries and payments are paid out of the ordinary accounts. The generals, captains in charge, and captains, in addition, receive money to maintain the soldiers. This is done because these captains provide food for the soldiers from their ships. The money given to them is entered under payments for salaries, but in reality is for food and for buying drink in the ports, as well as for meat, fish, and fruit, and almost everything else. This payment is necessary because it would take away other money from Your Majesty to support them, and because the salary for their nine months at sea ordinarily is very little. These expenses are listed as "ordinary" because, if this were not done, it would call attention to their low monthly salaries. In order to avoid this

---

2. The "north" was the cluster of outposts stretching from Chaul, Bombay, Bassein, to Damão and Diu.

problem, they were called payments for the room and board for soldiers and sailors. If one kept accounts more rigorously, these payments would not be called ordinary expenses since they are payments or salaries for the captains. These payments were charged under "extraordinary expenses" but should only be listed as grants. In not one of the six years when I ruled will it be found that I reached the limit of the forty thousand pardaus, but rather, these totals will be much lower, as is shown in the same account books in which the charges against me are made. In not one of the six years will the total come to thirty thousand cruzados. May God forgive he who first makes accusations against me, understanding what he says.

5. Because the intention of the law obliges more of those who wish to fulfill it than its words alone state, Your Majesty should inquire as to the motivation that moved the king, now in eternal glory, the father of Your Majesty, to make the referenced limitation. It will be easily understood from the words of his provision:

> Considering the great number of expenses that the viceroys of India entered into while they administered with wasteful abandon, exceeding in all limits of reason and good government. My treasury is left without the possibility of preparing the ships needed for its defense.

6. Faced with the intention and words of this law, Your Majesty should examine in particular and most closely the entries of the extraordinary payments that I made in the six years I governed India. It will be noted that I never made a payment to a relative, friend, servant, or any other person to whom I had an obligation or any personal reasons for doing so. All payments were made to noblemen and soldiers because of their military service to Your Majesty, or so that they would serve, or because they had returned from service penniless, wounded, or ill. Most of these payments were from ten to twenty pardaus, which is four to eight thousand réis in our money. Few payments were as high as fifty pardaus or fifteen thousand réis. Very few payments reach one hundred pardaus, and those were only for urgent reasons. In such cases, it was because the person was especially meritorious and had spent a great deal in performing royal service. When payments are so moderate, or made with such strictness and with such a tight fist, they stay well within the limits of good government. It is not possible, neither through reason nor conscience, to oppose a law or provision that one

encounters, except to outfit the necessary ships and war supplies. What I enacted has the same form and intention as the referenced law. In regard to the deceptive words in the report, it is clear that I fought so many wars and naval battles in so many kingdoms, with so many unexpected demands, so far from the royal presence, that I was not able to follow the rules on royal taxation as much as I had wanted or hoped.

7. All the payments that I made were for military service for the injured and poverty-stricken. The reason that I say this is that, Your Majesty will recall, there is no greater obligation than sustaining soldiers so that they do not die, ensuring sufficient manpower for warfare, and maintaining ships so that the wood does not rot.

8. For clarity, it is not possible to speak about these materials one by one and without first-hand experience. It was not possible for me to wage war or obtain victory by any other means [than those demonstrated in the account books]. If Your Majesty wishes to know these payments have been a service or a disservice, have each entry examined in detail and find those responsible for those which appear excessive, or for which payments can be approved. I state clearly that it will be shown that I did not make any more payments than those required and necessary for your service. If Your Majesty mandates a review of the entries of my time by people familiar with the subject matter, you will understand how inequitably Your Majesty has been served by other viceroys and governors. I could show also, by way of papers and signed notes, that in addition to the great sums of my own money that I loaned, I borrowed more on my personal credit and used all of this for Your Majesty's service. I made loans to noblemen and other individuals totaling more than fifteen thousand pardaus. These debts remain in India and I have little hope of ever being repaid. When these men told me of their great need and how none of them had been paid for their royal services, they agreed to take my money to save Your Majesty's, so that royal funds would be available for those who serve you. Now I understand deeply that these excesses of my zeal are the reason why God allows Your Majesty's ministers to accuse me of the troubles with which I have suffered for so many years.

9. In the end, the king, now in eternal glory, the father of Your Majesty, knew of my zeal and thus showed constant confidence in me. In the letter of 1594, signed by his own hand and sent by land, in one chapter he says as follows: "and because in these issues I have seen your vigilant service to

me, I commend you and remain knowing for certain that you will do more than I could."³ By saying this, the king, now in eternal glory, could not have had any more possible confidence in my person but to expect all that was possible. And in the same letter, he said, "because you have served me so well and with such zeal in my service as I have seen, it does not please me that you should return to Portugal so quickly." Later he says, "I commend you and encourage you to continue with this work of that government and its obligations with the great care and vigilance it needs, and in conformity with the great confidence that I had and have in you." In another letter sent to me in 1598 and signed by Your Majesty, who was prince at the time:

> and I commend you very much, knowing that the ships, without the Count there, would arrive empty. Originating from the obligations of the government, which you have been given and as you have continued to govern and do, I am very pleased. I remember profiting by your visit, as I have reason to believe that you will be returning to your home.

Having the confidence in me that these words show, the king, now in eternal glory, was persuaded by seeing and understanding my deeds and actions, which he affirmed. Without any change whatsoever on my part, however, I am burdened by the treatment done to me, being called to remain in my home every day, which unsettles me. During fours years of prison, I have asked Your Majesty's ministers to send me the accounts of those who governed in error. If I do not ask for them, and I pray to God to open their eyes so that they can see that there were no errors in my service to Your Majesty, but rather it seems that Your Majesty's ministers close their eyes, so that they do not see the service that cannot now be hidden. I ask for these accounts not because I want to ask or desire satisfaction from them, but because it is not possible to oblige more, so that the resolve and spirit of Your Majesty's subjects are not weakened in performing your service when they live in the prison of seeing their service discredited.

3. Correspondence between Lisbon and Goa was normally sent by sea on the annual fleets. In rare cases, some urgent messages could be sent overland through the Middle East, which was faster than the eighteen-month roundtrip sea voyage, but also risky. As Matias would have ended his three-year term in 1594 when the king's letter was sent (whereupon another viceroy would have replaced him), the need for a speedy letter was great.

10. Finally, so that all of the details of this material will be understood, I will quote here one chapter of a letter from the king, now in eternal glory, the father of Your Majesty, sent to me in the fleet of 1595, which says as follows:

> In regard to what you say, that the provision sent on the fleet of ninety-one seemed overly rigorous for the viceroys and governors of that state not to give pensions ... and that I will take away those already given and will order collected those that may have already been paid to people not authorized by me. The bishops and prelates of those parts all seem to believe that you should excuse, so far as you realized, what I learned was the truth and that I have understood in years past: that viceroys and governors were giving away pensions from my treasury to many people—whomever they favored because of private reasons or friendships—with great generosity and with so much harm to the income of the state that I ordered the provision with which you became aware. I appreciate your reminding me about this matter, because it has served me well when pensions are given to honorable widows in shelters, whose husbands have spent their savings in my service and the defense of that state and to the poor, the old, and the crippled, who have spent their lives in the same service.[4] As your letter reminds and informs me, I will accept the reasons you gave for doing this. It is for the best that pensions are given to widows and old men.

11. I copied this chapter to show two things. First, that many people as described in this chapter [i.e., widows, the elderly, the disabled] were given one payment to save Your Majesty's treasury from the need to make payments throughout their lives. Secondly, the provisions of His Majesty, now in eternal glory, were not followed by those under his service in India, because the haste of ruling by pen and paper obscured the reasons, which were so obvious there. The distance between the two places and shifting fortunes do not allow any foresight into circumstances and troubles that happen far away. With all of this, I have responded to the questions made to me on behalf of Your Majesty.

---

4. The City of Goa had a shelter for such women called the Shelter of Our Lady of the Mountain, which housed widows and orphans.

12. I served the best I knew how to and could have, with honor, love, and justice. I have been treated in a way which I did not anticipate, and I pray to God that time will not lead others astray who might well serve and keep the Catholic and royal person of Your Majesty for many and happy years.

13. Today the last day of April of 1603.

FURTHER READING

In addition to the sources cited in M. N. Pearson's foreword, see:

Charles R. Boxer, *The Portuguese Seaborne Empire*. This is the best one-volume overview of the early modern Portuguese Empire written in English. Boxer was a prolific historian of the Portuguese and Dutch Empires and produced many fine works. This is one of his very best.

Anthony Disney, *The History of Portugal and Its Empire*. This is a new two-volume history. It is concise, very well written, and very readable. It is certainly the best general history of Portugal and its empire in English, along with the works by Oliveira Marques (below).

Antonio Henrique de Oliveira Marques, *A History of Portugal*. Although now a bit dated, this is still an excellent work.

M. N. Pearson, *The Portuguese in India*. This is a short, very readable work discussing Portuguese society and interactions in India.

A. J. R. Russell-Wood, *The Portuguese Empire: A World on the Move, 1415–1808*. A global overview of the goods and peoples moving around the Portuguese world.

Sanjay Subrahmanyam, *The Portuguese in Asia*. The social and economic history of the Portuguese in Asia, written by a preeminent historian of South Asia.

George D. Winius, *The Black Legend of Portuguese India*. A short, interesting work that discusses the importance of *The Veteran Soldier* and the Black Legend the work created.

INDEX

Page numbers in *italics* refer to the glossary of foreign and archaic English terms, graphs, illustrations, and maps.

accountants: dishonest, 63, 74–76; in Goa, 72

accounting: books, 70; closing accounts, 41, 73, 75, 123; confusion in, 183; errors in, 23, 29, 72; house in Goa, 71, 74, 80; ordinary verses extraordinary expenses, 183; owing money to, 58, 73, 76; presenting accounts, 64; theft from royal accounts, 22. *See also* Casa dos Contos; treasury

Aceh, 19 20n31, 141, 159, 160, 161

advice: from council members, 65; from lawyers, 114; from soldiers, 49; rejected by the Children of Israel, 69; of others, 69; from those who know how to play the game, 34; of the viceroy, 91; of wise men, 13

Africa: affairs relating to, 17; cloth trade in, 164; connection overland from Mutapa to Angola, 165; missionary efforts in, 165; reasons for conquest of Mutapa, 166, 168; slaves in Goa from, 150; wealth of (compared to India), 168–73, 175, 177. *See also* Malindi; Mombasa; Morocco; Mozambique; Mutapa

Africanus, General Scipio, 50, 125, 139, 170

Agadir, 168, 170. *See also* Morocco

Ahab, King of Samaria, 38, 39

Albuquerque, Afonso de, *xxxv*, 97, 99, 118

Alexander (the Great), 9n9, 14, 16, 21, 49, 50, 51, 130, 133, 135, 139

Al-Kurdi, Amir Husain, 54, 55, 55n86, 176. *See also* Arabs; Ottomans; Straits of Mecca; Turks

Almeida, D. Francisco de, *xxxv*, 55n86, 99, 160, 176

Amadeu, Duke of Savoy, 42, 43n58

Antipater, 51, 53

appointments (as awards for service): for those absent, 148; in accounting house in Goa, 73; commoners not considered for, 65; of crown judges made first, 39, 40, 41, 42; delays in making, 19; dishonest dealings by those appointed, 60, 80; done by archbishop and viceroy (verses judges), 94, 95; as done in China, 122; as done by kings in past, 45, 114; emergency (of viceroy), 77, 105; to favorites, 19, 20, 122; as instructed by the king, 26, 97; letters of, not in order, 94, 96; loss of (as punishment), 74, 149, 154; as made by the viceroys in Goa, 26, 95, 121, 132, 158; how made in Portugal, 17, 126, 147, 148; nature of, 13; sale of, 39, 120, 129; too many for same position, 106–8; for the most troublesome, 145–47, 150; not trusting those appointed, 58; underhanded dealings in making, 46. *See also* kings; soldiers; viceroys and governors

Arabs: in antiquity, 84, 130, 162; in Iberia, 43n59, 44, 103; ruling Africa, 170; and trade, 20n31, 23n35; in warfare, 21. *See also* Islam and Moslems; Straits of Mecca

archives in Goa, 66, 66n96
Arzila, 168, 170. *See also* Morocco
Ataíde, D. Luís de, *xxxvi*, 70, 80
Athens, (ancient), 3, 9, 53, 61, 138
Atlas Mountains (north Africa), wealth in 169, 169nn32, 35. *See also* Morocco
Augustinians. *See* religious orders
Azamor, 168, 170. *See also* Morocco

Barreto, Francisco, *xxxv*, 119, 120n54, 165, 173
Bartolus, 34, 109
Bassein, 55, 58, 119, 127, 136, 175, 183n2
Bengal, 55, 62, 63
Bharuch, 54, 55, 59, 88. *See also* Cambay
boys: arriving on ships, 151; as pages, 109, 147, 151, 152, 155, 188. *See also* pages
bribery: in antiquity, 125; of governors, 34, 78, 85, 88, 89; of justices 8, 95, 113; of other officials, 42, 57, 149. *See also* justice; truth; virtue
brocades. *See* cloth

Cabral, Jorge, *xxxv*, 99, 110
Caesar, Julius, 16, 90, 124, 133, 134, 138
Calicut, 8, 20n31, 38, 86, 87, 126, 161n12. *See also* Malabar
Cambay, 19, 20n31, 54n85, 55, 100, 146
captains: characteristics they should possess, 123–27, 128–36, 137–38; their conduct in antiquity, 50-51, 61, 129, 131, 133, 135, 139; dishonorable actions of, 10, 13, 36, 37, 70, 78, 80, 136; of fleets, 144, 147, 149; inquiries conducted of, 11; giving their opinions in council, 91; purchasing office, 120; and registration books, 66–68; rewards after death, 12; salaries of, 60, 175, 183, 184; as sponsors of soldiers, 30n41; theft conducted by, 35, 38, 52, 56, 58, 62, 63, 69, 76; and treasury officials, 59, 60. *See also* soldiers
carpets, 34, 113, 174

cartazes, *xxix*, 117n47. *See also* fleets and ships; trade
Carthage and Carthaginians, 42, 49n72, 50, 86, 88, 170
Casa dos Contos, *xxix*, 64, 64n95, 72. *See also* accountants, accounting
Castro, D. João de, *xxxv*, 55, 80n104, 110
certificates: as paper debt, 52, 64; to cover illegal actions, 28, 30, 74, 75, 76, 120, 123, 130; in lieu of letters of appointment, 96, 97; and letters of appointments, 94, 95, 96, 106, 107, 108, 122; as proof of service, 32, 125, 144, 145; as registration of soldiers, 68. *See also* appointments
Charles V, King of Spain, 119, 139
Chaul, 55n86, 68, 175, 183n2
China and Chinese: emperors of, how they select their governors, 112; Macau, 174n51; trade to and from, 40, 55, 68, 69, 101, 113, 143, 160, 173. *See also* silver; trade
Christian duties: of kings, 16, 18, 45, 102, 114, 140; of individual soldiers, 61, 147; of viceroys, 27, 33, 51, 97, 98
Christianity: beliefs of, 82, 121, 165; Council of Trent, 47; in Ethiopia, 119; in India. 38, 79, 80, 107, 115, 118, 166, 167, 179; missionary efforts in Mutapa, 165; on island of Solor, 174. *See also* religious orders
Cicero, 111, 131
cloth (and trade), brocades, 174; damasks, 174, 175; in east Africa, 164, 166; embroidered, 34, 42, 54, 59, 72, 172. *See also* trade
clothing: names of pieces of, defined *xxix*, *xxx*; 157, *159*; new fashions and decline of Portuguese Asia, 101, 156, 157; suitable for a soldier, 156, 157. *See also* swords

INDEX

Cochin, 20n31, 87, 99, 101. *See also* Malabar

coins: bazarucos, *152*, 153; counterfeit, 153; drachmas, 131–34; escudo, 132; gold, 64, 99, 101; larins, 174; minas, 133; minting, 153; names of, *xxix–xxi;* nummus, 134; patacas, 22; réis, 72, 153, 174, 183, 184; tanga, 41; tostão, 29; xerafins, 22, 120, 152, 173. *See also* cruzado; gold; payments; salaries; trade

companies (of soldiers), how they should be organized, 66–70. *See also* captains; soldiers

compassion and mercy: importance of, 50, 89, 117, 123–27, 140, 141; God's, 11, 84, 101, 103, 104, 148, 171

councils: in Lisbon, 17, 56, 65, 90, 91, 97; manner in which they operate in Goa, 8–10, 110; proposed for India in Lisbon, 77; town council of Goa, 29, 77, 82, 83

cruzados: captains' rights to, 35; defined, *xxx;* dowry for D. Isabel, 169; from an estate, 29, 46; total income of Portuguese Asia in, 120; lackies receive, 23; marriage for, 155; needed for the conquest of Mutapa, 164; owed to king, 29; owed by renter, 30; in old payments, 53; profit from counterfeiting, 153; profit from India disappears, 12; saved with fewer justice, 113; spent on lady friends, 149; taken by fraud, 38, 40, 41; treasury officials and, 58, 64, 74; viceroys refuse to invest their own, 22; given to viceroys, 25, 132, 182, 184; value of jewels in, 172. *See also* coins; payments; salaries

Cunha, Nuno da, *xxxv*, 55, 176

cutter (ship), 120, 120n55, 154. *See also* fleets and ships; galleys

Dabhol, 8, 54, 55. *See also* Cambay

Daman, 55n88, 67, 175, 183n2

Darius, King of Persia, 18, 21, 38, 49, 51, 85, 130, 139. *See also* Persia, ancient

David (King), 69, 81

debts: in budget of Portuguese Asia, 182; of captains, 35, 58; of deceased, 29, 75; of governors, 22, 27, 28, 123; old, defined 58, 52–53, 72–76, 147; to governors, 185; to merchants, 52; payments made in old, 58; phony, 60, 74; in prison for, 25; to soldiers, 26, 60–69, 94, 148, 164, 183–85. *See also* accountants; accounting; expenses; payments; salaries

Devil, at work in Portuguese India 12, 13, 25, 33, 39, 61, 121, 149, 152, 175

Dionysius of Syracuse, 10, 132, 133

Diu: battles of, 55, *57, 62, 71, 98,* 99, 100n6, *106, 118,* 119, 161, 176; captains of, 64, 175; cloth from, 54. *See also* fleets and ships; Ottomans

doctors, 64, 120. *See also* hospitals

Egyptians: ancient, 9, 102, 110, 124n62, 175, 177, 178; Mamluk, 55, 176n56

enemies (of Portuguese Asia): Dutch and the VOC, 20n31; learn news of Portuguese plans, 8, 38, 128; king's ministers act as, 21, 22, 53; surrounded by, 79, 101, 110, 115; warfare against, 55, 99, 105, 125, 143, 146, 160, 178, 182. *See also* neighboring kingdoms (to Goa); Ottomans

Ephors (of Sparta), significance of, 45, 70

Estado da Índia (Portuguese Asia): idea of abandoning, 44, 167; documentation to and from, 66; expanding territory of, 55; fleets of, 117, 120; income of, 119, 165, 182; needs of, 152, 155; reputation of, 25, 90, 99, 129, 160, 167; shortfalls in income of, 32, 37, 53, 76, 162; shrinking area ruled by, 56, 101; great size

Estado da Índia (*continued*)
of, 91; traits needed to retain, 100, 101; selecting a viceroy for, 122; voyage to and from, 7. *See also* Goa; viceroys and governors

expenses: for the conquest of Mutapa, 164; extraordinary, 183–85; for fleets, 8; forts only create, 160; lavish, 60; the many of the Estado da Índia, 163, 172; ordinary, 25, 32, 58, 132, 133; paid by viceroy, 23. *See also* coins; cruzados; debts; payments; salaries

factor: appointed by viceroys to position of factor or lower, 26, 108; auditing their accounts, 73, 74; defined, *xxx*; handles expenses, 23, 71; fraud committed by, 29, 60, 63–64, 72, 75, 76; avoiding fraud committed by, 67; in Hormuz, 22n33; occupying post with bribes, 34, 35; relations with captains, 37; relations with treasury officials, 58. *See also* accountants; accounting; captains; viceroys and governors

favoritism. *See* appointments; viceroys and governors

Flanders, 60, 103, 162

flattery, 3, 6, 14, 15, 53

fleets and ships: captains of, 35, 36, 120, 144, 149; captured by pirates, 63, 115, 131, 143, 150; guarding convoys, 63; documentation regarding, 66, 71; financing, 38, 42, 71, 87; arriving in Hormuz, 23; to and from Lisbon, 28, 59, 77, 79, 108, 123, 147; Ottoman, 54, 55, 117–19; provisioning, 21, 52, 58, 76, 78, 80, 88, 104, 119, 129, 130; sending at right times, 8, 25, 37, 80, 87; serving on, 30, 38, 86, 105, 107, 110, 116, 149, 150; unavailable for duty, 80, 99, 120. *See also* cutters; Diu; galleys

food: awarded a position to sufficiently pay for, 108; in India, 177; for nobility, 78; payments for, 58, 63; for the sick, 164; for soldiers, 36, 66, 136, 155, 156, 164, 168, 183, 185;on voyage to Lisbon, 94. *See also* rice; wheat

forts: lack of a master list of appointments at, 108; captains and, 35, 52, 53, 137, 150, 178; documentation to and from, 66; factors and, 36, 60, 71, 72; in Hormuz, 22, 174; inquiry conducted for officials at, 11; judges and, 39, 40, 109; maintaining verses galleons, 119, 160–61; at Mozambique, 165; in Mutapa, 164; payments made in, 64; profits from, 12, 13, 175; provisions for, 21; soldiers' registration books at, 61, 67–69; staffing of, 63, 151; treasury officials at, 54, 57–59; viceroy appointing his man at, 95, 121, 122, 126. *See also* accounting; appointments; captains; factors; judges; treasury

Franciscans. *See* religious orders

fraud: accountants and, 76; avoiding, 114; deceiving the king, 29–32; deceiving men, 32–39; deceiving God, 39–48; deceiving all four, 48–56; factors and, 63; four types of, 29; judges and, 113; laws created for, 110; by viceroys, 28, 74, 147, 152–58. *See also* accounting; debts; expenses; loans; payments; salaries

galleys (ships), 9, 82, 116, 119, 120, 124, 149, 176. *See also* cutters; fleets and ships

Gama, D. Vasco da, *xxxv*, 169, 177

generosity, (the importance of), 32, 38, 124, 128–34, 162. *See also* compassion and mercy; virtue

Goa: accounting house in, 71; as tower

of Babel, 5; correspondence to and from, 186n3; golden era verses present, 104, 115, 119, 126; Inquisition in, 29n39; buying goods in, 58; horses in, 36, 150; rights of residents of, 14, 15, 24, 25, 77, 83, 89, 111; sedan chairs used in, 147; soldiers living in, 66–69, 156; town council of, 83, 111; winter in, 30. *See also* fleets and ships; soldiers; viceroys and governors

gold: in antiquity, 134, 135; chains, 34, 42, 149; in China, 143; importance of, 99, 101; from São Jorge da Mina, 169; in Mutapa, 161, 162n17, 166; given to Pope, 172; from Tivar (west Africa), 169; in SE Asia, 173; in trade, 59, 153; value of old payments in, 62. *See also* coins; cruzados; payments; trade

gossip, 8, 10

governors. *See* viceroys and governors

greed: its cure, 112; how it caused the end of the Roman Empire, 7, 29, 53, 54, 102; in Portuguese Asia, 88, 105, 113, 121, 128, 129, 177. *See also* virtue

Hannibal, 49, 50, 86, 99, 170n36
herbs, 18, 174, 175
Hindus, 29, 115
homage. *See* oath
Homem, Vasco Fernandes, 161, 162
honor: loss of in forts, 37; for the generous, 134; of governors, 28, 31, 47, 51, 73, 84, 89; of king, 38, 53, 74; of a married woman, 10;when misdeeds become, 11; nature of, 112, 126; of a deceased parent, 7; when presenting petitions, 6, 145; wanting rewards more than, 85, 86, 125, 126, 129, 130, 132; of soldiers, 61, 105, 108, 137, 138, 167; of a young woman, 49. *See also* obligations and duties; truth; virtue

Hormuz, trade in, 22, 23, 38, 41, 64, 65, 72, 107, 119, 161, 174, 175

horses: gifts of, 22; pricing of, 22, 23; as status, 27, 36, 109, 113, 148, 150, 155; trade in, 174; for warfare, 46, 131, 132, 133, 149, 151, 170

hospitals, 20, 64, 69, 80, 94. *See also* doctors; misericórdia

inquiries: by auditors, 72; by judges, 41, 115; by the king, 11; of the misericórdia, 83; secret, 76; by treasury officials, 59. *See also* justice; testimony in court

D. Isabel, Queen of Castile, 114, 163n18, 169

Islam and Moslems, 44, 45, 102, 119. *See also* Arabs; Ottomans; Straits of Mecca; Turks

ivory and elephants, 131, 173

Japan, 40n55, 55, 160, 167, 174, 175, 176
jewelry, 135, 169, 172
jewels: amethysts 172; diamonds 113, 172; jacinths, 172; rubies, 113, 172; robazes, xxxi, 172

Jews: awarding appointments to, 96, 97; should be forced to leave Portuguese Asia, 29, 44, 45, 103, 157

D. João II, King of Portugal, 27, 101, 119
D. João III, King of Portugal, 107, 169
judges: bribery of, 8, 22, 41, 111, 113; of the dead (Minos), 50; fewer in the past, 110, 113, 114, High Court, 24; homes of, always open, 33; of the orphans, 46, 53n82, 82; payment in afterlife, 12; power of appointments taken away from, 94, 95; in Portugal, 7, 97; to protect the people, 45; ready to occupy their positions, 34, 39, 108, 109, 158; relatives and, 122; rulings from, 13, 30, 40, 94, 115; special in Portugal to make

judges (*continued*)
   appointments, 96, 97; only the wealthy should act as, 41–43, 74. *See also* justice
justice: administration of in Goa, 8, 25, 40, 41, 45, 73, 109, 110, 152; affairs relating to discussed in Lisbon, 17; available at all hours, 34; bribery and, 8, 23, 24, 26, 41, 42, 56, 73, 95, 123; in ancient Greece, 45; as practiced by the ancient Persians, 113. *See also* inquiries; judges; testimony in court

Kanará, 54, 87, 156, 174
kings: councils advising, 7n5; deceiving by fraud, 29–32, 37, 123; duty to poor, 42, 43, 107, 108; duty of, 18, 44, 45, 107, 108; generosity shown by, 32, 33, 128, 130, 133, 148; honoring truthful men, 74; hearts are in God's hands, 5; ordering inquiries, 11, 12, 77; unaware of many things, 13–15, 28, 76, 80, 120, 121; meaning of the term, 15, 127; ministers should acts as, 16, 21–24, 27; and old payments, 62–70, 73; orders must be obeyed, 157–58; owing king money, 25; refusing to serve, 149–50; selection of viceroys, 56; treasury officials and their disservice to, 57–61; viceroys disservice to, 53, 54, 88, 89, 132, 152, 153; work on a schedule, 17–19. *See also* D. João II; D. João III; D. Manuel I; D. Sebastian

laws: merits of abolishing all, 114; in antiquity, 45, 110; changes in, 101; dishonest applications of, 34, 116; God's, 84, 121, 178; lack of in Mutapa, 165; of Portugal, 89, 90, 94, 114, 184; of nature, 15; applied against the needy, 24, 147; poor use of, 115, 116; regarding secrecy, 9; those trained in, 41, 95, 109; viceroy breaking, 89, 90, 183. *See also* judges; lawyers

lawyers, 24, 41, 109n27, 114, 115, 128
letters: from the king, 185, 186, 187; to the king, 56, 66, 76, 77, 79, 120, 147, 165
Lisbon: Casa da Índia in, 7n3; misericórdia of, 83; sailing to Goa from, 6n2, 147, 157, 164, 186n3
Livy, 85, 86, 132
loans: from governors, 36, 130, 185; to governors, 37, 53, 76; to judges, 40; made by king, 33; failure to repay, 41, 149. *See also* debts; expenses
lust, 49, 51, 92, 99. *See also* virtue

Macau. *See* China
Malabar: ambassadors sent to, 169; Basrur, 174; Calicut, 8, 38, 86, 87, 126; Cannanore, 87; Chalé (Chaliyam), 38, 161; Cochin, 87, 99, 101; defined, 8n7; fleet sent to, 8, 19, 36, 117, 120; forts in, 54, 183; located, *xxxii*; rulers of, 80, 87; peace in, 86–88; Quilon, 87; warfare in, 20n31, 37, 88, 143, 144, 150, 151, 157
Malacca: and Aceh, 20n31; captains of, 38, 150, 175; fort in, 119, 160; help sent to, 156; located, *xxxiii*; trade from, 87, 173
Malindi, *xxxiv*, 55, 62, 164, 165
mankind, his evil nature, 22, 49, 54, 74, 90, 104, 121, 157
D. Manuel I, King of Portugal, 100, 172
marriages, their deceptive nature in Goa, 10, 46, 47, 68. *See also* orphans
married men, their registration in books, 62, 68, 69
Mecca, 8, 45, 59, 117, 118, 154, 175n55. *See also* Arabs; Islam and Moslems; Straits of Mecca
medicines, 112, 113, 174. *See also* doctors; hospitals
Meneses, D. João de, 170, 171
merchants: Moslem, 20n31, 37, 41, 59;

failure to repay, 52, 76, 78; viceroys acting as, 130, 133
mercy. *See* compassion and mercy
merit: awards based on, 5, 105, 126, 184; ignored, 6; nothing awarded for, 120
Mesa da Consciência, 26, 45, 97
Mina, São Jorge da (west Africa), 60, 169, 172
mines: in Malabar, 143; in Mutapa, 159–66; in north Africa, 169–73
Misericórdia, Santa Casa de (Holy House of Mercy), 69, 69n99, 83, 94
missionary efforts, 115, 165. *See also* Christianity; religious orders
Moabites, 84, 102n17
Moluccas, *xxxiii*, 91, 143, 156, 160, 172n42
Mombasa, *xxxiv*, 55n90, 161
Morocco: Ksar el-Kebir, Battle of, 70n103, 104, 104n24, 163, 163n19; Portuguese outposts in, 107n26, *167*, 168, 170, 171; wealth of, 169
Moses, 44, 45, 69, 102, 103n21
Mozambique Island, *xxxiv*, 161–65
Mughuls, 12, 79, 148n1. *See also* neighboring kingdoms (to Goa)
Muscat, *xxxiv*, 146, 161, 175
Mutapa, kingdom of, *xxxiv*, 159–66, 173

Nagasaki. *See* Japan
the needy, 13, 18, 19, 24, 33, 43. *See also* obligations and duties
neighboring kingdoms (to Goa): Balagate, 22; Bijapur, 8; Vijayanagara, 172
nobility: actions on the council in Goa, 8; ancestry alone insufficient, 49; dishonorable acts, 10, 13, 36, 37, 52, 53, 78, 144, 146, 149; in jail, 25; of Malabar, 87; on the misericórdia, 85; giving their opinions, 65, 79; and their pages, 150, 151; paying those who serve the viceroys, 35, 36, 38, 52; feeding soldiers, 66, 67, 155, 184, 185; raised in the backwoods, 36; serving the crown loyally, 56, 59, 97, 104, 107, 125; serving the Spanish king, 162; too young to serve, 120, 155. *See also* obligations and duties; viceroys and governors

oath: in antiquity, 88; in court, 41, 114; meaning of term, 114; viceroy's, 23, 24, 31, 88, 90
obligations and duties: examples from antiquity, 49, 51, 84–86, 90; of the king's servants, 39; of king to his subjects, 18, 26, 32, 33, 38, 42, 186; to soldiers, 108, 146; of loyal subjects, 16; of viceroys and governors, 31, 84, 91, 130, 147, 152, 182, 184; to those who serve the viceroys, 47, 90
Ottomans, 59, 80n104, 117, 175, 176. *See also* Al-Kurdi, Amir Husain; fleets and ships; Straits of Mecca
orders: for fleet, 8; of the king, 11, 16; of the king ignored by viceroys, 14, 39, 89, 150, 157
orphans: female, 46, 47, 102, 123, 187n4; judge of, 46, 46n68, 82; needy, 26, 31, 51, 54, 91; obtaining loans from, 5. *See also* marriages, their deceptive nature in Goa

pages. *See* boys
patients, 31, 69, 164
payments: in afterlife, 12, 82; from captains, 35; from Hormuz, 22; to nobility, 26; old, 60–70; for service, 5; to soldiers, 26, 28, 94, 148, 164, 183–87; to treasury supervisors, 58, 59; from viceroy to his servants, 27; provided by villages, 46. *See also* debts; expenses; loans; salaries; soldiers
pearls, 95, 172, 175
D. Pedro I, King of Portugal, 114

Persia and Persians: in antiquity, 18, 21, 38, 84, 112, 113, 129n73, 162, 174; in the sixteenth century, 22, 23. *See also* Darius; Hormuz

Protestants, 47n71, 103, 140

pirates, 63, 87, 115, 131, 151. *See also* fleets and ships; Malabar

Plato, 10, 17n22, 69, 110, 128

Plutarch, 9, 15, 47, 126, 131–33, 137, 138

pepper, 7n4, 87, 101

petitions: to Casa da Índia, 7; Christ responding to, 18; king responding to, 19; to High Court, 34; presenting, 5, 17, 148; responding to, 6, 105; to viceroy, 28, 33, 48, 51, 64

Pope, 81, 95, 172, 175

porcelains, 173, 174. *See also* China; trade

prisoners, 33, 40, 186

Red Sea. *See* fleets and ships; Straits of Mecca

registration. *See* soldiers

relatives: in antiquity, 131; of nobility, 36, 52, 95; of viceroys, 54, 62, 78, 87, 97, 122, 123, 184

religious orders: Augustinians, 81; Dominicans, 81, 174; Franciscans, 81

rice, 37, 38, 52, 58, 76, 153–55, 160

Rome and Romans: emperors, 14, 41, 89, 114, 129; censor of, 15; dictators of, 45, 85; military strength of, 50, 86, 130, 170; tribune, 33; examples of virtue from, 50, 92, 139. *See also* truth; virtue

salaries: better spent on older officials, 112; factor to pay, 60; governors paying, 22; for nobles, 53, 158; nobles paying those who live with them, 26; old, 61, 62–70; for soldiers, 30, 148, 164, 183, 184; for treasury officials, 58; to various captains in Portuguese Asia, 183–84. *See also* payments

Sampaio, Lopo Vaz de, *xxxv*, 55, 176

D. Sebastian, King of Portugal, 70, 104n24, 163n19, 172

secrecy: bribes and, 42; and deals made by Jews, 157; God reveals his secrets, 48; the importance of, 5–16; and inquiries, 76; and orders, 87

secretaries: of the accounting house, 29, 59, 72; of a company of soldiers, 67, 68, 69; of a fort, 19, 63, 108; legal, 111, 128; writing letters of appointments, 96; as the source of problems, 112, 115; to the viceroys, 34

sedan chairs, 148–50

shortages, 21, 42, 52, 60, 115, 125n65, 153

Silveira, António de, 99–100

silver: boxes, 59, 120; decoration, 109, 155; Japanese, 40n55, 174; jewelry, 58, 157; mines in Morocco, 169; mines in Mutapa, 161, 162, 166; Pompey and his gifts of, 131, 132; thread from China, 173; trifles made of, 42. *See also* trade

slaves, 19n30, 29, 50n75, 120, 146n2, 150

Sofala, 91, 107, 150, 161, 163, 166, 167, 175

soldiers: activities of, in the past, 80; appearing before crown officials in Lisbon, 6, 17, 145; boys becoming, 151; captains place in harm's way, 125; captains provide moral examples for, 49, 50; proper clothing for, 156, 157; favors not awarded to, 21, 26; their hard lives on ships, 154; importance of generosity with, 131–36; importance of prudent speech with, 137–41; king should listen to experienced, 91; needed for the conquest of Mutapa, 164; needing assistance today, 80, 104, 110; old payments and, 60, 62–69; paying taxes in Lisbon, 7; pretending to fight, 146; registration process for, 66–70; salaries for, 30, 56, 182; sent from Lisbon, 79; sheltering in Goa, 36, 155, 183–85;

shortages of in Portuguese Asia, 80, 115, 160; importance of prudent for soldiers, 123, 137–42; valiant first Portuguese in Asia, 55, 100, 119; viceroys provided a poor example for, 101. *See also* appointments; captains; payments; salaries

Solon, 47, 61, 110, 115

the soul, 13, 73, 112, 121, 138

Spartans, 9, 16, 45, 70, 110, 113n35

speech: of Ahab, 38; given to the mute, 16; provided by truth, 48; Roman to the senate, 86; importance of prudent for captains, 123, 137–42. *See also* captains; truth; virtue

Sri Lanka: cinnamon from, 7n4; conquest of verses Aceh, 141, 159–72; forts in, 54; Kingdom of Kotta, 117

Straits of Hormuz. *See* Hormuz

Straits of Mecca (Bab el Mendeb, Red Sea Straits), 8, 117, 119, 120. *See also* Islamand Moslems; Mecca

Surat, 8, 38, 88. *See also* Cambay

swords: first Portuguese in Asia and their bloody, 55; golden, 109, 126; importance for Portuguese to remain in Asia, 99, 101; importance of having in hand, 110, 121; new styles, 101, 157; old fashioned, 100; practicing with, 80, 155; wounds from, 105, 145. *See also* clothing; soldiers

taxes: assessed by treasury officials, 60; captains avoid paying, 37; Casa da Índia, 7, 147, 148; new imposed by viceroys, 33, 38, 56

testimony in court, 41, 111. *See also* inquiries; justice

trade: in east Africa, 164; in Cambay, 8, 19; cartazes and, *xxix* 117n47; with China and Japan, 160, 174n51; in cloves, 7n4; King D. Dinis and, 33n44; in Hormuz, 22n33; in horses, 23, 36n48; in Malabar, 8, 38; spice, 19n31, 171, 174. *See also* cloth; gold; horses; jewels; porcelains

treasury: accounting house in Goa, 71; people appointed to positions in, 108, 158; costs to royal, 21, 22, 23, 25, 183; unnecessary expenses from, 26, 30, 34, 35, 38, 77, 121; fraud and, 42, 52, 72; increasing funds into, 96, 182; supervisors at northern outposts, 57–70. *See also* accounting; debts; fraud; payments; salaries

truth: giving testimonies and, 11; importance to retain Portuguese Asia, 98, 99; kings should seek those who speak, 14, 15, 76, 130, 147; nature of, 32, 48, 112; ridiculed on council, 9; plain and unvarnished coming from soldiers, 3, 31, 78, 90, 93. *See also* oath; obligations and duties

Turks: fighting, 19, 80, 99, 100, 146; in Europe, 103; in east Africa, 161. *See also* fleets and ships; Ottomans

vagrants, 33n45, 125, 125n65, 154

Vegetius, 49, 49n73, 132, 132n86, 133

viceroys and governors: appointing, 19, 122, 123; appointments made by, 37, 94, 95, 108, 120; how they should conduct themselves, 21, 33, 56, 70, 84, 101, 104; conduct leaving office, 28, 88; councils advising, 8n6, 91, 97; dishonest actions of, 12, 22, 26, 27, 34, 54, 73–80, 152, 153; dishonorable actions of, 10, 48, 49; many duties of, 143, 162, 184; edicts issued by, 35, 63, 72, 86, 111, 147, 150, 151; should follow royal orders, 157, 158; and the High Court, 116; interfere in town council of Goa, 83; inquiries regarding, 11; list of *xxxv–xxxvi*; loans solicited by, 37, 52, 130; make themselves

viceroys and governors (*continued*)
priests, 81, 82; marry orphans to poor men, 46; oath of office, 23–25, 114; rule as tyrants, 45, 47, 89, 90; relatives of, 131; seek profit before duty, 132–36; and soldiers, 67–69; underlings of, 39, 53, 56, 60, 149. *See also* appointments; debts; loans; oaths; obligations and duties; payments

virtue: in antiquity, 17, 19, 49, 84, 123, 125, 126, 130; appreciated, 92, 112; of captains, 50; duty as, 89; of kings, 15, 32, 127; laws made to reward, 111; of soldiers, 90; of viceroys, 33, 77; becomes a weakness in corrupt Goa, 11, 111. *See also* clemency and mercy; truth

voyages: from Goa to Lisbon and return, 6n2, 94, 96n1, 186n3; to Japan, 175; of soldiers, 19

wealth: of Asia, 173, 174; and generosity, 128; importance of, 13; of India, 172, 176, 178; in Mutapa, 162–65; nature of, 13; in Portuguese Asia, 160; royal, 73, 76, 80; viceroys retiring in, 88

wheat, 52, 58, 165, 174

widows: making needless payments, 75; poor, 18, 26, 33, 51, 54, 91, 123, 187; pretending to marry rich, 10, 46, 155; seeking redress, 29. *See also* marriages, their deceptive nature in Goa

witnesses, 11, 97. *See also* inquiries; justice; testimony in court

wood, 37, 52, 58, 76, 174, 185